# Victory in Limbo

*Imagism 1908-1917*

# VICTORY IN LIMBO

*Imagism 1908-1917*

———◆———

J. B. HARMER

ST. MARTIN'S PRESS

# Acknowledgments

◆

Many people have helped me. Some of them are dead, and I remember with gratitude Sir Maurice Bowra, Sir Herbert Read and Professor Geoffrey Tillotson.

Among the living I would mention in particular Harold Brooks, G. S. Fraser, J. F. Hendry, Patricia Hutchins, Denis Kelly, Wallace Martin, Walter Roberts and Ian Willison.

Kate Lechmere, Mary Storer, Christopher Tancred and others allowed me to interview them.

Librarians were invariably helpful. I worked mostly in the British Museum, but used also Birkbeck College, the Bodleian, Keele University, the University of Leicester, the Humanities Research Center, Austin, and drew from the resources of Yale and the University of Chicago.

My final typing was done by Mrs Barbara Nelson-Smith, who showed great skill in deciphering a raddled text and much energy in helping me to meet deadlines.

This book began life as that most melancholy of documents, a thesis for the title of doctor. If it has grown into something better thanks are largely due to the taste and insight of Jenny Craven. The rigorous editing of the text was largely her responsibility; and most of the ideas added in this published version are hers, not mine.

For permission to use copyright material grateful acknowledgment is made to the following:

Richard Aldington—Mme Catherine Guillaume; Joseph Campbell—estate; Hilda Doolittle—Norman Holmes Pearson; Keith Douglas—Faber & Faber Ltd and the Chilmark Press Inc., New York; Edward Dorn—Grove Press, New York; John Gould Fletcher—literary estate; F. S. Flint—Mrs Ianthe Price; Ford Madox Ford—Miss Janice Biala; A. E. Housman—estate; Rudyard Kipling—A. P. Watt; D. H. Lawrence —estate of Frieda Lawrence; Amy Lowell—Houghton Mifflin Co., Boston; Jim Morrison—estate; Michael Palmer—Black Sparrow Press, Los Angeles; Ezra Pound—Faber & Faber Ltd and New Directions Publishing Corporation, New York; Edward Storer—estate; Dylan Thomas—David Higham Associates.

# Note

Various of the terms of art used here have never been stabilized. They belong to a nomenclature that shifts between literary and cultural history and the differing jargons of aesthetics and the 'practical' critic. The rationale of their varying forms can to some extent be explained, however.

*Imagist* and *Imagism* refer to the whole development of which this book is a discussion.

*Imagiste* and *Imagisme* are reserved for Pound's group and its cognates between 1912 and 1914.

*Symboliste* and its derivates refer to writers or work belonging to and viewed from within the French tradition of that name.

*Symbolist* implies the larger tradition of conscious literary and artistic symbolism, French or otherwise.

*symbolist* in lower-case is concerned with properties, not movements and becomes part of the thin vocabulary of the aesthetics of literature.

*Romantic*, *Classical* and *Impressionist* are other terms that sometimes earn a capital initial, at other times not. Decision is discretion and in these instances must often be *ad hoc*.

In all quotations from unpublished documents I have preserved the original spelling and punctuation, without resort to silent correction or the time-honoured use of *sic*.

# Contents

———◆———

> . . . out of key with his time
> He strove to resuscitate the dead art
> Of poetry; to maintain 'the sublime'
> In the old sense. Wrong from the start—
>     Ezra Pound, *Hugh Selwyn Mauberley*
>       (*Life and Contacts*)

> The age demanded an image
> Of its accelerated grimace,
> Something for the modern stage,
> Not, at any rate, an Attic grace; . . .
>     Ezra Pound, *Hugh Selwyn Mauberley*
>       (*Life and Contacts*)

> There is a kind of gossamer web, woven between the real
> things, and by this means the animals communicate. For
> purposes of communication they invent a symbolic language.
> Afterwards this language, used to excess, becomes a
> disease, and we get the curious phenomena of men
> explaining themselves by means of the gossamer web
> that connects them.
>     T. E. Hulme, 'Cinders',
>       *Speculations*

> Clouds lift their small mountains
>     Before the elder hills.
>                 Ezra Pound, *Canto LXXXIII*

# Index of Poems

◆

* = Poem quoted in part.

# Preface

———◆———

The opening years of the twentieth century initiated an exciting period for the arts in Europe. In every aspect of art and its ideologies there was ferment, much of it on an unprecedented scale. If this 'modernism' sometimes looks frenetic in retrospect, the vigour and enthusiasm that marked it can still be enjoyed, as can the talent that, in many countries and various of the arts, went into its effective manifestations. It was an epoch of doctrines and movements. Theories and manifestoes flourished, sometimes in advance of the work they proclaimed, sometimes in retrospect or as justification. The new art was everywhere a celebration of urban man. It came out of the great European centres, Paris, Vienna, Berlin, St Petersburg, Moscow—and even London.

England, seemingly at the height of its Imperial opulence, had begun to lag in ideas and artistic impetus, just as it was beginning to trail Germany and America in industrial matters. In artistic impulse the U.S.A., the great English-speaking power outside Europe, was even more backward at that moment. 'A half-savage country, out of date,' was how Ezra Pound was to judge his homeland at this time. Given this cultural lag, the strenuous modernism of the Continent was not easily acclimatized in Britain and America. In painting these countries were notably in arrears. English advanced taste as represented by Bloomsbury had limped as far as late Impressionism at a time when the triple ferocities of Futurism, Expressionism and Cubism were being unleashed in Europe. In music the story would have been similar but for the emergence of a unique folk-art deriving from the American negro. It had begun as ragtime and continued as jazz.

Even in poetry, the one medium in which the English imagination had continued to work relatively unfettered by the dullness and middle-class posturings of Anglo-Saxon culture, there seemed little prospect of change. The French Symbolists had created a new method, as some British and American writers had not been slow to recognize. But the creative dimension of the Anglo-Saxon response had been slight.

In these conditions it is hardly surprising that modernism came tentatively and partially to writers in English. The one literary movement in Britain and America that reflected the energies of modernism was the short-lived series of groupings that came to be known as Imagism.

# I

## The Dead Art

Critics are still undecided about the value of Imagism. About the nature of the situation which provoked it there is less disagreement. Poetry in English in the early years of the twentieth century remained seriously dislocated from living speech. Too often the form was mechanical; diction archaic; content varied between clichés and the journalistic immediacy of such writers as William Watson and Henry Newbolt. Compared with prose fiction English poetry was a dying art. Byron was almost the last man who wrote poetry as speech (with the possible and very different exception of the Brownings). Wordsworth's claim to do so is not confirmed by his work. A powerful exception was Burns in his dialect poems but, even more than D. H. Lawrence, he had reverted to literary idiom when composing in standard English. The vernacular is rediscovered in Wilde's 'Ballad of Reading Gaol':

> He does not die a death of shame
>   On a day of dark disgrace,
> Nor have a noose about his neck,
>   Nor a cloth upon his face,
> Nor drop feet foremost through the floor
>   Into an empty space.
>
> . . . . . . . .
>
> He does not sit with silent men
>   Who watch him night and day;
> Who watch him when he tries to weep,
>   And when he tries to pray;
> Who watch him lest himself should rob
>   The prison of its prey.
>
> He does not wake at dawn to see
>   Dread figures throng the room,
> The shivering Chaplain robed in white,
>   The Sheriff stern with gloom,

1

And the Governor all in shiny black,
   With the yellow face of Doom.

He does not rise in piteous haste
   To put on convict-clothes,
While some coarse-mouthed Doctor gloats, and notes
   Each new and nerve-twitched pose,
Fingering a watch whose little ticks
   Are like horrible hammer-blows.

He does not know that sickening thirst
   That sands one's throat, before
The hangman with his gardener's gloves
   Slips through the padded door,
And binds one with three leathern thongs,
   That the throat may thirst no more.

He does not bend his head to hear
   The Burial Office read,
Nor, while the terror of his soul
   Tells him he is not dead,
Cross his own coffin, as he moves
   Into the hideous shed.

But, lacking his particular experience of suffering, other poets of the day continued on the roundabout of artificial idiom. Hardy, though elderly, was not yet fully valued as a poet; the Edwardian age was primarily a prose age. At first glance the decline of poetry in England seems involved with the failure of the Decadence of the nineties and the early deaths of the writers in that movement (Dowson, Lionel Johnson, Francis Thompson and Beardsley himself). This, however, is not the whole story. Decadence was a self-defeating attitude in a society which allowed little scope for Bohemian divagations (or at least for their public manifestation). 'The atmosphere of London is not the atmosphere of movements or of societies,' wrote Arthur Symons in his memorial notice of Ernest Dowson.[1] The attitudes of the nineties, or at least of the poets who gathered in the Rhymers' Club and who found an occasional market in *The Yellow Book* and *The Savoy*, were to a large extent an attempt to transplant Parisian modes of behaviour into English ground. This failed, not least because European café-life had little place in London. In the lives of the writers most typical of the period, it is not hard to see a theme of defeat that could only have been changed by a more favourable environment. The trial and conviction of Oscar Wilde in 1895 and the failure of *The Savoy* in 1896 mark the virtual extinction of Decadence in England both as movement and doctrine. The Decadent writers continued a few years longer; still young but already mostly shadows of themselves. Yeats, who had never been more than a part-time Decadent, survived the downfall of his friends.

In terms of personality, the nineties (as Yeats understood) represent a tragic episode in cultural history. In terms of art and technique the Decadents' achievement was minor; yet the better poets of the nineties, small writers though they were, worked with great care and respect for their medium. But Johnson's Latin severity and decorum, Symons's impressionism, Dowson's recourse to Verlaine could not save them from remaining largely overshadowed by the tradition of Tennyson and the Pre-Raphaelites. They took the lyrical forms of their predecessors, refined them and distilled from them something of their own. In a sense, Dowson and Symons did in poetry what the eclectic Beardsley did in black and white illustration, but they lacked his demonic energy. (Beardsley's contempt, although in most ways unjustified, for Symons suggests that he was well aware of this difference.) 'At Dieppe' is characteristic.

> The grey-green stretch of sandy grass,
> Indefinitely desolate;
> A sea of lead, a sky of slate;
> Already autumn in the air, alas!
>
> One stark monotony of stone,
> The long hotel, acutely white,
> Against the after-sunset light
> Withers grey-green, and takes the grass's tone.
>
> Listless and endless it outlies,
> And means, to you and me, no more
> Than any pebble on the shore,
> Or this indifferent moment as it dies.

Ford Madox Hueffer (later Ford Madox Ford), who was virtually of their generation (he was six years younger than Dowson, a year junior to Beardsley), summarized these writers in phrases that are still worth quoting:

> ... the slouch-hatted, bearded, inverness-caped, mouthing—but extremely slovenly-writing—poets of the '40's to '90's of the last century had so exceedingly bored whilst they browbeat the Public, that the Public had practically finished with Poetry by the time of the men of

the 'nineties. The men of the 'nineties wrote infinitely better ...
infinitely! ... the Dowsons, Johnsons, Thompsons, Davidsons, and
the rest. Only—*par pur snobisme!*—they found it necessary to indulge
in, to promote, vices and bad habits of the cigarette, Soho-absinthe
type. They revelled professionally in squalor .... And it rendered them
infinitely provincial—to Soho.[2]

Here, as often with Hueffer's judgments and memories, there is a flavour
of picturesque exaggeration. But the underlying force of his criticism is
sound. On the technique of poetry in the nineties he had this to add:

I had to make for myself the discovery that verse must be at least as
well written as prose if it is to be poetry .... The Victorians killed the
verse side of poetry .... The men of the 'nineties had 'sensed this out.'
They wrote. On the whole their sentences, when they wrote in verse,
were as well constructed as prose sentences. They aimed at a nervous
style and a compact form; they tried to distil picturesqueness from the
life that was around them.[3]

Hueffer's dismissal of the poets of the high Victorian period is too sweep-
ing to have value. He calls the Victorian poets slovenly, but it could
equally be argued that form, as the nineteenth century proceeded, became
a mania. This mania, with whatever differences of emphasis, reached its
zenith with Swinburne and his younger contemporary, Hopkins. The
lesser poets of the eighteen-seventies and eighties revived various traditional French forms such as the *rondeau*, the *triolet* and the *ballade*.[4]
The concern with form, whether in art or behaviour, was of dominant
importance for the Decadent group. They often brought their work and
their lives to a point at which only form could retain any significance.

In his feeling that Victorian poetry had exhausted itself Hueffer was on
surer terrain. Uncomplimentary references to the poets and poetry of
the age are frequent in Hopkins' correspondence. William Morris
complained:

Poetry goes with the hand-arts, I think, and like them has now become
unreal; the arts have got to die before they can be born again.[5]

By the beginning of the twentieth century many people would have agreed.
The high Victorian tradition had worn itself out; the Decadent movement subsided in suicidal failure. One writer from the nineties who
survived, solitary and gifted, with an increasing readership was A. E.
Housman. His popularity did not make him a model for other poets:

4

Far in a western brookland
That bred me long ago
The poplars stand and tremble
By pools I used to know.

There, in the windless night-time,
The wanderer, marvelling why,
Halts on the bridge to hearken
How soft the poplars sigh.

He hears: long silence since forgotten
In fields where I was known,
Here I lie down in London
And turn to rest alone.

There, by the starlit fences,
The wanderer halts and hears
My soul that lingers sighing
About the glimmering weirs.

The major Victorian poets were rejected by the young. 'For us in 1902 Tennyson was out-of-date, and we therefore underestimated his poetry ...'[6] wrote Leonard Woolf of his own generation who were then arriving in London fresh from Cambridge or Oxford. The better poets among the younger writers of the nineties were inactive or dead. Beardsley died of consumption in 1898; Dowson of the same disease complicated by poverty and alcohol in 1900; Lionel Johnson from a fractured skull after falling off a bar stool in 1902; Thompson, also of consumption (he had been cured of his opium addiction) in 1907; Davidson, the last of them, drowned himself in the English Channel in 1909. Arthur Symons had lost much of his momentum as a poet after the publication of his collected *Poems* in 1901. In 1908 he suffered a mental breakdown while in Italy and was out of action for two years. He finally recovered his sanity, but never his creative ability. Although Yeats was reaching a new level of achievement, he was, according to Pound a decade later,

already a sort of great dim figure with its associations set in the past.[7]

As an assessment, Pound's remark has little merit. As an indication of his state of mind and of how the younger writers of the period felt about Yeats, it is highly pertinent. The Edwardian epoch was the period of Yeats's maximum involvement with the theatre in Ireland. Much of his

5

imaginative energy was absorbed by the Dublin Abbey Theatre. His preoccupations now drew him further from London and his English contemporaries than at any previous time in his career. The pronounced national flavour of so much of his work no doubt weakened his influence on English writers. Hueffer, while praising Yeats in 1913, admitted that for the previous 'ten or twenty years' he had regarded him as a 'merely "literary" poet; an annoying dilettante'.[8] This opinion reflects more unfavourably on Hueffer's taste than on Yeats's work, but it is significant as a contemporary assessment.

Of course, Wilfred Blunt, Robert Bridges, C. M. Doughty and Thomas Hardy were still writing. Though they were already in their sixties, some of their best work was being done at that time. But their age and aloofness, coupled with the idiosyncrasies of their language (particularly that of Doughty and Hardy) prevented any of them from being widely appreciated. Even so correct a poet as Bridges had few followers. He remained relatively little known until his appointment as Poet Laureate in 1913. Bridges, however, appealed to a certain quasi-academic taste:

... the *Shorter Poems* of Mr. Bridges gave him at once a place among our poets which is second only, among the living, to that of Mr. Swinburne.[9]

This was the opinion of John C. Bailey of the *Times Literary Supplement*, a fairly influential literary journalist and scholar of the period.

In such a literary climate, the poets who flourished tended to have certain predictable qualities. Patriotism and moral orthodoxy were virtues that gained approval. Poets who wanted any sort of attention seem to have resigned themselves to writing for a bourgeois audience. There are many examples of such writers, notably Kipling, Newbolt and William Watson—all of them contemporaries of the Decadents. Kipling was a writer of exceptional talents, greater perhaps in prose than in poetry, but still among the more considerable poets of his epoch. The rest were not in the same class. Newbolt was a subtle and intelligent critic, who wrote one of the most acute early studies of Futurism to appear in English.[10] Watson had the courage to oppose the Boer War, though his work was indifferent. If these men, particularly Watson and Newbolt, are to be faulted, it is not for their nationalism or their imperial sentiments (attitudes now dead that seem no more ridiculous than the left-wing politics of some of the English poets of the nineteen-thirties) but rather for their insufficiencies of technique, their often mechanical attitude to poetic form, the inadequacy of their language. Many of what are now their less intelligible postures were the guarantees of popularity in their own era. This may reflect a coarsening in the tastes of the bourgeoisie, or at least in the poetry-reading sections of it, compared with the early Victorian period when Tennyson's *In Memoriam* had been a popular success. On the other hand, the early Victorians, in spite of their admiration for Tennyson, had helped to make bestsellers of Bailey's *Festus* and Tupper's *Proverbial Philosophy*, both the work of laughably bad writers. Matthew Arnold's poems did not sell. Browning remained a commercial failure throughout most of his life. Swinburne was consistently successful, but for reasons that may have been in part outside literature, such as his supposed daringness and the fact that he offered an age of severe repression the illusion of the erotic.

If a deterioration of public taste did exist, it is indicated by the readiness with which these Edwardian writers offered pre-fabricated attitudes and adopted ready-made techniques, and by the respect their productions gained among the critics of the period. In terms of technique Kipling and Watson were a long way apart. Watson was a belated Miltonic, perhaps the last English poet so far to attempt a bad style in the grand manner. Some of Kipling's most effective poems are his ballads and soldier-verses ('Danny Deever' is a superb example). In these verse-narratives of the army Kipling manipulates a pseudo-Cockney idiom with extraordinary versatility. When he adopts a more serious literary persona he becomes more conventional. Poems such as 'Recessional' or 'Cities and Thrones and Powers' have undeniable quality, but their diction has a disproportionate weight of archaisms:

> So Time that is o'er-kind
>    To all that be,
> Ordains us e'en as blind,
>    As bold as she:
> That in our very death,
>    And burial sure,
> Shadow to shadow, well persuaded, saith,
>    'See how our works endure!'

The poem (written in 1905) is effective in spite, rather than because of, various of its locutions. Kipling's control of form is, as always, skilful and assured. But nothing in its language or technique would have seemed surprising to Wordsworth or Tennyson.

This poem was much admired by Rupert Brooke, a representative figure of the generation that followed. Kipling had been contemporary with the nineties writers, Brooke was a contemporary of the Imagists, and became identified with the Georgian movement that appeared around the same time as Imagism. The organ of this new movement was the anthology *Georgian Poetry*, edited by Edward Marsh, at that time private secretary to Winston Churchill. The title *Georgian Poetry* is of questionable accuracy, as the poets who appeared in Marsh's first anthology for the years 1911 and 1912 were Edwardians. Fourteen of the seventeen writers included already had published collections during the reign of Edward VII. Several had produced their first books of verse in the last years of the previous century. Georgian poetry existed *avant la lettre*, before the conscious formulation of Georgianism.

Among the contributors to Marsh's five anthologies were D. H. Lawrence, Isaac Rosenberg, Robert Graves, Siegfried Sassoon, John Masefield, Walter de la Mare, Ralph Hodgson, W. H. Davies and, of course, Rupert Brooke—who was a much better writer in his ironic metaphysical vein than when he later attempted the grand manner in his war sonnets:

*Sonnet (suggested by some of the Proceedings of the Society for Physical Research).*

> Not with vain tears, when we're beyond the sun,
>      We'll beat on the substantial doors, nor tread
>      Those dusty high-roads of the aimless dead
> Plaintive for earth; but rather turn and run
> Down some close-covered by-way of the air,
>      Some low sweet alley between wind and wind,
>      Stoop under faint gleams, thread the shadows, find
> Some whispering ghost-forgotten nook, and there
>
> Spend in pure converse our eternal day;
>      Think each in each, immediately wise;
> Learn all we lacked before; hear, know, and say
>      What this tumultuous body now denies;
> And feel, who have laid our groping hands away;
>      And see, no longer blinded by our eyes.

Although Wilfred Owen admired and was admired by some of the Georgians—in 1917 he wrote to his mother 'I am held peer by the Georgians; I am a poets' poet'—he did not figure in *Georgian Poetry*.[11] Neither did Edward Thomas. Many of the poems printed by Marsh now seem trivial or faded, and so strong is the blurring effect of more than half a century that it is difficult to understand why the Georgians were at first regarded as dangerous, even radical, innovators. They saw themselves in terms of a significant reaction against Victorianism. To the Imagist writers the whole development appeared petty:

The Georgians were regional in their outlook and in love with littleness.

They took a little trip for a little week-end to a little cottage where they wrote a little poem on a little theme.[12]

The Georgians tried to remain within one aspect of the English tradition, its Romantic-Victorian line, by adhering to received form while attempting a renewal of diction. The best of them were good poets; few of them lacked a measure of talent. But the prevailing tone of Marsh's anthologies suggests a failure to solve the problem of language in poetry. Poeticisms abound, diction veers unstably from the Miltonic to fey attempts at colloquialism, that echo the worst of Wordsworth without the redeeming fineness of his insight. The laxity of the Georgians becomes a dangerous diffuseness in their longer poems. Thinness of language is accompanied by poverty of ethos. It is as if the old rural England that Wordsworth and Arnold had celebrated, and which twentieth-century industrial and social changes were rapidly making into an archaeological phenomenon, found in these poets a last unreal celebration:

### Of Greatham

For peace, than knowledge more desirable,
    Into your Sussex quietness I came,
When summer's green and gold and azure fell
    Over the world in flame.

And peace upon your pasture-lands I found,
    Where grazing flocks drift on continually,
As little clouds that travel with no sound
    Across a windless sky.

Out of your oaks the birds call to their mates
    That brood among the pines, where hidden deep
From curious eyes a world's adventure waits
    In columned choirs of sleep.

Under the calm ascension of the night
    We heard the mellow lapsing and return
Of night-owls purring in their groundling flight
    Through lanes of darkling fern.

Unbroken peace when all the stars were drawn
    Back to their lairs of light, and ranked along
From shire to shire the downs out of the dawn
    Were risen in golden song.[13]

The world they praised and which so many of them tried to inhabit was already dying before 1914. The Georgians must be seen as a final aberration from the Victorianism which they thought they were attacking. As Bernard Shaw said, those who make half-revolutions dig their own graves. The Georgians represent an attempt to renew English poetry out of its native resources. In this they mark a reaction against the more cosmopolitan interests of the nineties. Whatever their merits they suggest a dwindling of poetic horizons. In place of the cultural diversity of the Decadents or the Imperial vastness of Kipling they offer a world of almost suburban cosiness. The best British poets of the period, Hardy and Yeats, remained aloof.

*       *       *

Shaped by American history, American poetry had taken a very different path. The emergence of American literature from its colonial dependence had been slow and not always comfortable. American writers had long remained in uneasy apprenticeship to English literature. National independence was attained by the U.S.A. almost half a century before its writers were able to achieve literary autonomy. America, unlike England, did not fully experience the Romantic movement. The New England poets of the nineteenth century, with the exception of Emerson, seem often to have suffered from the fustian of the Victorian age without its redeeming emotional intensity. Only two or three American poets of the early and middle nineteenth century escaped the prevalent anemia, most notably, the important figures of Edgar Allan Poe and Walt Whitman.

Ezra Pound's view was that the American Civil War was a cultural watershed, after which the quality of the national life underwent a drastic decline:

A national American culture existed from 1770 till at least 1861. Jefferson could not imagine an American going voluntarily to inhabit Europe. After the debacle of American culture individuals had to emigrate in order to conserve such fragments of American culture as had survived.

.   .   .   .   .   .   .   .   .

There is no inferiority sense in the Jefferson-Adams letters. Till at least 1850 the U.S. was respected. The American as such was not at a disadvantage.[14]

There may be overstatement in Pound's assertion of the early flowering of America's culture. There can be no dispute about the cultural decline that set in after the War between the States:

10

... by 1850 the great fortunes had been made (in the rum, slave, and milling industries), and New England became a museum. The whatnots groaned under the load of knickknacks, the fine china dogs and cats, the pieces of Oriental jade, the chips off the leaning tower of Pisa. There were the rare books and the cosmopolitan learning. It was all equally displayed as the evidence of a superior culture. The Gilded Age had already begun. But culture, in the true sense, was disappearing.[15]

There were few poets of any ability at work in the United States during the last third of the nineteenth century. Even such a conventional academic critic as F. L. Pattee saw 1866 as the 'low-water mark' of American literature.[16]

The one American poet of importance to appear between Whitman and the last decade of the nineteenth century was Emily Dickinson. Like Hopkins in Britain, to whom she has otherwise little similarity, Emily Dickinson remained almost unknown in her lifetime and for some while afterwards. She died in 1886. The first collection of her poems appeared in 1890 and had an immediate public success.[17] But the duration of this success was limited to about a decade. In the first ten years of the twentieth century the reputation of her work declined and she reverted to semi-obscurity.[18] Pattee's judgment is characteristic:

The poems are disappointing .... . Emily Dickinson has figured, often at length, in all the later histories and anthologies, but it is becoming clear that she was overrated.[19]

He concludes that Emily Dickinson's poems are 'mere conceits .... . They should have been allowed to perish as their author intended.' The confusion of this judgment is a reminder of the level of academic criticism prevailing in America at that time.

The significance of such wrong canons of taste in university circles must be emphasized. Outside the universities America had not developed an effective apparatus of culture, except at a debased popular or market level. If the universities failed there were no other agencies to correct them. Pattee's opinions become the more unfortunate when one considers the poets whom he discussed with respect.[20] In all of them there is a fatal lack of distinction and effective imaginative energy. Almost all were copyists of copyists. Only the latest of the poets mentioned by Pattee shows a different range of preoccupations and a more eclectic use of sources. This was Richard Hovey (1864-1900), a contemporary of the English Decadents of the nineties, related to them by his taste for the

11

French Symbolists, like them under the remote influence of Swinburne, but distinguished from them by a more virile energy (or at least by aspirations to a more virile style in language as in life).[21]

With Hovey, whose first significant volume *The Laurel: An Ode* appeared in 1889, we come to the American nineties. This period was in some respects a transatlantic reflection of what was occurring in London. There was a brief emergence of Decadence. Decadence in America began its public life, encouraged by the example of *The Yellow Book*, in 1894. That year saw the appearance of *The Chap Book*, which started as the work of two Harvard undergraduates and was soon transferred to Chicago, where Herbert Stone was joined as editor by the Canadian poet Bliss Carman. The example of *The Chap Book* was followed by various other reviews, most of them ephemeral. They failed, but their failure was significant. They showed the hunger for new developments in sensibility that had been concealed behind America's provincial facade; and their origin in a number of centres was a reminder of the regionalism that, properly handled and understood, could become a major strength in America's cultural evolution.[22] Apart from *The Chap Book* two of these reviews were of some importance: *The Bibelot*, which first appeared edited by Thomas B. Mosher at Portland, Maine in January 1895 and *M'lle New-York*, edited by the critic Vance Thompson, which appeared in August 1895. *M'lle New-York* introduced the work of the French Symbolists to the American literary public. It marked the beginning of the involvement with French literature that has affected so many twentieth-century American poets. Mosher, though he later refused to publish Pound's first collection *A Lume Spento*,[23] played a valuable role in re-issuing for the American market the work of English writers of the Decadent movement.

Although Decadence in America was short-lived, it was important in several ways. For the first time American writers had responded by imitative participation to a development currently occurring in Europe. For the first time conscious resort was made to French literary models. The agencies of this process were reviews of a kind that can properly be regarded as 'little' magazines. In actual poetic achievement the American Decadence was disappointingly slight. It was more fertile in criticism and in its response to foreign literary sources. By the turn of the century Decadence in America was exhausted. Most of the reviews launched in the nineties did not outlive their decade. Small magazines that attempted to follow them in the first years of the twentieth century had an even shorter existence. A reaction against Decadence had set in, a reaction intensified both in England and America by conventional moralistic disapproval. The critical interests of the nineties were largely enveloped in a smog of puritanism, consequently the knowledge of French literature communicated by such critics as Vance Thompson and James G. Huneker had to be rediscovered by the writers of the generation that followed. Almost the only American poet of any merit who continued to work under French influence in the early years of the century was Stuart Merrill, who, however, lived in France and wrote mostly in French. Merrill's most interesting work in English is his translation of Judith Gautier's imitations of Chinese poetry in her *Le Livre de Jade*. His versions, published as *Pastels in Prose* (New York, 1890), may have had some share in the formation of the taste of the American Decadents, but Kenneth Rexroth's claim that 'All the Imagists were familiar with Judith Gautier's *Livre du Jade* . . . ' seems hardly tenable.[24]

Edwin Arlington Robinson and Stephen Crane, the only poets of any significance who appeared in America in the nineties, were never involved with the Aesthetic coteries. Robinson published his first two volumes in the nineties. His second book, *The Children of the Night* (1897), includes the well-known 'Richard Cory':

> Whenever Richard Cory went down town,
> We people on the pavement looked at him:
> He was a gentleman from sole to crown,
> Clean favored, and imperially slim.
>
> And he was always quietly arrayed,
> And he was always human when he talked;
> But still he fluttered pulses when he said,
> 'Good-morning', and he glittered when he walked.
>
> And he was rich—yes, richer than a King—
> And admirably schooled in every grace:
> In fine, we thought that he was everything
> To make us wish that we were in his place.
>
> So on we worked, and waited for the light,
> And went without the meat, and cursed the bread;
> And Richard Cory, one calm summer night,
> Went home and put a bullet through his head.

This fine poem shows one American poet, at least, had already been able to free himself from derivative literary clutter. Robinson's reputation was slow to grow; he was ignored by the Imagist writers a decade and a half later. Although his methods and technique were very different from theirs, his work was by no means less effective.

Stephen Crane, who died young in 1900, published two books of verse in his lifetime, *The Black Riders and Other Lines* (Boston, Mass., 1895) and *War is Kind* (New York, 1899). In recent years he has attracted attention as a poet; his contemporaries seemed interested only in his prose. The critical claims made for him as a poet seem exaggerated. It is difficult to agree with the opinion that his poetic work 'must stand at the beginning (although in a rather unformulated relation) of any discussion of modern American poetry'.[25]

Crane, as his biographer John Berryman has remarked, was a 'primitive' in poetry, 'deeply uninterested in manner'.[26] His poems lack a personal rhythm; they are fables in manner and content; Crane's treatment of his material is aphoristic:

> The wayfarer,
> Perceiving the pathway to truth,
> Was struck with astonishment.
> It was thickly grown with weeds.
> 'Ha', he said,
> 'I see that none has passed here
> In a long time.'
> Later he saw that each weed
> Was a singular knife.
> 'Well,' he mumbled at last,
> 'Doubtless there are other roads.'

The recent criticism that has praised Crane's poetry seems to have missed the point that this, like all Crane's poems, is the work of a prose sensibility using prose techniques. Crane represents an interesting breach with nineteenth-century literary decorum. As a poet he had little to contribute to the impending new developments. Ford Madox Hueffer, who was among Crane's friends, was a warm admirer of *The Red Badge of Courage*, but he seems to have shown no interest in his poems.

In America, as in England, bad taste in poetry was at a premium at the beginning of the new century. There was not merely a dearth of good poets but the few who were writing found no ready market. The bad taste of the Edwardian period found different local forms of expression between England and America, but this was little better than a choice in rotten apples. American popular middlebrow taste was pseudo-*völkisch* where British taste was imperial, but the qualitative differences were less remarkable than the local variations in tone:

> Go among all kinds of people and love 'em whether you want to or not. Get rightly acquainted and the boor's even a gentleman. God gets along with him, it seems. He listens.[27]

14

This reads like an excerpt from a sales promotion handout. In fact it was written with serious intention by James Whitcomb Riley, who was probably the most popular American poet in the eighteen-nineties. Riley was a skilful writer with a particular aptitude for handling a literary stylization of his native Indiana dialect. But the falsity of his suggested programme is unpleasant. Rudyard Kipling, a much more powerful writer than Riley, showed a far greater objectivity in his attitude to his work. He lived and worked in North America during the nineties, and had it not been for his unshakeable involvement with Britain and her Imperial Destiny his writing might easily have seemed what was called 'American' in its relentless concern with toughness and efficiency.

Two American poets of real promise who died young were William Vaughn Moody and Trumbull Stickney. Neither of them succeeds fully as a poet. There are brilliant flashes of neo-romantic imagery in Stickney, but none, even of his shorter poems, sustains itself to the end. Moody shows a more interesting talent. Among the débris of his more ambitious poems, with their belated and inconsistent use of a nineteenth-century Miltonic diction, can be found a few attempts at a relaxed and idiomatic language such as Edwin Arlington Robinson had already begun to restore into English. Both Trumbull Stickney and Moody died too early to show what they might have done. What survives of their work is outdated and was, indeed, obsolete even in its moment of composition.

A few years later, parallels with the Georgians can be found among some American poets of the years immediately before 1914, but these writers (some of them litter the early files of *Poetry* [Chicago]), unlike the Georgians in England, have found no place in the history of twentieth-century American poetry. John Masefield and Rupert Brooke gained many admirers in the United States. Masefield's *The Everlasting Mercy* (first published in 1911) was popular in America as well as in Britain. The only poet of importance to have strong affinities with the Georgians was Robert Frost. His friendship with Edward Thomas had possibly a decisive effect in encouraging the English writer to turn to poetry in 1914. Frost, like Thomas, found his way to poetry rather late in life. Both of them were some years older than the majority of the writers with whom they were associated. The poets who began to appear in America in and after 1912 showed far more radical approaches to technique than Frost. These were the years of the early poems of Carl Sandburg, T. S. Eliot (who, although unpublished until 1915, had written some of his most characteristic poems as early as 1911), Hilda Doolittle and Ezra Pound (1912 was the year in which Pound wrote his first modernized poems). This is the period that American critics often like to call the American Renaissance. The phrase is inapposite, but it is a reminder of the energy

15

suddenly and unexpectedly released into literature in America. It is from this period that modern American poetry can properly be said to begin.

\* \* \*

To separate taste from fashion is always difficult. When the dramatic critic William Archer, friend of Shaw and translator of Ibsen, Hauptmann and Maeterlinck, compiled his influential anthology *Poets of the Younger Generation* (London and New York, 1902) he included a good selection of American and Canadian writers. The British poets to whom he gave most attention, apart from Kipling and Yeats, were John Davidson, Henry Newbolt, Stephen Phillips and William Watson. By 1903 G. K. Chesterton already regarded Watson as obsolete. In less than a decade the Georgians were to consider him a boring survival.[28]

The failure of the Decadence, followed by the gradual rejection of the tradition represented by William Watson, should have meant that the way was clear for new poets, but poetry seems to have occupied a relatively small place in Edwardian culture. The strength of the novel and the return to life of the English theatre absorbed more and more of the response of the public. The new poets who appeared both in England and America were minor figures. In England especially the rhetoricians did not yield without a struggle. (In America they were driven to take refuge in universities and high schools.) English writers had to carry a weight of the past that gave the wrangles between Georgians and their conservative detractors a significance it is now difficult to comprehend. America may have been, as Pound called it, 'half-savage'; but it had space, energy, and an increasing confidence. It was not burdened with the literary pretentiousness of London or the attitudes of Oxford and Cambridge, attitudes that W. H. Auden stigmatized more than twenty years later:

> And through the quads dogmatic words rang clear,
> 'Good poetry is classic and austere.'[29]

# II

## The Age Demanded

We ... fought in the decade spreading—roughly—over the years 1908 to 1918. We called ourselves 'Imagists'; but the name does not matter, and in any case it was adopted as a joke rather than the challenge it finally became. We had our principles and our precepts. We did not like the tumpty-tum of hurdy-gurdy verses; and we said so. We wanted free verse, which is a mistranslation of the French phrase, *vers libre*. We did not like rhyme; we thought it an intrusion into the expression of poetry. And we had a doctrine of the image, which none of us knew anything about.[1]

This ironic summary was made by the English poet F. S. Flint in a lecture he delivered in the fateful summer of 1940. Flint may not be an ideal witness; but he was the only man who went through each of the phases of Imagism from its beginnings in 1909 to the last of Amy Lowell's anthologies in 1917. The development of Imagism involved a succession of small groups. In all there were three: one fostered by T. E. Hulme in 1909; a second led by Ezra Pound from 1912 to 1914; a third organized by Amy Lowell from 1914 to 1917.

While these groups directly descended from one another, they were by no means identical in aim or operation. The 1909 meetings seem to have functioned chiefly as a study group. Pound's Imagistes of 1912 were engaged in propaganda and publication as well as dialogue. The little magazines that began to appear, particularly in America, helped them in this. The 'Amygists' who continued after 1914 were no more than a publishing consortium. Their point of focus was the annual anthology *Some Imagist Poets* of which three volumes appeared between 1915 and 1917. The members of the third group were widely dispersed geographically. If brought together it is doubtful they would have achieved even the temporary unity or comradeship of the earlier groups. Their personalities and interests were too disparate.

The first group, virtually unknown during its short lifetime, had the hardest task and the largest share of failure. It was only Pound's flair for publicity in 1912 and 1913 that finally put Imagism on the cultural map. As he later remarked:

Take our groups in London. The group of 1909 has disappeared without the world being much the wiser. Perhaps a first group can only prepare way for a group that will break thru.
The one or two determined characters will pass through 1st to 2nd or third groups.[2]

In the end Imagist history pivots on the activity of those 'one or two'.

Among the amateur cultural organizations in Edwardian London was the Poets' Club. This had been founded by Henry Simpson, a Scottish banker, who remained President from 1907 to at least 1930. Simpson, who has been described as a man of considerable personal charm, was a mediocre poet.[3] One of those marginal figures who so often infest artistic circles, an unlikely person to have much to do with any striving towards the original or the dynamic in literature. Nonetheless, the Poets' Club was valuable in the low state of poetic activity that prevailed in Edwardian London. It provided a meeting-ground for writers. Ezra Pound, then fresh to London, was introduced to it by the publisher Elkin Mathews at the Club's dinner on 23 February 1909. The Irish poet Joseph Campbell, who figures in the early history of Imagism, was also a member at that time.[4]

Among those who found their way to the Poets' Club was an ex-student of mathematics named T. E. Hulme. Hulme had been an undergraduate at St John's College, Cambridge, but was sent down at Easter 1904, after a boat-race night brawl in which he apparently hit a policeman and spent the night 'or weekend' in gaol.[5] In protest, he organized an impressive mock funeral as a farewell gesture.[6] He then entered University College, London to prepare for the Indian Civil Service examination, which he failed two years later. After that he spent some months in Canada and Belgium, returning to settle in London early in 1908. His wanderings on the Canadian prairie had awakened him to imaginative possibilities which he had previously ignored. He began to develop an interest in poetry. What are possibly his earliest writings to survive, the notes 'Language and Style', testify to this interest. The unpublished manuscript of these notes suggests that Hulme had begun thinking about language and literature during his stay in Brussels. He seems to have started to write verse during 1908,[7] and that year he joined the Poets' Club, becoming for a while its secretary, though Henry Simpson complained that he found him a 'very trying one'.[8] The assertion, still often made, that Hulme founded the Poets' Club is an error,[9] which seems to have originated with F. S. Flint. When Flint came to write a short 'History' of Imagism in 1915 he managed to forget what he must have known in 1909:

18

Somewhere in the gloom of the year 1908, Mr T. E. Hulme, ...
excited ... by the propinquity, at a half-a-crown dance, of the other
sex ... , proposed to a companion that they should found a Poets'
Club.[10]

The gloom that Flint refers to is an attribute of human memory, a
reminder of the fallibility of all history founded on personal reminiscence.

Nevertheless, whether founder of the Club or not, Hulme was still
among its members in the first weeks of 1909. Members of the Club had
published a pamphlet entitled *For Christmas MDCCCCVIII*, though it
did not in fact appear until January 1909. Among the contributors was
T. E. Hulme with two poems, 'Autumn' and 'A City Sunset', his first
published work. The pamphlet, which is now a rarity, attracted little
attention. It was reviewed with much condescension by F. S. Flint in
*The New Age*, a radical weekly edited by A. R. Orage. The opening
sentence of Flint's review establishes its tone:

> I have before me the two volumes of *Poètes d'Aujourd'hui* and two little
> plaquettes by members of the Poets' Club—almost an antithesis, but
> not quite.[11]

The other 'plaquette' consisted of the *Poems* (published by William
Blackwood in 1907) of F. W. Tancred.

Flint did well to praise *Poètes d'Aujourd'hui*, the fine anthology edited
by Adolphe Van Bever and Paul Léautaud. (It is, incidentally, a further
reminder of England's cultural backwardness that this could be reviewed
as a novelty in 1909. The original edition had been published in Paris
in 1900.) He was probably right to dismiss *For Christmas MDCCCCVIII*,
though it is odd, in view of his later admiration for Hulme, that he gave
only limited approval to 'Autumn', which he called a 'quaint conceit'.
In earlier reviews in *The New Age* Flint had been calling for a 'revaluation
of all poetical values'.[12] Yet when offered an original poem he proved unable to recognize it. Indeed, he denounced the Poets' Club as more
concerned with social niceties than art, added that it was 'death', and
said that 'almost the only poetry' in the two books under review had been
written by Lady Margaret Sackville.

This one stanza, from an ode to Aphrodite, outweighs almost the whole
of the print of the other members:–

> Wherefore the shrine that is to her most meet
> Is one bright gleaming on some dangerous shore
> Where the slow dancers on gold-sandalled feet

May feel the sea-wind sweep across the floor;
Where every cloud of the storm-laden skies
Shall cast its shadow, and the sullen rain
Enter at will, and the soft dove's low call
Be mingled with the sea-gulls' mournful cries—
Where, when the flickering altar fires are vain,
The flaming storm may light her festival.[13]

This is representative work of the period. Now, after sixty years, it is without any interest or value. However odd Flint's praise may seem, his aberrations of taste cannot be condemned as purely personal. A little later, Ezra Pound, writing to his friend William Carlos Williams, mentioned Margaret Sackville's work with equal enthusiasm:

... if you'll read Margaret Sackville, Rosamund Watson, Ernest Rhys, Jim G. Fairfax, you'll learn what the people of second rank can do, and what damn good work it is.[14]

Nonetheless, it is surprising that Flint could not recognize the originality of 'Autumn':

A touch of cold in the Autumn night
I walked abroad,
And saw the ruddy moon lean over a hedge
Like a red-faced farmer.
I did not stop to speak, but nodded;
And round about were the wistful stars
With white faces like town children.[15]

Hulme's reply to Flint was prompt and effective, appearing the following week in *The New Age*, under the title 'Belated Romanticism'.

When Mr. Flint compares the unclassed lyric assembly of the Poets' Club with that of Verlaine and his companions in obscure cafés—he laughs. I can hear that laugh: sardonic, superior, and rather young.

When, oh, when, shall we finish sentimentalizing about French poets in cafés! One hoped that with Mr. George Moore's entry into middle-age the end of it was nigh. But now comes Mr. Flint, a belated romantic born out of due time, to carry on the mythical tradition of the poetes maudits. Nurtured on Mürger, he is obsessed by the illusion that poets must be addicted to Circean excess and discoloured linen.

With all the sentimentality of an orthodox suburban, he dwells with pathetic fondness on perfectly ordinary habits, and with great awe reminds us how Verlaine hung his hat on a peg. We, like Verlaine, are natural. It was natural for a Frenchman to affect cafés. It would be dangerous as well as affected for us to recite verse in a saloon bar.

Mr. Flint speaks with fine scorn of evening dress. It is time to protest against the exclusiveness of the Bohemian, that exotic creature of rare and delicate growth. Why should we be treated as outcasts by the new aristocracy of one suit?

Historically, Mr. Flint is inaccurate. The founders of the modern 'vers libres' movement were Kahn and Laforgue, the latter a court functionary 'épris de ton londenien,' Kahn entertained at a banquet where Mallarmé (alas for the granitic Flint) in evening dress formally proposed his health.

I hereby invite Mr. Flint to come to the next dinner, on the 23rd, in any costume that suits him best, when that 'correct person'—Professor G. K. Chesterton—will lecture 'portentously.'

T. E. Hulme, M.P.C.[16]

Café Tour d'Eiffel.

The initials 'M.P.C.' appended to his signature are presumably an assertion of his continued membership of the Poets' Club. The letter is addressed from the Café Tour d'Eiffel, the restaurant that was to become the meeting-place of the first Imagist group. As Flint had sourly noted, the Poets' Club met in South Audley Street, which was socially and geographically quite a distance from the fringes of Soho. Even on this point of location the factual record is unclear. Flint referred confidently to meetings in 'suave South Audley Street',[17] but reports in *The Times* in 1908 and 1909 all refer to dinners of the Club as taking place in the United Arts Club in St James's Street.[18]

It is not known whether Flint went to the dinner to which Hulme had invited him. Certainly, in some way, he took up Hulme's challenge and the two men met; within a month Hulme was writing to Flint as follows:

Dear Mr. Flint,
    Can you come to the Tour Eiffel Thursday at 7.30. Only poets this time, Ernest Radford, Rhys, Seosamh MacCathmoil, the man Storer, whose poems you reviewed in the new Age and 4 or 5 other 'versers.'[19]

This letter is undated but postmarked 24 March 1909. This confirms

Flint's 'History' which states that the first meeting of the group took place at the Tour d'Eiffel on 25 March. According to Flint those present, apart from himself and Hulme, were Edward Storer, F. W. Tancred, Joseph Campbell, Florence Farr and 'one or two other men, mere vaguements to my memory . . . .'[20] While the two lists do not tally, they agree about four of the participants, Hulme, Flint, Edward Storer, and Joseph Campbell. These four were the central figures of the Tour d'Eiffel meetings.

The Café Tour d'Eiffel was at No. 1 Percy Street, a side-street joining Charlotte Street to the Tottenham Court Road at the north end of Soho. The Tour d'Eiffel was a well-known artists' rendezvous. In 1909 it was cheap. Later, it was decorated with murals by Wyndham Lewis and became semi-fashionable. It was advertised in Wyndham Lewis's shortlived review *The Tyro* in 1922. By then it had mutated into the Hôtel-Restaurant de la Tour Eiffel, 'the only Vorticist saloon in London, painted by Mr. Wyndham Lewis, and Vorticist ante-room by Mr. William Roberts.'[21] Wyndham Lewis's murals have disappeared, but the Tour d'Eiffel still survives, under its changed name of the White Tower, as one of the more luxurious Greek restaurants in London. When Hulme settled on it it was cheap and tolerant, a suitable meeting-ground for young and impecunious writers. Perhaps Hulme, who was a brilliant and confident talker, had already set up his *Stammtisch* there before the formation of his group. Only a few weeks earlier he had been the defender of the Poets' Club. Now, like many defenders of faiths, he changed position. In a letter written in the autumn of 1909 he refers to the publication of work by members of his 'little secession'. Hulme's use of the term has overtones. It offers at least a side-glance at the *Sezession* painters in Germany, a group who anticipated the Expressionists. More than most Englishmen of his generation, Hulme showed awareness of contemporary artistic developments on the Continent. What provoked his defection can only be guessed. No doubt he found the Poets' Club too tepid and too genteel. Simpson's complaint about him might suggest that Hulme, in his turn, found Simpson not altogether agreeable as a colleague. Hulme was by temperament a leader. It was not in his nature to be subordinate. The gatherings at the Poets' Club were presumably as tedious as such affairs usually are. It is unlikely that they allowed Hulme much opportunity to govern conversation. Nor would the Poets' Club have given him opportunity to discuss the literary doctrines he was acquiring from the French Symbolists. Whatever the qualities of the writers who met at the Tour d'Eiffel, it is certain that several of them shared Hulme's literary tastes. For a while it might have seemed that he had found the colleagues and disciples he was looking for.

F. W. Tancred and Florence Farr may have contributed something tangible to the discussions but were not themselves primarily concerned with new developments in poetry. Ernest Rhys and Ernest Radford were survivors from the Rhymers' Club of the nineties. (Rhys, in fact, had been its co-founder with W. B. Yeats.) Finally, there were a number of writers who appeared sporadically, among them Ezra Pound, Desmond Fitzgerald, and possibly Padraic Colum, but there is no evidence that any of them went very assiduously to the Tour d'Eiffel.

The appearance of Rhys or Radford at Hulme's table would have been a pleasant gesture of continuity. However, it is unlikely that either could have had anything effective to say to any group of younger writers, particularly to a group concerned with the break-up of the formal properties of metre and diction in which the poems of these older men were embalmed. Rhys maintained his interest in literary colloquia and his memoirs refer to regular meetings of writers in his house at this time.[22] Ford Madox Hueffer, during his editorship of *The English Review*, introduced D. H. Lawrence there, probably in the summer or autumn of 1909. Ezra Pound also found his way to Rhys's drawing-room. But there is no evidence that discussion at Rhys's evenings ever took the more urgent tone it seems to have had for Hulme and some of his colleagues.

Francis Willoughby Tancred, though a decade older than Hulme or Flint, was of a younger generation than Rhys or Radford. In his life as in his work Tancred was sad and ineffectual:

> The sex enchants me, and I like to view
> Their knacks and laces, or run through
> The silks in folio, and brocades
> Unfurled to show their glistening shades:
> Not missing coats of rich effect,
> Or beauty-linked creations flecked
> With chosen lace, or tier on tier
> Of silk-veined fabrics, from Cashmere.
> But come! if you want charming frocks for June,
> For Ascot, Court fêtes, tea, and suave devoirs,
> I'll manage—but the pearls had best wait over
> Till land improves, and things all round recover.[23]

Flint observed that Tancred spent 'hours each day in search for the right phrase.'[24] He could perhaps have added that Tancred usually failed to find it. Tancred's main function in the group seems to have been that of loyal friend and disciple to Hulme, and Hulme thought well enough of Tancred as a critic to quote his opinion in a letter to Flint.

If you think what I've sent is rot, the (enclosed poems I mean, just say so. Tancred says one is. So should like confirmation.)

This letter, which is undated but was probably written in the autumn of 1909, suggests that Hulme took both Tancred's and Flint's advice in the selection of his poems for *The Book of the Poets' Club*. It is a reminder that the living element of a relationship between writers can never be adequately inferred from their work alone. So much of a group relationship must consist in conversation and the interplay of minds and ideas. Where no record of those conversations remains only stray inferences are possible. Tancred's papers are not available. What remained of them was burned as rubbish by his relatives after his sister's death in 1965. Without the letter quoted above, surprisingly humble in its tone, something of Hulme would have been lost to us and Tancred would have seemed a more negligible figure than it appears he was at that time to his intimates.

Florence Farr was now in her late forties, and had had a career of some distinction in the theatre. By profession an actress, the friend of Shaw and Yeats, she was by avocation a mystic and a writer. The hermetic groups of which she was a member in the nineties had had an important role in the development of Yeats's interest in magic. Later she became a Buddhist and died in Ceylon in 1917. Her short novel *The Dancing Faun*, published in 1894 with title-page and cover design by Aubrey Beardsley, is still worth reading. Something of her interests can be guessed from the range of references in *A Calendar of Philosophy*, which she compiled and edited in 1910, with its quotations and epigraphs from Bergson, Nietzsche, Rémy de Gourmont, Laforgue, Lao-Tzu and such British writers as Yeats and Arthur Symons. A later novel, *The Solemnization of Jacklin* (1912), has references to Rimbaud and de Gourmont, while at one point the central character Dorus remarks:

Sometimes I think that the bridges of sound, the little intermediate slurs one hears so much more in speech than in song, are what gives Tragedy its quality.[25]

This remark gives a clue to what Florence Farr may have contributed to the discussions at the Tour d'Eiffel. She was interested, unusually so for the period, in the nuances of the spoken language, and she gave stage performances and recitals of verse, accompanying herself on a kind of lyre called a psaltery, made for her by Arnold Dolmetsch. Dolmetsch later became a friend of Ezra Pound, who wrote several appreciations of the German musician's work.[26]

Florence Farr's interest in the auditory properties of language links her with Yeats and Pound, both of whom conceived poetry as a predominantly spoken art. Hulme on the other hand, as his posthumously published 'Lecture on Modern Poetry' confirms, distinguished rather arbitrarily between verse to be spoken and that to be read in the study. This, of

24

course, was part of Hulme's campaign against the exhausted regular metres of his contemporaries.

> Starting then from this standpoint of extreme modernism ... verse at the present time ... is read and not chanted. We may set aside all theories that we read verse internally as mere verbal quibbles. We have thus two distinct arts. The one intended to be chanted, and the other intended to be read in the study .... I am not speaking of the whole of poetry, but of this distinct new art which is gradually separating itself from the older one and becoming independent.[27]

Hulme's argument is typically forceful and dogmatic. Part of its over-emphasis may be ascribed to a reaction against the large place that recitation, often of a very banal sort, held in the middle-class culture of the period. However, Florence Farr's interest in the possibilities of the spoken word led in a more fruitful direction. Only by recognizing language as speech could the rhythms of poetry be renewed. Florence Farr was not herself a good poet. Her poems, few in number, were competent exercises without much intrinsic interest.[28] The value of her contribution was that of an executant. She extended her interest in the rhythms of language to prose as well as verse. (There are arrangements of prose maxims by that very unpoetic writer Bernard Shaw for her particular kind of chanted delivery in her pamphlet *The Music of Speech* [London, 1909].) Of course, against the respect she earned from Yeats and Pound there is the more sceptical view of her 'ping-wanging' offered by D. H. Lawrence,[29] but Lawrence was something of a professional demolisher of his friends and acquaintances. What Florence Farr's work meant to those who listened to her in 1909 is better gauged from Flint's tribute more than thirty years later:

> I have never yet heard verse read in any way pleasing to me except perhaps Miss Florence Farr's speaking to Psaltery of W. B. Yeats's verse.[30]

Of the writers who formed the core of this first Imagist group T. E. Hulme has received most attention. In both life and work Hulme had the elusive but essential quality of personality. His range of preoccupations —poetry, art criticism, politics and aesthetics—was broader than that of his colleagues. The interests of the other members of the group were more narrowly limited to literature. Nonetheless, each of them had done creative or critical work of some originality before they came to the meetings at the Tour d'Eiffel. Campbell (as an Irish nationalist he preferred the Gaelic form Seosamh MacCathmhaoil) had begun to publish his poems in 1904.[31] By 1906 he had already experimented with free verse. An indifferent poem in free verse 'O Beautiful Dark Woman' is included in his collection *The Rushlight* published at Dublin in that year.[32] W. B. Yeats had already praised this collection in qualified terms:

... The *Rushlight* man knows better than the others what a poem is, though not a very interesting sort of poem, but he has not written it yet.[33]

Several of the poems in a more ambitious volume, *The Mountainy Singer*, are also in free verse:

### Darkness

Darkness
I stop to watch a star shine in the boghole—
A star no longer, but a silver ribbon of light.
I look at it, and pass on.[34]

The independence of Campbell's work is worthy of notice. It is almost certain that 'Darkness' was written before the meetings at the Tour d'Eiffel. Hulme's group did not meet before the last days of March 1909. *The Mountainy Singer* was published in July. While Hulme and Campbell had both been members of the Poets' Club, the tone of Hulme's letters in the summer of 1909 suggests that his closer acquaintance with Campbell came only through the new group. His attitude to Campbell, at first friendly, became increasingly irritable as the summer went on. In one letter he complained that Campbell was imitative of him and added: 'He imitates everything.' This included even Hulme's boots.[35]

Unlike Hulme, Flint and Storer, Campbell was largely indifferent to French literature. The diction of his poems is far less cluttered with, literary detritus—clichés or archaisms—than those of his colleagues with the exception of Hulme. Their sometimes rather limited registration in terms of visual perception brings them surprisingly close to one aspect of Imagist doctrine.

Edward Storer was both a poet and a critic. In retrospect his criticism seems more valuable than his verse. His only premeditated statement on poetry is the 'Essay' which he appended to *Mirrors of Illusion*. This embodies the first coherent argument for free verse produced by any writer in English. Storer's argument has flaws, it is often tentative and fumbling, but it is a serious attempt at metacritical statement. In the nineties, a more important critic than Storer, Arthur Symons, had found free verse almost incomprehensible.[36] Here, for the first time, in English the arguments for the existence of free verse were put on a rational basis.

The value of Storer's 'Essay' has been sadly overlooked. The meagreness of his poetic achievement no doubt tended to obscure his abilities as a critic, particularly in Britain. He was a self-effacing, almost a defeated man, who had little contact with the pioneer developments in literary modernism after 1909. He was not helped by his prose style, which is careful, thoughtful and honest, but without any charm or excitement. Storer was a rather unusual phenomenon among writers; a thinker with little gift of style. His labyrinthine formulary prose may owe something to his profession. (He was a solicitor, though he gave up legal practice after 1908.) Unfortunately in the 'Essay' he lists and praises good and bad poets with equal approbation. Both Verlaine and Richard Le Gallienne are quoted with no apparent discrimination. This failure of taste was no doubt an integral part of Storer's failure as a poet.

*Mirrors of Illusion* was published in November 1908, and reviewed in *The New Age* by Flint during the same month.[37] Storer did not at that time know Hulme and was probably not a member of the Poets' Club. Until the meetings at the Tour d'Eiffel got under way, Hulme had not read Storer's work. One of Hulme's letters to Flint, written in the early spring of 1909, says:

> ... If you have a copy of that book of verse by 'Storer' (in loose metres) that you reviewed some time ago, would you bring it along, as I have never been able to see it anywhere.

Storer's theory of poetry is in some ways a blueprint for subsequent Imagist formulation. Its elements are impressionism and free verse (a term Storer does not use). He argues that impressionism is unavoidable, a *donnée* of literary method, but he does not regard impressionism as an end in itself. Instead he uses it as a technique by means of which a world of symbols is to be evoked. Poetry, he insists, should be brief and condensed. This presupposes a functional activity which he calls 'separatism.' By this he means:

> ...we must ... strip our poetry of all unessential and confounding branches of literary art ... .[38]

For Storer, impressionism was use of significant detail. He argues that only fragments of a literary work carry its essential meaning. He wishes to release poetry from superfluity by changes in form based on the adoption of what he calls *vers-libre*. In support of this theory he appeals to the French *vers-libristes*, while at the same time noting the provenance of free verse in the English poetic tradition. His argument is weakened by two inaccuracies: first, because he identifies English free verse with

French *vers libre*, a dangerously inexact attempt at assimilation of the poetic genius of two languages; secondly, as he over-simplifies, and reduces the concept of free verse to 'blank verse ... cut up and spaced'. These criticisms should not obscure Storer's historical importance. Before the initiation of the meetings at the Tour d'Eiffel he was advocating and practising free verse, brevity, and selective use of impressions as the means by which poems should be written.

Whether Storer had any influence on later and better-known theorists cannot be proved. What is more interesting is that some of the mature formulations of Ezra Pound (who, of course, came to know Storer and professed little respect for him) and T. S. Eliot (in the days of his close association with Pound) show no advance on the positions argued by Storer in 1908. Here is Storer's attack on the mechanical utilization of poetic forms:

> Form even stimulates thought, as Flaubert said, but form must not be allowed to domineer over thought. Form should take its shape from the vital inherent necessities of the matter, not be, as it were, a kind of rigid mould into which the poetry is to be poured, to accommodate itself as best it can. There is no absolute virtue in iambic pentameters as such ... . Indeed, rhythm and rhyme are often destructive of thought, lulling the mind into a drowsy kind of stupor, with their everlasting regular cadence and stiff, mechanical lilts.[39]

And this is Pound's credo written early in 1912:

> I believe in an 'absolute rhythm', a rhythm, that is, in poetry which corresponds exactly to the emotion or shade of emotion to be expressed ... some poems may have form as a tree has form, some as water poured into a vase ... a vast number of subjects cannot be precisely, and therefore not properly rendered in symmetrical forms.[40]

Three years later, Pound stated:

> ... Emotional force gives the image ... .
> ... Emotion is an organiser of form ... .
> The rhythm form is false unless it belongs to the particular creative emotion or energy which it purports to represent ... . There is no form of platitude which cannot be turned into iambic pentameter.[41]

Equally, T. S. Eliot's 'Reflections on *Vers Libre*,' written in 1917, seem sometimes only to echo what Storer had worked out nearly a decade earlier. Storer had written:

28

It is quite possible that a nuance of suggestion may lie in a rhyme, and the added musical effect may give the actual meaning of the words a kind of spiritual iridescence or perfume . . . some rhyming must surely be allowed?[42]

Eliot develops this argument as follows:

'Blank verse' is the only accepted rhymeless verse in English—the inevitable iambic pentameter ... . There is no campaign against rhyme. But it is possible that excessive devotion to rhyme has thickened the modern ear.

. . . .

And this liberation from rhyme might as well be a liberation *of* rhyme. Freed from its exacting task of supporting lame verse, it could be applied with greater effect where it is most needed. There are often passages in an unrhymed poem where rhyme is wanted for some special effect.[43]

Storer, as his later career shows, was a pioneer who gained little encouragement or recognition.

F. S. Flint was already ardently committed to the notion of change in poetry, though his own work was still surprisingly old-fashioned in form and attitude. He was a self-taught man of impressive learning, who became one of the most remarkable linguists of his generation in Britain. Flint had been reviewing verse for *The New Age* since the summer of 1908, and he continued as poetry reviewer for Orage's journal until September 1910. Most of his public statements about poetry were made in the capacity of a literary journalist. As a reviewer Flint was anchored to the books given him to report on, most of which were bad. Hence his more original comments could only appear in the gaps between his appraisals of individual authors. His verse of this time, the poems published in November 1909 under the title *In the Net of the Stars*, shows him held in traditions reaching back through the nineties to Keats and Baudelaire. It is formally-worked, late Romantic poetry of some slight accomplishment but of very limited interest. Flint was a mediator of ideas and information, a kind of middleman rather than an original critic, but he brought to the group the valuable qualities of intelligence, learning and discontent.

T. E. Hulme, like his colleagues, came to the Tour d'Eiffel, with work of some significance already to his credit. It is obvious from 'Autumn' that he had found his own kind of poetic maturity with surprising certainty and speed. Hulme published little literary criticism or commentary in his lifetime. There are some notes on the function of language in poetry in one of his essays in *The New Age* in 1909. He wrote a review of a French study of the Symbolist poets for the same periodical a couple of years later. These are almost the only discussions of literature that Hulme himself prepared for publication.[44] His principal statements on poetry and its language were first printed a number of years after his death. They are contained in the notes 'Language and Style', printed in part in 1925 under the title 'Notes on Language and Style', an emendation by Hulme's editor, Herbert Read. A fuller edition was compiled by Michael Roberts in 1938, as an appendix to his study of Hulme.[45] There is also the 'Lecture on Modern Poetry', first published as another appendix to Roberts's study.[46] These are the principal documents from which inferences can be made about Hulme's critical position in 1909. Hulme's interests are those of the aesthetician more than the literary critic. The 'Lecture' offers a somewhat dogmatic programme for a modernization of poetry. The ingredients of Imagism are already contained in this programme: the emphasis on free verse, the appeal to the visual, the advocacy of the image both as a way to refreshment of language and as the essential source of poetic knowledge. Its tone and interests are those of Hulme's earlier work, and from internal evidence it seems reasonable to ascribe it to the period 1908-9. (It was perhaps intended for delivery to the Poets' Club.) The 'Lecture' survives as a typescript, probably the fair copy of a manuscript now lost, and it is likely that this represents a revision of an earlier draft. It begins with an argument for impressionism not unlike that developed in Storer's 'Essay'.

> We are no longer concerned that stanzas shall be shaped and polished like gems, but rather that some vague mood shall be communicated.[47]

To communicate mood Hulme advocates the

> method of recording impressions by visual images in distinct lines . . . .
> . . . .
> Regular metre to this impressionist poetry is cramping, jangling, meaningless, and out of place.[48]

He ends his argument with the challenging statement: 'This new verse resembles sculpture rather than music . . . .'[49]

Even if this paper was not known to his colleagues there can be little doubt that its arguments represented the elements of the doctrine that Hulme proclaimed across the dinner-table. The notes 'Language and Style' record Hulme's thinking about the uses of language in poetry in somewhat more detail, and seem to belong to the earliest period of his

30

literary activity. They include comments obviously deriving from his spell as a teacher of English in Brussels in 1907.[50] In themselves the notes are confused and self-contradictory. The order imposed on them by Hulme's editors is specious and has given them a gnomic significance that is somewhat less evident in the muddle of the manuscript. Yet one theme does emerge, whether one reads the public version or the original text (now in the library of the University of Keele). Hulme was concerned to make language more physical. He had already found his key to this by the use of visual images. Storer and Flint had similar intentions but lacked Hulme's capability. Of all of them, Hulme was the only one who could effectively illustrate his poetic theories.

Other figures came and went to the Tour d'Eiffel, but little record of their attendance remains. It is known that Pound came to a meeting when the group had been established for a month. As reported by Flint, he read his 'Sestina: Altaforte' so thunderously that the waiters discreetly put screens around the poets' table.[51] However, at that time, Pound had little to offer to the discussions. His poetic interests remained predominantly Victorian-medieval for another two years, at least until the publication of *Canzoni* in 1911.[52]

Another possible participant in the meetings, the Irish poet Padraic Colum, still remained in Pound's fertile (though not always accurate) memory more than a decade later.[53] In a note about the origins of Imagism written to Flint in 1921 Pound included Colum's name with a question mark in the list of those present. Padraic Colum, like Joseph Campbell, belonged to the Irish National school. Like Campbell, he is more important among the Irish than among the English poets of his generation. Colum made a number of experiments in free verse and his interest in biblical rhythmic modes may link him with the members of Hulme's group. But his characteristic manner has little in common with that desiderated by the Imagist writers. If emotion is left implicit or, as sometimes, withheld in Imagist verse it flows with almost disconcerting ease in Colum's work:

> Mavourneen, we'll go far away
> From the net of the crooked town,
> Where they grudge us the light of the day.[54]

In later career Colum experimented with prose poems, a genre honourable in French, though seemingly never quite acclimatized in English. One of his early poems demonstrates Colum's technique in 1906 or 1907:

### The Trees

There is no glory of the sunset here.
Heavy the clouds upon the darkening hills.

And heavy, too, the wind upon the trees.
The trees sway, making moan
Continuous, like breaking seas.
O! impotent, bare things,
You give at last the very cry of earth!
I walk this darkening road in solemn mood.
Within deep Hell came Dante to a wood.
Like him I marvel at the crying trees!

Pound remembered and sometimes alluded to Colum's well-known poem
'I Shall Not Die For Thee', a translation from Gaelic:

O woman shapely as the swan
On your account I shall not die;
The men you've slain—a trivial clan
Were less than I . . . .

It would be consistent with Pound's habits of mind if his own admiration
for this poem encouraged him to assume Colum's share in the Tour
d'Eiffel meetings. Other than this, there seems no evidence for Colum's
presence there.

These, then, were the writers who gathered at the Tour d'Eiffel. It is
easier to examine their work and ideas than their meetings. The surviving
letters among Flint's papers give hints as to the pattern of the meetings,
but have little to say about what happened at them. Flint's mention of
Pound's sonorous reading of his 'Sestina: Altaforte' suggests that public
reading of poems occurred sometimes. This is unlikely to have been a
regular happening. The Tour d'Eiffel was, after all, a restaurant with a
duty to its other and perhaps more profitable customers. It appears that
the group met weekly, loosely organized with Hulme as convener,
throughout the spring and summer of 1909. In August and September
Hulme was writing to Flint from Devon. He had complied with the
conventional ritual of pre-1914 England and left London in August. His
letters of those months suggest the temporary dispersion of the group.
It is probable that of all of them only Flint was obliged by poverty to
remain anchored to the town where he earned his meagre living (unlike
his colleagues he had a wife and family to maintain). By early autumn
Hulme was in London again. In what was perhaps his last letter from the
country that year Hulme asked for Storer's new address, added that
Florence Farr was back in London, and ended by inviting Flint to tea
'at the I.L.S.' the following Saturday. The initials conceal the Irish
Literary Society, a Nationalist cultural organization, with London
premises at 20 Hanover Square, of which Joseph Campbell was the some-
time Secretary. Hulme's letters for the later months of 1909 indicate that

32

he had now adopted the Irish Literary Society as a teatime arena. It appears that the evenings of the Tour d'Eiffel were over.

Flint, in his 'History', says 'the group died a lingering death at the end of the second winter.'[55] What he meant is not altogether clear. There is no evidence for the continuance of the group after the autumn months of 1909. Such groups are by nature short-lived, even conspiratorial. The mainspring was Hulme whose enthusiasm, at least at this stage of his career, was intense although brief in duration. Hulme's interest in poetry dwindled after 1909. Of the five poems printed in 1912 as his 'Complete Poetical Works' three had already appeared in 1909. 'Mana Aboda', though not published until 1912, had been written in 1909. Only for 'Above the Dock' is the date of composition uncertain.

The Tour d'Eiffel meetings seem to have ended unfortunately for all the participants, with the possible exception of Flint. Both Campbell and Edward Storer gave up their experiments in free verse after 1909. Campbell's *Irishry* (Dublin, 1913) shows a regression in form from which he did not free himself until after 1914. Storer's retreat must have already started during his involvement with the Tour d'Eiffel. *The Ballad of the Mad Bird*, a small collection which he brought out in the autumn of 1909, is an uninteresting exercise in fake Orientalism of imagery and theme. It was a decade before Storer returned to free verse. Hulme's fate is equally puzzling. During 1910 he withdrew from public literary activity. In 1911 he reappeared as a critic of philosophy. By 1912 he had become the proponent of a kind of classicism, prophesying an era of 'dry, hard, classical verse', a prediction by no means fulfilled in the years that followed.[56]

But for Flint's example one would be tempted to dismiss the meetings as counter-productive. He, if anyone, would seem to have been the immediate beneficiary. His book reviewing in *The New Age* during 1909 and 1910 acquired a sharper tone. There is a suggestion of Hulme's energy in remarks like these: 'Every new image made is a violation of the language'; and 'The language has become a set of newspaper counters.'[57] There is more tangible evidence in the change in his poetic work after 1909. His first poems in free verse formed the sequence 'Moods', which appeared in a magazine called *The Tramp* (edited by Ford Madox Hueffer's friend Douglas Goldring) in November and December 1910.[58] Flint's growing involvement with French literature joined with the arguments of Hulme and their colleagues to provide the mixture of encouragement and direction that he needed to get fresh impetus for his own work. Where they stopped or back-tracked he continued.

Storer and Campbell appear to have dropped out of Hulme's milieu, though Storer remained friendly with Hulme and was perhaps the only one of his contemporaries to commemorate him. 'Caravan', the first poem in Storer's *Terra Italica* (1920), is dedicated 'To the memory of T.E.H.'[59] On the evidence of their correspondence Flint and Hulme maintained a rather ambivalent friendship, characterized by some bullying touches on Hulme's side. Some of the surviving letters do not show Hulme in a very pleasant aspect:

> I have just received your wire which upsets me considerably. I have got myself in a position now where I must have a little further help to finish the thing off. I cannot wait until you come back from your holiday. You must *come round tomorrow if only for a couple of hours in order to finish* the job off, otherwise I shall be left in a most awkward position. It is not a question of money this time for I have told you I will pay you for it extra—but simply that having gone so far I must have you to finish the thing off. Everything is ready for you, there are only a few difficulties to discuss. Now do make an effort—I really require you.[60]

Much of their correspondence during 1912 is concerned with the translation from Bergson that was published under Hulme's name in 1913 as *An Introduction to Metaphysics*. Flint, as Pound noted, did 'a good deal of the sweating' over the translation.[61] It would appear that Flint resented Hulme's attitude to him, but lacked the confidence to make the ripostes that Hulme might have respected. More to the point, after 1909 there is virtually no mention of poetry in the correspondence between the two men. Hulme's interest in poetry declined almost as swiftly as it had developed. The evenings in Frith Street, Soho, with which he replaced the Tour d'Eiffel meetings around 1911 appear to have been cultural 'at home' occasions. The house in Frith Street where they were held was the London home of Mrs Ethel Kibblewhite, a lady who may or may not have been Hulme's mistress.

*       *       *

Ezra Pound, who was usually generous in his attitude to his literary colleagues, went to some pains to insist that he learned little of value from the 1909 discussions.

> My own impression of 1909 is that there was very little agreement. I seem to remember Hulme vainly trying to convince people of something. There was little or no formulation.[62]

In a still later letter, also written to Flint, Pound reiterated his view of the situation he encountered in 1909. About Hulme's group he was by no means flattering:

... pre-existence of French of french symbolists—each unknown to someone of the cenacle—and most of them rather dim to all.[63]

If Pound's memory was accurate, and if he was writing without undue bias, this would suggest he had observed in discussion the rather fragmented knowledge of French literature that Hulme, Storer, and Flint display in their writings. (Flint became a specialist in modern French poetry as neither Storer nor Hulme ever was. But this was later. In 1909 he was still laying the foundations of what became an exceptional scholarly knowledge.) Into this group Pound erupted.

my incursion—if such it was—Browning'd, Yeats'd, stuffed with undigested middle ages, barbarian zeal, Xtianity etc.[64]

While willing to admit his own insufficiencies, Pound was reluctant to acknowledge that he owed any particular debt to Hulme:

Hulme's talk, of which I remember d—d little, save that he talked about Image and hustled Tancred with immitating Herrick .... [65]

Consideration of Pound's debt to Hulme has tended to limit itself to specific discussion of ideas. While Hulme may have had little direct effect on Pound's theories, it could be that his impact on Pound's imagination was far greater than the American could allow himself to recognize. This might explain much of Pound's subsequent vehemence. Only towards the end of his long life was Pound able to do justice to Hulme. In response to praise of the poems of his London period in an interview in 1968 Pound merely replied, 'How about that poem Hulme wrote on "The Embankment"?'[66]

Pound left England in the early summer of 1910 to go back to America. He stayed there almost a year, returning to London in the spring of 1911. During the next few months he travelled on the Continent, visiting Paris with W. B. Yeats and the Rhineland with Ford Madox Hueffer. He settled again in London in the autumn of 1911. There he began the pattern of casual encounters that led to the formation of what Pound named the Imagiste group. These meetings occurred at the Kensington home of Brigit Patmore. Those taking part soon came to form a smaller and more cohesive group than that of Hulme and his colleagues. In addition to Pound the chief participants were Hilda Doolittle, always known publicly as H.D., a friend of Pound and William Carlos Williams during their student days in Philadelphia, and the young English writer Richard Aldington, whom she married in 1913. Many years later Brigit Patmore (who was married to a son of Coventry Patmore) became Richard

Aldington's mistress. The private lives of some of the Imagist circle were almost as complicated as their literary relations.

H.D. and Aldington had begun to write in free verse before their meetings with Pound. Flint, who soon became a member of the group, had experienced a conversion to the new doctrine after the meetings at the Tour d'Eiffel. He was now immersed in his study of French literature, a study that Pound, although he despised the rather ineffectual Englishman, did not fail to profit from:

> Flint in return for having been ressurrected, has put me on some very good contemporary French stuff: Remy de Gourmont, De Regnier, etc.[67]

Moreover, Flint was not merely a scholar with exceptional scope of knowledge in modern French poetry and literary criticism. He was the one member of the Imagiste group who had taken part in the Tour d'Eiffel evenings from beginning to end. He remained far closer to Hulme than Pound ever was.

A whole range of experiences seems to have urged Pound to his new formulation: his travels, his conversations with Yeats and Hueffer, the example of the poems of H.D. and Aldington, the French writers he was hearing about from Flint and—it may be—the remembered enunciations of Hulme. A simple notion of linear cause and effect cannot apply to something so complex as a literary development.

During 1912 Pound gained colleagues, sources and theoretical models to give effect to his impulse to modernity. Until then almost all his work had been a hangover from the Victorian. Through the strenuous two years' work between 1909 and 1911 that produced three books of verse, *Personae*, *Exultations* and *Canzoni*, and the essays in *The Spirit of Romance*, there persists a note of the archaic, both in theme and language. One influence that helped to break this habit was undoubtedly that of Ford Madox Hueffer. Pound had at various times emphasized the importance of Hueffer's criticism for his personal development as a poet:

> The critical light during the years immediately pre-war in London shone not from Hulme but from Ford (Madox etc.) in so far as it fell on writing at all.[68]

In his obituary notice of Hueffer, Pound recalled how Hueffer had reacted to his pre-Imagiste poems in 1911.

> And he (Ford) felt the errors of contemporary style to the point of rolling ... on the floor of his temporary quarters in Giessen when my

third volume displayed me trapped, fly-papered, gummed and strapped down in a jejune provincial effort to learn, *mehercule*, the stilted language that then passed for 'good English' in the arthritic milieu that held control of the respected British critical circles . . . .

And that roll saved me at least two years, perhaps more. It sent me back to my own proper effort, namely, toward using the living tongue. . . .[69]

It is curious that when Pound was first in England in 1909 Hueffer seems to have made no particular impression on him. He acted as Hueffer's secretary for a while in Germany in 1911[70]—but still found little to impress him. In August he was back in London, and writing to his mother that he disagreed 'diametrically' with Hueffer on every question: 'art, religion, politics . . .'[71] Within a few months, probably by the beginning of 1912, his attitude was to change radically. What prompted this can only be guessed. Of that slightly later time Brigit Patmore remarked:

Pound and Hueffer used to discuss interminably the styles and faults of writers past and present, raising up gods and pulling them down.[72]

Regardless of their personal dealings, the Imagistes had one important advantage in opportunities of publication which Hulme's circle had lacked. *The New Age* was now more accessible. During 1911 and 1912 Orage published Hulme's 'Complete Poetical Works' as well as Pound's articles 'I Gather the Limbs of Osiris' and his *Patria Mia*.[73] Of even greater importance was the rise of the little magazines, reviews aimed deliberately at a minority market. Without *Poetry*, which first appeared in Chicago in October 1912, and *The New Freewoman* in London (later *The Egoist*) which began publication in June 1913, the history of Imagisme would have been very different.

In 1909 no little magazine was available and no systematic attempt at periodical publication was undertaken. In 1912 and 1913 Pound launched his propaganda for Imagisme by means of a series of manifestos and pronouncements. This was done through a variety of periodicals, but in particular through *Poetry* and *The New Freewoman*. It was no doubt as a result of these activities that Pound gained the notice and encouragement that enabled him to bring out the anthology *Des Imagistes* in 1914.[74] The manuscript of *Des Imagistes* had been ready for publication in the summer of 1913 when Pound sent it to the American poet and chess master Alfred Kreymborg.[75] The list of contributors is an interesting reflection of what Pound and his allies had achieved since his first announcement of Imagisme in *Poetry*, some months earlier. Aldington, with ten poems, received the largest allocation of space in *Des Imagistes*. The other members of the Imagiste group, Pound, H.D., and Flint— whose early adherence turned the original trio into a quartet—were also well represented. With twenty-eight poems between them, these four took most of the space of the anthology. Seven other contributors had one poem each: James Joyce, William Carlos Williams, Ford Madox Hueffer, Allen Upward, Amy Lowell, Skipwith Cannell and John Cournos. Four of these seven were American, and the Irishman Joyce was already in Trieste, a permanent exile from Britain. The balance of the new development was beginning to shift away from Britain and towards America. Moreover, the poems by Joyce and Hueffer were reprinted from previous collections of their work, Joyce's fine poem 'I Hear an Army' having first appeared in his volume *Chamber Music* in 1907.

The contributors to *Des Imagistes* represent a mixed bag of talents and interests. Upward was a learned eccentric, a friend of Pound and Hulme, and a man whose thinking seems to have had some importance for Pound. He was in no serious sense a poet. Joyce was uninterested in the Imagistes, as he was in anything save the development of his own work. Both Cannell and John Cournos came under Pound's influence, and Cournos became a follower and imitator of Imagiste poetic practice. Hueffer as a poet is to be linked with the followers rather than the begetters of Imagisme. He was influenced for a time by his association with Pound and the Imagiste group, but his experiences during the war years seem to have been of far greater importance to his development. Pound's lifelong friend William Carlos Williams became one of the more influential American poets of the present century. The influence of Imagism on his work was considerable, though his talent was strong enough to absorb it and to continue to go its own way. His direct affiliations with Pound's Imagisme were tenuous. Amy Lowell appears to have been included in *Des Imagistes* for business reasons. She was rich and was beginning to manifest an interest in Pound's movement. Pound, chronically impecunious, was looking for a backer. If this was his motive for bringing Amy Lowell into the Imagiste group he was soon to have reason to regret it.

So far the history of Imagisme had been one of rapid development. The movement had progressed in a far more businesslike way than Hulme's group. The first meetings at Brigit Patmore's home in the early weeks of 1912 to the initial announcement of the existence of the Imagistes had been a matter of some ten months. Little more than half a year later the manuscript of *Des Imagistes* had been made ready for publication. Pound's work, both in his poems and his thinking about his art, was in process of rapid evolution. The personal development of his colleagues, as evidenced in the poems of Aldington and H.D. seems to have been more tentative.

There are indications that the speed and intensity of Pound's enthusiasms were resented by the other members of the Imagiste group. H.D., for example, wrote with some irritation to Harriet Monroe, the editor of *Poetry*:

> Mr. Pound writes me that you are using the other poems I sent you!— If they are not already in type, will you please sign with the simple initials *H.D.*—I feel that the 'Imagiste' in the first series has sufficiently identified me.

In another letter she repeated this request:

> I saw your announcement in the end of *Poetry* anent my poems. When you publish them will you be so good as to sign the 'H.D.' simply, cutting out the affectation of 'Imagiste'.[76]

Aldington, while continuing to assert his admiration for Pound as he had then known him—

> He gave me Villon, he gave me Verlaine, he gave me the Symbolistes, he gave me Flaubert, and carelessly threw in the Neo-Latins. We have come to differ over a lot of things but—I find I'm a bit like Yeats in this respect—I can't go back on the Ezra of 1912-14.[77]

echoed H.D.'s criticism of Pound's methods as an entrepreneur:

> I didn't like his insistence that the poems should be signed: 'H.D. Imagist,' because it sounded a little ridiculous. And I think H.D. disliked it too. But Ezra was a bit of a czar in a small but irritating way, and he had the bulge on us, because it was only through him that we could get our poems into Harriet Monroe's *Poetry*, and nobody else at that time would look at them.[78]

Pound's dictatorial ways annoyed his Imagiste colleagues in other respects. Aldington remarked how irritating he found Pound's choice of some of the contributors to *Des Imagistes*. In particular, he objected to the inclusion of Amy Lowell. This was to prove ironical, in view of the direction that the Imagiste enterprise was soon to take.

Pound had arrogated to himself the leadership of the group of 1912. His force and energy of personality, and the range and diversity of his interests, no doubt fitted him for this role. But it is apparent from many comments that he had the knack of irritating colleagues by his mannerisms and assumptions of superiority. Pound and Flint, though sometimes friendly, seem never to have been on very comfortable terms. In a letter of much later date Flint renewed his hostility:

> Before August 1912, Ezra Pound used to say that he knew no French poetry after Villon. After August 1912, he became like a cat in heat. He told my wife in the Ristorante Italiano, Soho, that if I didn't write the book (on modern French poetry) *he* would. He could not hold himself.[79]

This has a note of plausibility, though one might question the accuracy with which Flint refers to a specific month in 1912, particularly as he claimed that his personal papers were totally destroyed by air raid in 1940. (Even this claim is incorrect. Much of Flint's material survives, most of it in the collection of the Humanities Research Center, Austin, Texas.) The precision of Flint's statement may be explained by the fact that this was the month *Poetry Review* appeared as a special number on contemporary French poetry, written entirely by Flint. In the letter already quoted Flint again insists that Pound got the name of his new school by 'taking the *Image* from T. E. Hulme and the *ism* from my August number'.

No doubt Flint believed this. His ground of complaint seems underlined by the fact that *Ripostes* came out in October 1912, and would therefore have been in proof at the time when, on Flint's view, Pound was engaged in filching from Hulme and himself.

Flint's continuing hostility to Pound is unfortunate; equally, Pound's attitude to him was far from attractive. 'Frankie—victim of milieu. At any rate sunk.'[80] This judgment, of which he delivers himself in a letter, is ungraceful, terse—and accurate.

The beginnings of Imagisme in 1912 coincided with Pound's personal drive to modernization. In that process all Pound's circle was ruthlessly involved. Those who could help or serve his needs were made to do so. Those less advanced than himself were put under instruction. As he put it:

> after all I am a spoiled professor, with a pedagogic urge hybris, mania or what you will.[81]

Pound's urgency of involvement with his work cannot have made him easier to deal with. Effective group-collaboration among writers is particularly hazardous, the personality required for creative literary work does not blend comfortably with collective activity. Pound's medico-legal history is well-known; H.D. suffered at least one severe emotional breakdown, and only attained psychic equilibrium in middle life following

40

a period of analytic treatment with Freud in Vienna; Aldington's estrangement from Britain and his attitude to his contemporaries in his later years shows a hostility that bordered on paranoia; Flint, in superficial appearance and life-style the most balanced of the group, abandoned poetry as suddenly and dramatically as Hulme had done; and his frequent attacks on Pound suggest an enmity excessive to the point of obsession.

It is hardly surprising that the Imagiste group did not last long in its original form. Finally it was undermined through a takeover bid by Amy Lowell, who descended on London in the late summer of 1914 and, almost literally, seems to have purchased the allegiance of Pound's colleagues. She organized what Aldington called 'a Boston Tea Party for Ezra',[82] a manoeuvre that led to his removal from the Imagiste group which in consequence mutated into little more than a publishing consortium. Amy Lowell had much to help her in the dispute that now developed. Aldington and H.D. were ready to join forces with her. They were, as one of Pound's biographers has put it, her 'chief aiders and abettors'.[83] Flint soon joined them. So did D. H. Lawrence, who never had much liking or respect for Pound. The group found a new colleague in John Gould Fletcher, another American expatriate settled in London, who had refused to contribute to *Des Imagistes*.

Pound, not surprisingly, was indignant about this turn of events. The Imagist rift was swamped in the beginnings of a much greater struggle, but Pound found time to write in detail to Amy Lowell on 1 August 1914:

> The present machinery was largely or wholly my making. I ordered 'the public' (i.e. a few hundred people and a few reviewers) to take note of certain poems.

> You offer to find a publisher, that is, a better publisher, if I abrogate my privileges, if I give way to, or saddle myself with, a dam'd contentious, probably incompetent committee. If I tacitly, tacitly to say the least of it, accept a certain number of people as my critical and creative equals, and publish the acceptance.

> I don't see the use. Moreover, I should like the name 'Imagisme' to retain some sort of a meaning. It stands, or I should like it to stand for hard light, clear edges. I can not trust any democratized committee to maintain that standard.[84]

Between this view and that of Amy Lowell there could be no compromise. As she wrote to Harriet Monroe:

> You ask about the quarrel between Ezra and the rest of us. It is not a quarrel now, it is a schism.[85]

41

It is hard not to sympathize with Pound in the situation that now developed. He had nursed the new movement with unremitting care. Even the word 'Imagisme' carried some proprietary rights in Pound's mind. Legally he had no case. Morally he had considerable grounds for outrage. The simple fact was his former colleagues did not want him.

They were able to maintain working relations with Amy Lowell for the next two and a half years, through the three issues of the new anthology *Some Imagist Poets*. This final Imagist group was in effect a publishing venture. Shared literary ideals seem to have been submerged in the common desire to find a market. Amy Lowell was well placed to ensure the market that her colleagues needed. She was of Boston Brahmin family, rich, enthusiastic, dictatorial. She had a much more astute head for business than Pound. Her talents were smaller than his, but she had energy, determination and the upper-class habit of getting what she wanted.

It must be admitted that the three volumes of *Some Imagist Poets* which appeared from 1915 to 1917 represent a more satisfactory editorial job than *Des Imagistes*. Pound, with all his gifts as poet and critic, had been too violent and personal in his tastes to be a convincing editor of poetry anthologies. The *Catholic Anthology*, which he edited in 1915 as an answer to *Some Imagist Poets*, contained some excellent work, but it included too many indifferent poems by writers with whom Pound had ties of personal sympathy. A more impressive compilation is *Profile*, published in a limited edition in Milan in 1932. This was a retrospective collection of poems that had personal significance for Pound; or, as he put it:

> poems which have stuck in my memory and which may possibly define their epoch, or at least rectify current ideas of it in respect to at least one contour.[86]

It may be worth adding that the five poems of Hulme's 'Complete Poetical Works' are included in this anthology.

\*     \*     \*

With the formation of the group who contributed to *Some Imagist Poets*, the focus of Imagist activity shifted to America, where it became part of an energetic campaign of public relations, conducted by Amy Lowell on behalf of the new poetry as she understood it. This campaign, which Amy Lowell continued until her death in 1925, outlasted Imagism by some eight years. The movement itself formally ended with the final volume of *Some Imagist Poets* in 1917. In England, under the impact of war and with Pound's transfer of interest to Vorticism, Imagism gained no new adherents and quickly lost most of the few it had acquired. It would be incorrect to say, as Hueffer did,[87] that Imagism was killed by the war. The war of 1914 was destructive of much in English culture, but Imagism was not among its victims. The Imagist movement died of its own inner contradictions, in particular of the tensions and rivalries among the members of the Imagiste circle. What survived from that movement was a new and changed attitude, an attitude that was in itself part of a development in the art of poetry and that became the reagent of further developments in the poetic evolution of the decades that followed.

As reconstituted under Amy Lowell's management, the Imagist group became a kind of Rump. Soon, the war dispersed the Imagist poets. Amy Lowell went back to Boston. John Gould Fletcher returned to America before the opening of unrestricted submarine warfare by the Germans helped to bring the U.S.A. into the struggle. Aldington joined the British army in 1915 and was posted to the Western Front. D. H. Lawrence and Frieda left London for Cornwall and began the tormented wanderings that were to end with Lawrence's death fifteen years later. Only H.D. and Flint (before he, too, was called to the army) were left in London. Pound had already shifted his allegiance to Vorticism.

Vorticism had begun to attract Pound's enthusiasm some while before his rupture with the Imagistes. A letter that he wrote in December 1913 already refers to 'The Vortex'.[88] For Pound the Vortex meant London. Vorticism in its metaphysical inception was an attempt to create an aesthetic and an art that would express the consciousness of contemporary urban man. As such it was much nearer to Futurism or to German Expressionism than Imagism had been. In terms of personnel Vorticism was predominantly a painterly movement. The Vorticist group included seven visual artists, among them Wyndham Lewis, Henri Gaudier-Brzeska, and Edward Wadsworth. Among the half-dozen painters linked with it were David Bomberg and C. R. W. Nevinson. In a note written in 1915 Wyndham Lewis was explicit about the pictorial emphasis of the movement:

> This is the first exhibition of a group of painters, to whom the name Vorticist has been given ... . BLAST was started principally as a vehicle for the propagation of their ideas, and as a sort of picture-gallery, too.[89]

Pound seems to have had a large share in the formation of the Vorticist aesthetic and his essay on Vorticism, first published in *The Fortnightly Review* for September 1914, is the principal statement available of the Vorticist position.[90]

Vorticism announced itself in a more dramatic and spectacular way than

43

any of the Imagist groups had done. Its medium was the review *Blast*, with its magenta cover, bold typography, and ferocious brilliance of phrase and design. Only two numbers of *Blast* appeared, and the magazine, like the Vorticist movement itself, may be regarded as an early casualty of the war in a far more tangible sense than Imagism. The first number of *Blast* is dated 20 June 1914. It actually appeared some three weeks later, a fortnight before the outbreak of war. The second issue of *Blast* came out in July 1915, in time to record the death in battle of Gaudier-Brzeska. Pound was to remember him in *Canto XVI*:

> And Henri Gaudier went to it,
>   and they killed him,
> And killed a good deal of sculpture . . .

Pound continued to describe himself as a Vorticist until 1919. The term had still some currency, though debased to advertising uses, in 1922, when it appeared in a restaurant announcement by the Tour d'Eiffel in Wyndham Lewis's periodical *The Tyro*.[91] It is as if the history of Imagism and Vorticism begins and ends with an obscure café.

# III

◆

# Poems and Poets

In terms of theory it is difficult to define the Imagist poem. Writers involved in the movement seem themselves to have been bemused by this problem. Remarks made by the Imagists and their contemporaries show how far this confusion went.

In 1914 Richard Aldington wrote in *The Egoist*:

> ... let me say from memory what I, as an Imagist, consider the fundamental doctrines of the group. You will see that they are all practically stylistic.
>
> (1) Direct treatment of the subject. This I consider very important. We convey emotion by presenting the object and circumstance of that emotion without comment. ...
> (2) As few adjectives as possible. ...
> (3) A hardness, as of cut stone. No slop, no sentimentality....
> (4) Individuality of rhythm. We make new fashions instead of cutting our clothes on the old models. Mr. Hueffer says that the unit of our rhythms is the unit of conversation. I daresay he is right.
> (5) A whole lot of don'ts, which are mostly technical, which are boresome to anyone except those writing poetry, and which have already been published in *Poetry*.
> (6) The exact word. We make quite a heavy stress on that. It is most important. All great poetry is exact. All the drearyness of nineteenth century poets comes from their not quite knowing what they wanted to say and filling up the gaps with portentous adjectives and idiotic similes....
> (7) I know there are a lot more but I can't remember them now.[1]

Ezra Pound in a letter to F. S. Flint in 1915:

> ... when on a certain evening in, I think 1912, I coined the word Imagisme, I certainly intended it to mean something which was the poetry of HD and most emphatically NOT the poetry of friend Storer....[2]

Flint in a letter to Pound:

> ... You have never done Storer justice. His *Mirrors of Illusion* are the work of a poet. Generally, it can be said of them that they are 'Imagist' in tendency, i.e. direct speech or simple current speech .... That being so, Storer had a right to be considered in a history of Imagism ... .[3]

Pound to Flint:

> ... As to being a good or bad imagist, let us not confuse matters. A good lyrist is a person who writes good lyrics when trying to write lyrics, not necessarily a person who writes nothing but lyrics.[4]

1916—some remarks in the 'Preface' to *Some Imagist Poets:*

> ... We have decided ... to explain the laws which govern us a little more fully. A few people may understand, and the rest can merely misunderstand again, a result to which we are quite accustomed.

> In the first place 'Imagism' does not mean merely the presentation of pictures. 'Imagism' refers to the manner of presentation, not to the subject. It means a clear presentation of whatever the author wishes to convey. Now he may wish to convey a mood of indecision, in which case the poem should be indecisive ... .

> The 'exact' word does not mean the word which exactly describes the object in itself, it means the 'exact' word which brings the effect of that object before the reader as it presented itself to the poet's mind at the time of writing the poem. Imagists deal but little with similes, although much of their poetry is metaphorical ... .

> ... the Imagists have the greatest admiration for the past, and humility towards it. But they have been caught in the throes of a new birth ... .

> It is not what Imagists write about which makes them hard of comprehension; it is the way they write it ... . That the Imagists base much of their poetry upon cadence and not upon metre makes them neither good nor bad ... .

> ... a cadenced poem is written to be read aloud, in this way only will its rhythm be felt. Poetry is a spoken and not a written art ... .

> Poetry is the vision in a man's soul which he translates as best he can with the means at his disposal.[5]

46

Ford Madox Hueffer in an article in *The Outlook*:

> I differ therefore from my Imagist friends in one very important
> particular. They dismiss 'prose' with a sniff. That is wrong, since they
> only exist by descent from the great prose writers—and I will go so far
> as to hazard the dogma that the prose form is the only satisfactory
> vehicle for expressing the poetry of life .... .[6]

After all this there is relief in the gloomy epigram of Bela Zold, a modern
Hungarian novelist:

> The trouble with him is that he has no sense of rhythm.
> Nowadays without that you can only write poetry.

Whatever the confusion of their theories, the Imagist writers attempted
to illustrate them in their poems, but it is hard to be sure when they wrote
poems to fit their theories or theories to fit their poems. Theories may
offer a fascinating parlour-game, or as Hulme said, 'All theories as toys'.
Ultimately the importance of any artistic movement lies in the work of
art itself.

\* \* \*

Of the writers who gathered at the Tour d'Eiffel, three had already
made various experiments with free verse: Edward Storer, T. E. Hulme
and Joseph Campbell. On the whole, Storer is an ineffectual poet, a writer
of far less merit than Hulme or Campbell, but his historical primacy
cannot be denied. Already in *Inclinations* (published in November 1907
and predating by nearly a year the better-known *Mirrors of Illusion*)
nearly half the poems are in free verse.

### Blue Lotus (*Perfumes*)

If this be the Lotus' breath
I would lie
Close to the Lotus' mouth
That I might drink it all.

From what roots sprung?
By what strange nourishment of blood,
And whose,
Can such a flower come to creep and steal
So silently
Into the Night's white arms
From its lone dark cave
Of Nothingness?[7]

This is curiously like H.D.'s work of a few years later. Unlike her, Storer did not know when to stop. 'Blue Lotus' drags on for another eighteen lines until its initial impact is destroyed. In *Mirrors of Illusion*, his later but less successful volume, there are unfortunate evidences of his readings of Baudelaire:

*Thuribles: I*

Think! an enchanted isle,
Where music like a scythe
Sickles the sallow fancies of the soul,
And voices of strange birds
Burn like mysterious tapers
Of an antique rite,
In groves of shade.

His work was handicapped by a fatal lack of personality, a note of something muffled and unrealized. Pound, in an angry moment, referred sneeringly to Storer's 'custard'.[8] This was unjust, but Storer too often blurs the situation with trite adjectives: 'plaintive gasp', 'tiny lips', 'faint effulgence' and so on.[9]

Storer represents an early stage of free verse in English, a stage at which the sanction given by the French writers is expressed through rhythmic patterns derived from Henley or Matthew Arnold. His vocabulary shows no development from the poets of the nineties (and earlier) on whom it largely depends. His programme and justification for free verse is of more importance than his practice. Storer's theory was not substantially improved on by the later formulations of Pound and Eliot, but he lacked the confidence of his intentions. For a decade after 1909 he reverted to traditional verse forms. In these he shows very slight capacity. If his free verse is struggling pioneer work, his more formal poems are negligible. In two much later collections *Terra Italica* (1920) and *I've Quite Forgotten Lucy* (1932), while not abandoning received form, he again uses free verse, though this shows little advance on the work of his earlier years. As an appendix to *I've Quite Forgotten Lucy* he printed some sadly unamusing jokes. This lack of humour is manifest throughout his work. It is a significant gap. Humour implies criticism or self-criticism. Storer's lack of humour is bound up with a failure of self-criticism.

After 1918 Storer lived mostly in Italy, and his work came to no real fruition. His chief later distinction is to have been Pirandello's first English translator. Storer not only translated Pirandello. He also wrote the first critical study of Pirandello by a British writer.[10] His middle age was prosperous but clouded. He lived to be sixty-three, but his literary gift had died a dozen years before.

*       *       *

Storer's frustration is paralleled by that of two writers of more original talent. The first is Joseph Campbell, who called himself Seosamh MacCathmhaoil. Campbell was of Northern Irish origin and a fervent nationalist, culturally and politically. Like Storer he was born a Catholic. Campbell's upbringing and education had exposed him to the full ethos of the Irish literary and cultural movement. His earlier poems are full of sentimental Irishry. (He later used the word as the title of one of his verse collections.) He seems to have come to free verse by way of Whitman and the Bible rather than through French examples. In 1909 he was living in London where he acted as Secretary of the Irish Literary Society. He was a member of the Poets' Club, and read there Pound's 'Ballad of the Goodly Fere'. In an unpublished letter to his parents, now in the Yale collection, Pound wrote:

> The Poets' Club? the dinner was very like the first dinner of the club I attended only instead of G.B.S. and Hillaire Belloc jawing the gang, your precocious son effused & listened to his immortal works being rendered with different degrees of competency. Cambell, the 'dark man from the narth' read the 'Goodly Fere' splendidly. I wish I had his voice.[11]

Before 1909 Campbell had already begun to work out a free verse method of his own. This at first owed a good deal to Whitman; for example the opening lines of 'A Thousand Feet Up':

> A thousand feet up: twilight.
> Westwards, a clump of firtrees silhouetted against a
> bank of blue cumulus cloud;
> The June afterglow like a sea behind.
> The mountain trail, white and clear where human feet
> have worn it,
> zigzagging higher and higher till it loses itself in
> the southern skyline.

Or, in its earliest stages, to Biblical examples:

> O Beautiful Dark Woman, weep no more.
> Weep not for thy princes who have gone from thee:
> They shall come again.
> Cease thy crying and thy lamentation.
> Thou shalt be raised up as a star-cluster.
> Thy hair shall shine as a river in the dust, and thine
> eyes as the blue-bough when the summer is full.

Thy neck and thy breasts shall smell as hazel-saplings
   fresh peeled.
Thy paps shall flow as well-streams.
   ....

Yet as early as 1909 he had found something of his characteristic manner,
as in the three-line asyntactical poem, 'The Dawn Whiteness':

   The dawn whiteness.
   A bank of slate-grey cloud lying heavily over it.
   The moon, like a hunted thing, dropping into the cloud.

In July 1909 he published *The Mountainy Singer*, a collection which
includes a number of poems in free verse. Publishing, like public trans-
port, was quicker then than now, but it is clear that the composition of
these poems must have preceded the Tour d'Eiffel meetings. Moreover,
Campbell, like all his colleagues with the sole exception of Flint, showed
only a negative response to the discussions in Percy Street. Like Storer,
he reverted to stricter forms, as his next collection *Irishry* (published
in 1913) confirms. He returned to free forms in or after 1914.[12] His
work of the war years shows a rhythmical tightening, an advance into
economy of organization which makes him more truly an Imagist than
in his earlier phase. A short poem like this is far nearer to Imagist canons
than the more florid efforts of John Gould Fletcher or Amy Lowell:

*How Still the Night*

How still the night!
The air, a fragrance fallen
   from unseen wings;
The pine-trunks, stones of some dark
   and secret temple;
Venus, a lantern burning without flame.

But my soul is not still.
The wind blows bitterly;
The pines groan on their rock-nourished
   roots;
The stars are blotted out.

Campbell had no formal ties with the Imagist groups of 1912 or 1914,
but the slight yet durable lyrical quality of his work did not go unnoticed.
In *The Egoist* in 1917 *Earth of Cualann* was favourably reviewed and
Campbell acclaimed as:

50

one of the half-dozen or so of writers who are responsible for there being any contemporary poetry. He has established his own style of *vers libre*.[13]

That praise may seem excessive. But Campbell has been unjustly neglected.

### The Dead

The shadow stirs on the moondial:
Nuts drop from heavy hazel boughs.
*Only the dead are quiet.*

Water, without end,
Springs in the dark hollow of stone.
*Only the dead are quiet.*

Thought will not sleep,
Or, sleeping, talks to itself like a tired child.
*Only the dead are quiet.*

After the establishment of the Irish Free State in 1922 Campbell suffered a fate common in revolutionary situations. He was held in military internment at the Curragh for two years. He settled in New York in 1926 and did not return to Ireland until 1937.[14] His fate was ironical, but the irony was a tragic one, for the resulting sense of injustice disfigured the rest of Campbell's life and work.

Campbell was to a notable extent independent of contemporary influences. His imagination had been fed by the Irish Movement. His technique, as he developed and remodelled it, seems to have been his own. The rather primitive free verse of his earlier career matured within half a dozen years into work of much greater subtlety. He outgrew his derivation from Whitman, whose long, indolent but sinewy lines are so often the inspiration of Campbell's rhythms in *The Mountainy Singer*. In his later work the lines are shorter, the rhythms more compact:

### The Revealer

Not by prayers, not by songs
Are men reborn,
But by sacrifice.
Sacrifice is the revealer:
We see all things clearly
In the glazed mirror of blood.

\*     \*     \*

While Campbell's place among the writers of his time should be assured it must be stressed that this place is gained on a body of work very small in quantity. Paucity of output seems a characteristic of all the earlier Imagist writers. Perhaps however, a distinction should be made between writers of small output (like Hulme or Flint) and those who, like Storer and Campbell, wrote readily in traditional forms but became less fluent when using free verse. The difficulty and newness of free verse may be largely responsible. As Hulme suggested, it does not (or at that time did not) offer the possibilities of mechanical composition available to the poet supported by a set rhythm and with a ready-made vocabulary to accompany it. In those days poetry that had been negotiated through existent forms and through the sensibility of other writers was easier to compose than free verse. Much verse has been written only because the poet had examples to draw upon. This is true even of some good poetry. In proportion as there were few models for free verse in English, it was more difficult for these pioneers to write other than small numbers of short poems. There was also the question of confidence. Without critical approval and with few easy opportunities of publication, writers could get little encouragement. When the group they had formed collapsed their source of encouragement ended. None of them was determined enough or obsessed enough to continue in such hostile circumstances. This helps to explain their restricted output, the curious starts and retreats of their poetic activity and the general atmosphere of apology or even defeat that accompanied it. In particular, this atmosphere engulfed the most gifted of them, Hulme, a writer of potentially major talent who gave up poetry in a fruitless search for intellectual satisfaction. Hulme has been regarded primarily as a man of ideas. It is by his poems that he will survive. These are few, only twenty-four in all, and many of them were not available until fairly recently. They had appeared, both during his life and after his death, only in tantalizing handfuls until A. R. Jones edited them in 1960.[15]

The prevailing tone of Hulme's poetic work is wistfulness, a poignant lyric charm that contrasts oddly with the aggressive dogmatism that pervades his prose. As a poet he seems oddly out of time. During his life he was largely unregarded; and it is perhaps part of his tragedy that his talent was undervalued, even stultified by himself. Almost the only notice of his first published poem (in *For Christmas MDCCCCVIII*) was the doubtful praise from Flint in *The New Age*[16]; the only contemporary comment that has been discovered on the 'Complete Poetical Works' was in *The Quest*, a periodical sympathetic to Hulme. It was edited by his friend G. R. S. Mead, a figure of note in the quasi-philosophic and mystical fringe activities of the period. The reviewer in *The Quest*, commenting on the brevity of Hulme's poems, classified them as 'scraps'.[17]

The poems themselves deserve the attention they have received since Hulme's death. T. S. Eliot remarked that Hulme was the author of 'two or three of the most beautiful short poems in the English language'.[18] Their rhythmic variety is, as Alun Jones has said, 'impressive'. There is, for example, the well-known 'Autumn' with its delicate variations from the banality of the pentameter. Finer examples are 'Conversion':

### Conversion

Light-hearted I walked into the valley wood
In the time of hyacinths,
Till beauty like a scented cloth
Cast over, stifled me, I was bound
Motionless and faint of breath
By loveliness that is her own eunuch.
Now pass I to the final river
Ignominiously, in a sack, without sound,
As any peeping Turk to the Bosphorus.

and the epigrammatic 'Above the Dock':

### Above the Dock

Above the quiet dock in midnight
Tangled in the tall mast's corded height,
Hangs the moon. What seemed so far away
Is but a child's balloon, forgotten after play.

Sadly, only a handful of Hulme's poems were available for over forty years after his death. Poems of equal interest remained unpublished. 'Madman', for instance, is a remarkable small achievement.

### Madman

As I walk by the river
Those who have not yet withdrawn pass me
I see past them, touch them.
And in the distance, over the water,
Far from the lights,
I see Night, that dark savage,
But I will not fear him.
Four walls are round me.
I can touch them.
If I die, I can float by.
Moan and hum and remember the sea
In heaven, Oh my spirit,

53

Remember the sea and its moaning.
Hum in the presence of God, it will sustain you.
Again I am cold, as after weeping.
And I tremble—but there is no wind.

This poem offers a clue to much that might otherwise be mysterious about Hulme, a point that may become clearer if it is compared with the schizophrenic poem quoted by R. D. Laing in *The Divided Self*:

There! There is no cave.
It is gone.
But when did I go?
I cannot find me.
Where am I?
Lost.
And all I know is that I am cold,
    and it is colder, than when I was in the cave.
So very, very cold.
And, the people—they have walked on me,
    as though I wasn't there, among them—
    by mistake, I think, I hope,
Yes, I want the cave,
There, I know where I am.
I can grope, in the dark,
    and feel the cave walls.[19]

This comparison suggests that Hulme carried within him an unbalance or at least an awareness of unbalance such as exists, if only as a possibility, in the personalities of many artists. In him it was denied or repressed.

Hulme's period of poetic activity was regrettably brief. His interest in poetry seems to have developed relatively late. It is unlikely that he wrote verse before 1907 or 1908. He himself said:

... the first time I ever felt the necessity or inevitableness of verse, was in the desire to reproduce the peculiar quality of feeling which is induced by the flat spaces and wide horizons of the virgin prairie of western Canada.[20]

A Cambridge contemporary affirms that he showed no concern with poetry as an undergraduate.[21] The beginnings of his active literary interest date from his subsequent stay in Belgium. The earliest known draft is written on a hotel bill dated 26 May 1908.[22] The poem is 'Sunset', which represents Hulme in the first stage of his poetic development. His progress, if hesitant, was rapid. His first published poems, 'Autumn' and 'A City Sunset', appeared in *For Christmas MDCCCCVIII*. 'Conversion' and 'The Embankment' followed in *The Book of the Poets' Club* (to which Pound also contributed) less than a year later. 'Mana Aboda', unpublished until 1912, had been written during 1909. (He sent a first draft of the poem to F. S. Flint on a postcard dated 7 September 1909.)

> Mana Aboda, whose bent form
> The sky in arched circle is,
> Seems ever for an unknown grief to mourn.
> Yet on a day I heard her cry:
> 'I weary of the roses and the singing poets—
> Josephs all, not tall enough to try.'

These short poems are characteristic examples of Hulme's style and method. From them it is evident that Hulme's Imagism was already mature by 1909. The pity is that it did not develop further. During 1910 he published nothing. The publication of his highly selective 'Complete Poetical Works' in *The New Age* in January 1912 has about it a note of finality, however humorous. There is no evidence that he continued to write poems after 1910. By 1914 he had decisively abandoned verse. In an article that year, published in *Poetry and Drama*, he wrote almost with contempt of his own poems:

I have written verse of that kind myself, I understand the process. The result is immediately recognisable. Qualities of sincere first-hand observation may be constantly shown, but the result is not a poem.[23]

This judgment seems disproportionately harsh. It is as if Hulme misunderstood the nature of his own gift. His verse is stamped with a sensitive exactness of perception, a quality to be differentiated from the demand for precise observation set down in his lecture on poetry. He preached sensory registration and practised emotional statement. This refusal to believe in himself seems to have been deep in his makeup. Perhaps he mistrusted the childlike wistfulness that is revealed in various of his poems. A letter written during the war, when he was campaigning to save the sculptor Epstein from military service, suggests a streak of heroic pessimism and self-depreciation. 'There will unfortunately always be plenty of writers, but there are not more than 3 or 4 sculptors.'[24] Earlier, he had remarked 'I could have written more poems but I don't want to write poems. I'm going to be a philosopher, a heavy philosopher.'[25] Maybe poetry had become too dangerous, more menacing than the tangible perils which he endured, with grim detachment, on the Western Front.

## At Night

At night!
All the terror's in that.
Branches of the dead tree
Silhouetted on the hill's edge.
Dark veins diseased,
On the dead white body of the sky.
The tearing iron hook
Of pitiless Mara.
Handling soft clouds in insurrection.
Brand of the obscene gods
On their flying cattle,
Roaming the sky prairie.

Within himself Hulme had to balance many dissonances. He was the son of a fairly wealthy family in the Potteries and a strenuous critic of society; a Cambridge mathematician and a wanderer who knew many cities and people; a brilliant art critic and a would-be metaphysician. His diversion to philosophy seems regrettable. Pound shrewdly noted that Hulme's 'evenings were diluted with crap like Bergson'.[26] Perhaps Hulme should have remembered his own early dictum: 'Philosophy is about people in clothes, not about the soul of man.'[27]

At some point inside himself Hulme encountered great lassitude and sadness. He experienced the world as barren, 'A landscape, with occasional oases'.[28] Philosophy was safer than poetry. It was a challenge only to his intellect, an escape from such insight as this:

A melancholy spirit, the mind like a great desert lifeless, and the sound of march music in the street, passes like a wave over that desert, unifies it, but then it goes.[29]

Yet the poems remain. Of all Hulme's casually-used talents it is his disregarded lyric self which will continue to live. Perhaps 'In the Quiet Land', written with great simplicity, reveals more clearly than any of his other poems Hulme's awareness of the problem he was never to resolve:

In the quiet land
There is a secret unknown fire.

Suddenly rocks shall melt
And the old roads mislead.

Across the familiar road
There is a deep cleft. I must stand and draw back.
In the cool land
There is a secret fire.

*　　*　　*

The Imagist movement in 1909 was unable to outlive Hulme's interest in poetry. Without him it had lost its pivot. Imagisme as a conscious movement re-emerged in 1912 under the leadership and promotion of Ezra Pound. The vital human link between the two groups was F. S. Flint.

Though only twenty-three in 1909, Flint was already working towards critical standards more exacting than those of the periodical journalism of the day. His reviews of poetry in *The New Age* from 1908 to 1910 breathe discontent, but he was rather slower to find a coherent outlet for his feelings. His first book of poems, *In The Net of the Stars*, is by no means an interesting collection. Though there are occasional small hints towards a dislocation of form, the poems in this volume are conventional productions, both in shape and utterance. Flint's personal development as a poet started slightly later, which places him among the Imagiste group of 1912. The history of Flint's poetic career suggests that he, if anyone, was the immediate beneficiary of the 1909 meetings. In 1910 his poetry underwent a radical change.

The beginning of this change is signalled by his publication in *The Tramp*[30] in November and December 1910 of some short poems called 'Moods'. These include Flint's first published experiments in free verse or, as he later called it, unrhymed cadence. Too often they read like drafts or sketches for poems; almost never are they adequately worked out. Here is an example, the opening lines of an early version of the poem published in *Cadences*, his Poetry Bookshop Pamphlet of 1915:

*Moods: I*
O Golden red and tall chrysanthemums,
You are the graceful soul of the china bowl
Wherein you stand
Amid your leaves.
O flowers of flame, O quiet room,
You are the symbols of my quiet heart
And of the eternity that nestles there.
O flowers of flame, O tall chrysanthemums,

57

My love who comes
Will wave wide ripples of disquiet there,
And a great tide of the eternal sea
Will rise at her approach,
And surge—perhaps to God—
And surge to song.[31]

Revised three or four years later, this became:

*Chrysanthemums*
O golden-red and tall chrysanthemums,
you are the graceful soul of the china vase
wherein you stand
amid your leaves.

O quiet room,
You are the symbol of my patient heart.
O flowers of flame. O tall chrysanthemums,
my love who comes

will wave wide ripples of disquiet there,
and a great tide of the eternal sea
will rise at her approach,
and surge to song.[32]

Flint's revisions have improved the poem, but they still leave many imperfections. The ugly internal rhyme in line two of the earlier version is avoided in the later version. The 'eternity that nestles' and the cliché reference to God are deleted. However, 'wherein' and 'amid' are kept instead of the normal 'in which' and 'among'. The reference to the 'eternal sea' is a stock poetic device. The antithesis between 'quiet' ('my quiet heart') and 'disquiet' is so ineffective as to suggest that it is based on unconscious repetition rather than a deliberate play of language. The announcement of the room as a symbol is clumsy. Even in its later version this is not a satisfactory poem.

Another poem of Flint's Imagiste phase shows his characteristic weaknesses of diction. These lines are taken from 'Regret', first published in *Cadences* in 1915:

. . . .
Pardon me, maidens,
all you whose bosoms
my arms might have encircled,

58

> whose lips
> my own lips might have kissed.
>    . . . .

The chief weakness of Flint's work at this period was inertness, both of rhythm and language (so far as these are separable). He is, however, important in another way. Though the last of the 1912 group to become formally affiliated to the Imagistes he had a considerable role in supplying Pound with ideas and information. Yet in Pound's view Flint's status as an Imagist was always suspect. This emerges in Pound's accusation after the two men had quarrelled over Flint's 'History' in 1915:

> On the whole however you seem to see no difference between imagisme and impressionism. Now when on a certain evening in, I think, 1912, I coined the word Imagisme, I certainly intended it to mean something which was the poetry of H.D. and was most emphatically NOT the poetry of friend Storer whom I do not despise. And on that definition the other two original imagists most certainly concurred, and if you have never understood that distinction you were in error to subscribe yourself a fourth or fifth to our agreement.[33]

Behind this challenge lies a prolonged wrangle, with its origins in Pound's attempts to differentiate Imagisme from Impressionism. The distinction involved appears slim today, but it was apparently important to Pound. He seems to have been concerned to lump Flint with Hueffer as an Impressionist. Pound had no high opinion of Flint's poems. Much later, he wrote to William Carlos Williams:

> ... If they must blither about Flint/Tancred and Stoer it is is unjust to OMIT Ernest Rhys, Newbolt, Hewlett, Robt. Bridges who at any rate WROTE something now and again, and however much one disagreed with 'em, one was at least disagreeing with something.[34]

If Pound meant to equate Impressionism with the softness he so vehemently rejected, his comments on Flint become more pointed. In the same letter to Flint, Pound added:

> The only reason, or at least a very strong reason for inventing a new term is to have a term with a precise meaning, a term which makes it unnecessary to discuss with every Frank, John and Amy, whether 'hardness' for example is or is not a virtue in itself.[35]

Pound was not altogether wrong. There is more than a hint of Impressionism, particularly in some of Flint's later work. Poems like the following (from *Otherworld: Cadences* (1920)) are typical and indicate in what ways and to what extent his talents developed.

*Houses*

Evening and quiet:
A bird trills in the poplar-trees
Behind the house with the dark-green door
Across the road.

Into the sky,
The red earthenware and the galvanised-iron chimneys
Thrust their cowls,
The hoot of the steamers on the Thames is plain.

No wind;
The trees merge, green with green;
A car whirs by;
Footsteps and voices take their pitch
In the key of dusk,
Far off and near, subdued.

Solid and square to the world
The houses stand,
Their windows blocked with venetian blinds.

Nothing will move them.

Flint's most ambitious volume, *Otherworld*, was also his last collection of verse. He did not altogether give up poetry and published a few further poems in periodicals in the twenties. These later poems remain uncollected. Flint had nursed his own rather fragile gift through many vicissitudes, material and emotional, for a dozen difficult years. Why he abandoned it at mid-point in his career remains a puzzle.

Flint's literary career, like those of his colleagues of 1909, appears to have ended in frustration. At one time an admired figure in advanced literary circles, he now seems a man of wasted or thwarted potential. He was more a critic than a poet, and more a scholar than either. Yet as a poet he was highly praised by Hueffer:

... Of the six poets printed in this anthology, only two—H.D. and Mr. F. S. Flint—have the really exquisite sense of words, the really exquisite tranquillity, beauty of diction and insight that justify a writer in assuming the rather proud title of Imagist .... [36]

A personal sidelight was given by Miss Kate Lechmere. When interviewed for her recollections of Hulme she was able to quote from memory Flint's 'London' after more than half a century. Here are some lines from that poem:

> London, my beautiful,
> it is not the sunset
> nor the pale green sky
> shimmering through the curtain
> of the silver birch,
> nor the quietness;
> ....
>
> London, my beautiful,
> I will climb
> into the branches
> to the moonlit tree-tops
> that my blood may be cooled
> by the wind.

Flint's ambition was to become a recorder of urban sensibility, perhaps in the tradition of the French *Unanimistes*. His work was advancing considerably in the fulfilment of that objective when he vehemently and inexplicably turned his back on poetry. This is from his final volume published in 1920:

> *Cones*
>
> The blue mist of after-rain
> Fills all the trees;
>
> The sunlight gilds the tops
> Of the poplar spires, far off,
> Behind the houses.
>
> Here a branch sways
> and there
>     a sparrow twitters.
>
> The curtain's hem, rose-embroidered,
> Flutters, and half reveals
> A burnt-red chimney pot.

The quiet in the room
Bears patiently
A footfall on the street.

\*    \*    \*

With the exception of Pound, the remaining Imagist writers had had no share in the Tour d'Eiffel meetings. In 1909 Hilda Doolittle was in Philadelphia and Richard Aldington was a schoolboy. It is natural to bracket Aldington and H.D. Not only did they marry; not only did they constitute with Pound the original Imagiste trio; but their artistic interests and intentions in those early days had many features of similarity. Aldington and H.D. seem to have evolved their individual styles without reference to one another. Once they came together a considerable mutual influence was exercised. Despite the influence and the converging effect of the Imagist affiliation, in the end they emerge as very dissimilar writers. For some of her contemporaries H.D. was the archetypal Imagist poet. Hueffer thought so, as did Pound, who quoted her short poem 'Oread' on several occasions. Edward Storer, in his review of *Some Imagist Poets*, called her 'the most truly imagistic' and 'certainly the most delicate' of the Imagist writers.[37] In *Blast* Pound even tried to bring her within the ambit of Vorticism by quoting 'Oread' as a sample of Vorticist poetry. (For Pound words often meant what he wanted them to mean.)

In reality, H.D.'s relationship to Imagisme was always ambivalent. In two letters she asked Harriet Monroe to ensure that her poems were signed with the initials H.D. 'cutting out the affectation of "Imagiste".'[38] And it is by no means easy to fit 'Oread' into the demands of Imagist propaganda.

Whirl up, sea—
whirl your pointed pines,
splash your great pines
on our rocks,
hurl your green over us,
cover us with your pools of fir.[39]

Rather, this poem is a minor but perfect example in the Orphic tradition. The apparent remoteness of H.D.'s work, its recourse to Greek themes or classical properties, is only a mask for powerful but unformulated emotions. The use of classical settings is a distancing device. Only by this means could she release and articulate feelings that might otherwise have threatened to overwhelm her. (Sometimes her poems read like lesbian love poems in which both the love and the lesbianism are left out.) The cathartic notion of poetry finds ample confirmation in her situation. The

62

Orphic view of poetry presupposes symbolism as a starting-point for poetic significance. Symbolism in its more restricted sense (as among the *Symbolistes*) was an attempt to recover something of the mystery that Orphism takes for granted. It may be that with the collapse of official Christianity poetry could again begin to assume the vatic or quasi-religious function that Christianity had denied it.

In H.D. these possibilities appear only in germinal form. The symbols tend to be self-regarding. An example is 'Heat', one of her better early poems:

> O wind, rend open the heat,
> cut apart the heat,
> rend it to tatters.
>
> Fruit cannot drop
> through this thick air—
> fruit cannot fall into heat
> that presses up and blunts
> the points of pears
> and rounds the grapes.
>
> Cut the heat—
> plough through it,
> turning it on either side
> of your path.

There is little resemblance here to the work of Hulme or Storer, except for a strophic similarity which may be accounted for by common sources. (No doubt both H.D. and Storer had read Arnold's experiments, such as the unrhymed choruses of *Empedocles on Etna*, first published in 1852). Painting is not to be aligned with poetry, but there are parallels of attitude between H.D. and the French painters of the *Orphiste* movement, a development from Cubism initiated by Delaunay in 1912. In both there is a dislocation of surface reality in the interests of another and supposedly more meaningful reality. Years later Raymonde, the heroine of one of H.D.'s prose narratives, asked herself why she continued writing and answered: 'It's the thing behind my writing that I cling to.'[40] An example of how H.D. used the properties of the classical world to suggest the 'thing behind' her words is the opening of 'Hermes of the Ways':

> The hard sand breaks,
> And the grains of it
> Are clear as wine.

Far off over the leagues of it,
The wind,
Playing on the wide shore,
Piles little ridges,
And the great waves
Break over it.

But more than the many-foamed ways
Of the sea,
I know him
Of the triple path-ways,
Hermes,
Who awaiteth.

It would be easy to be lulled by the rhythms of this poem; but the image of

The hard sand breaks,
And the grains of it
Are clear as wine

is hardly acceptable in visual or any other terms. This was one of the twenty-eight short poems which make up *Sea Garden*. ('Oread', incidentally, was omitted from that volume. But it is included in her *Collected Poems*.) *Sea Garden* stands with *Cathay* as the chief memorial of the Imagiste group, but its existence implies a formidable critique of Imagist theory by Imagist practice. If the reading of H.D.'s work offered here is right, the Imagist formula of 'direct treatment' or 'direct presentation' must yield to Symbolist method. H.D. herself implied this in one of her rare critical utterances. In 1916 she reviewed John Gould Fletcher's *Goblins and Pagodas* in terms that become an assertion of a Symbolist poetic:

In the second section of his book, Mr. Fletcher deals with a more difficult and, when successfully handled, richer form of art; not that of direct presentation, but that of suggestion . . . .

. . . It is no static vision that Mr. Fletcher seeks to give us . . . . He uses the direct image, it is true, but he seems to use it as a means of evoking other and vaguer images . . . .

His poetry is not static, as I say—it is moving, whirling, drifting.[41]

H.D. may have been over-praised by her contemporaries, but some of her

64

early poems show a considerable gift. After *Sea Garden* her work declined. She began to retreat into tradition. Presumably she felt she had exhausted her ability to utilize the originality of her earlier format. H.D.'s initial impetus preceded the formation of Imagisme. It did not long survive the movement. The good poems in her next collection, *Hymen* (1921), are few. Sometimes she seems to be living on her own manner, reworking old themes and images without any renewal of intensity. These are the opening lines of the title poem:

> From the closed garden
> Where our feet pace
> Back and forth each day,
> This gladiolus white,
> This red, this purple spray—
> Gladiolus tall with dignity
> As yours, lady—we lay
> Before your feet and pray:
> . . . .

Here the rhythms are becoming mechanical, with a tendency to decompose into alexandrines. The tautness and subtle physicality of her language have dwindled into mannerism. There is far less pressure of experience. Pound had demanded that poetry be precise, but precision is what this example lacks. The first stanza of 'Why Have You Sought', from the same volume, shows other weaknesses:

> Why have you sought the Greeks, Eros,
> when such delight was yours
> in the far depth of sky:
> there you could note bright ivory
> take colour when she bent her face,
> and watch fair gold shed gold
> on radiant surface of porch and pillar:
> and ivory and bright gold,
> polished and lustrous grow faint
> beside that wondrous flesh
> and print of her foot-hold:
> Love, why do you tempt the Grecian porticoes?

The form is hesitant and unsatisfactory. The whole poem is fatigued, an amalgam of clichés created by her own practice. The war and the failure of her marriage seem to have had a crucial effect in precipitating H.D.'s withdrawal to Geneva and into a privacy that was a refuge rather than a workshop for art. After 1920 she entered a long period of seclusion, mediated by friendships and—much later—by psychoanalysis with Freud. Later still, her poetic gift renewed and strengthened itself in her war trilogy *The Walls Do Not Fall* (1944). Her psychoanalytical experiences are described in *Tribute to Freud*, a book that deserves to become a classic. Success in the Imagiste years came quickly to H.D., perhaps too quickly. In even the best of her early poems there is more intensity than substance. After *Sea Garden* the intensity dwindles with no corresponding gain in substance. The discipline of the more traditional forms that she attempted in the twenties and thirties brought little achievement in itself but served her well in the more complex developments of her late work.

In America she remains an important poet and one of the central figures of Imagism. In England, where she first gained success, she is today little known.

\* \* \*

Aldington had studied classical subjects at school and university: Greek mythology, in particular, seems to have influenced him.

> They have torn the gold tettinx
> From my hair;
> And wrenched the bronze sandals
> From my ankles.
>
> They have taken from me my friend
> Who knew the holy wisdom of poets,
> Who had drunk at the feast
> Where Simonides sang.[42]

These, the opening lines of 'Captive', suggest the central defect of Aldington's Hellenism compared with that of H.D. Sometimes his attempts at re-interpreting the classical world are distinctly unfortunate:

> *In the Via Sestina*
> O daughter of Isis,
> . . . .
> A manifest harlot.
> Straight and slim art thou
> As a marble phallus; . . .

Such language had no doubt a shock value in 1914. When the shock effect was exhausted the appeal of the poem was lost with it. This judgment must apply to much of Aldington's work at other stages of his career.

Aldington was by several years the youngest of the Imagists, but he had been a copious writer of verse as a schoolboy before he started to experiment with free forms in 1910 or 1911. His gifts, and perhaps his precocity, impressed many people. Orage gave him a commission to visit Italy to write prose articles for *The New Age* in 1913.[43] Pound though more sceptical, allowed him some merit. In a letter to Harriet Monroe he wrote:

> Aldington has his occasional concentrations, and for that reason it is always possible that he will do a fine thing. There is a superficial cleverness in him, then a great and lamentable gap, then the hard point, the true centre, out of which a fine thing may come at any time.[44]

Throughout his life Aldington was a prolific writer and his poetic output was considerable. Not only Pound but Herbert Read put high value on Aldington as a poet.[45] He has been praised by critics, themselves practising writers who were not necessarily sympathetic to modernist developments in poetry.[46]

In spite of his interest in classical literature, Aldington's tone and temper were anything but classical. He had a certain lyrical gift, but the characteristic tone of his work is anger. This is the *indignatio* of the Romans, but it is not *saeva*. Aldington is satirical and combative, in a way only paralleled among the Imagist writers by some of Pound's squibs and satires, but in personal bitterness Pound never equalled Aldington. (Hulme, by contrast, while aggressive and dogmatic, sometimes particularly so in his art criticism, kept his ideas and his dogmatism out of his poetry.) As a writer of verse satire or protest Aldington seems to fail, above all because of his inability to transmute personal bitterness into more objective statement. In his prose he was sometimes more effective. There is a further reason why Aldington's poetic fulminations are often ineffective. Verse satire needs the benefit of a recognized form, such as the couplets of Pope and Dryden or, failing that, an established rhetoric as with the Latin satirists, Martial and Juvenal. Free verse with its lyrical implications is a questionable medium for pure satire. Moreover, satire as rhetoric requires a public alignment. That alignment may be political or social. It cannot be merely personal. Satire is grounded in anger and hate; and hate without a counterpoise of purpose is sterile. Aldington lacks the complex blending of satirical and lyrical motifs, a technique of which Eliot, at least in his earlier work, was master. The result is a vehement note of personal hostility which suggests the 'Angry Young Men' of the 1950s were not as novel as they imagined. These lines are from a longer poem about Aldington's early life:

I hate that town;
I hate the town I lived in when I was little;
I hate to think of it.
There were always clouds, smoke, rain
In that dingy little valley.
It rained; it always rained,
I think I never saw the sun until I was nine
And then it was too late;
Everything's too late after the first seven years.
. . . .

It was all so dull—
Except a few grey legs under shiny black umbrellas
Running along the grey shiny pavements;
Sometimes there was a waggon
Whose horses made a strange loud hollow sound
With their hoofs
Through the silent rain.

I was like a moth—
Like one of those grey Emperor moths
Which flutter through the vines at Capri.
And that damned little town was my matchbox,
Against whose sides I beat and beat
Until my wings were torn and faded, and dingy
As that damned little town.

The old gibe that free verse is chopped-up prose seems to be justified here. Even bitterness does not give Aldington any marked rhythmical intensity. The language is unattractive: the effect is of an outburst of rage, a quarrel that lacks even the specious dignity of a war. As a poetic method the crude linearity is unsatisfactory.

Aldington took to free verse, as he himself stated:

partly because I was fatigued with rhyme and partly because of the interest I had in poetic experiment. I didn't know Heine or Patmore's 'Unknown Eros', and never suspected the existence of the French vers librists. I got the idea from a chorus in the Hippolytus of Euripides.[47]

Whatever a poet takes from foreign sources, his rhythms and vocabulary will depend principally on the matching of his own sensibility with models among the predecessors in his own language. Aldington's dependence on his English predecessors was considerable. No doubt he also learned something from H.D.; but not enough to give his lyrical work any distinct individual flavour. Aldington was frequent and energetic in his denunciation of Wilde, Francis Thompson, the English Aesthetes and the nineties poets. But something of Wilde and Aestheticism, mediated through their vociferous opponent W. E. Henley, had penetrated Aldington's work:

> The ancient songs
> Pass deathward mournfully.
>
> Cold lips that sing no more, and withered wreaths,
> Regretful eyes and drooping breasts and wings ...
> Symbols of ancient songs
> Mournfully passing
> Down to the great white surges,
> Watched of none
> Save the frail sea birds
> And the lithe pale girls
> Daughters of Okeanos.

These are the opening lines from 'Choricos' (Χορικός), a poem much admired in his own circle (the Imagistes at this early stage got little approval outside their own group) as modern and original. It may have had the temporary glitter of novelty, but the language is faded or trite; the rhythms are borrowed. Much of it could be realigned and written in slack pentameters. Aldington came closer to success in some of his attempts to write about contemporary life. The opening of 'In the Tube' is characteristic, though marred by one unfortunate line:

> The electric car jerks;
> I stumble on the slats of the floor,
> Fall into a leather seat
> And look up.
>
> A row of advertisements,
> A row of windows,
> Set in brown woodwork pitted with brass nails,
> A row of hard faces,
> Immobile,
> In the swaying train,
> Rush across the flickering background of fluted dingy tunnel;

69

A row of eyes,
Eyes of greed, of pitiful blankness, of plethoric
                                    complacency,
Immobile,
Gaze, stare at one point,
At my eyes.

. . . .

He is at his best when he abandons his desire to shock. In these 'Images'
perception and feeling join in a way rare in his more ambitious poems.

I

Like a gondola of green scented fruits
Drifting along the dark canals at Venice,
You, O exquisite one,
Have entered my desolate city.

III

A rose-yellow moon in a pale sky
When the sunset is faint vermilion
On the mist among the tree-boughs
Are you to me.

V

The red deer are high on the mountain,
They are beyond the last pine-trees.
And my desires have run with them.

VI

The flower which the wind has shaken
Is soon filled again with rain;
So does my heart fill slowly with tears
Until you return.

Here the poetic statement is limited to the moment of lyrical response
with no time for additions of thought or comment. These short sentences
are examples of what Pound called the presentation of image, but the
images Aldington offers are lyrical (emotional and rhythmical) rather
than visual in origin.

Aldington continued to write verse throughout most of a long literary
career. After the war, in which he served unwillingly but with distinction,
his poetic canons changed. In a letter to Herbert Read he renounced his
earlier allegiances:

70

I abandon, cast off, utterly deny the virtue of 'extreme compression and essential significance of every word.' I say that is the narrow path that leads to sterility. It makes a desert and you call it art. Pound, Flint, both went down on that; I saw them go . . . .[48]

Yet the technical principles of Imagism remained with him even in the long poems with which he experimented in the nineteen-twenties and early thirties, *A Fool i' the Forest* (1925) and *A Dream in the Luxembourg* (1930). These seem faded now, like much of Aldington's poetic output, but something of his own angry vitality and his odd half-hidden but genuine sensibility can be found, if only at moments, in most of what he wrote. In later life Aldington's claims for his own poetic importance were modest. In his anthology *Poetry of the English-Speaking World* (1947) he includes Pound, H.D., Ford Madox Ford and Hulme, though not himself. He gives a generous selection of D. H. Lawrence but excludes Flint, Amy Lowell and J. G. Fletcher among his colleagues of *Some Imagist Poets*. In the introduction to his own collected poems he wrote:

. . . I claim no share whatever in the so-called 'revolution of 1912'. It was a mere accident that what I was writing then chanced to meet with the approval of the verse revolutionaries, just as the publication of the poems in America was an accident. I am not ambitious to be known as the introducer or part introducer of some novelty in writing.

And he continues:

Willy-nilly I have been associated with the 'revolt of 1912,' and I think it appropriate to say a few words to dissociate myself from attitudes towards poetry which are not mine. I have already implied that I do not believe in willed or self-conscious 'originality.' I do not believe either that poetry is a matter of technique.[49]

Behind these changes of public attitude lay Aldington's unceasing bitterness and disappointment. In private life a man of great charm and generosity, he seems to have changed radically whenever he sat down to write. His hurt and angry feelings were always with him, though no doubt the war intensified them. Sometimes he attained a genuine statement of feeling unaffected by the mannerisms and excesses of his literary personality. The humanity of this short war poem is a fitting place at which to leave and to remember Aldington:

*Battlefield*

The wind is piercing chill
 And blows fine grains of snow
  Over this shell-rent ground;
Every house in sight
Is smashed and desolate.
But in this fruitless land,
Thorny with wire
And foul with rotting clothes and sacks
The crosses flourish—
Ci-gît, ci-gît, ci-gît. . . .
'Ci-gît i soldat Allemand,
*Priez pour lui*'.

\*     \*     \*

Ezra Pound was no beginner in poetry when he started his propaganda for Imagisme. *Ripostes* is often regarded as his first modern collection. In fact *Ripostes* is a transitional volume, joining the old-fashioned literariness of the early work[50] with the conscious modernism of *Lustra* and *Cathay*. Most of the poems of *Ripostes* offer wry commentary on Pound's own doctrine of revolution or renovation in literature. From his first published work Pound had experimented with rhythm and metre.[51] By the beginning of 1912 he was the author of five volumes. The majority of poems in these disprove the comfortable notion that even the immature work of a man of talent is always interesting. Not only is the achievement in Pound's early work often slight, its whole atmosphere is musty. The deliberate skill with which he changed his style from 1912 onwards is remarkable and presents a situation with which there are few parallels. In 1909 he must have seemed a reactionary figure beside Hulme or even Flint. His interests were medieval; his culture outmoded. At the beginning of 1912 he was still rather old-fashioned compared with his new colleagues. In Brigit Patmore's drawing-room Pound learned about Gautier and encountered the new excitement of H.D.'s poems. From Flint he gained knowledge of recent French poets. Flint's scholarly knowledge often outran his taste. This may explain Pound's acquaintance with and preference for some of the less considerable French poets. For example, Gautier rather than Baudelaire, Henri de Régnier rather than Mallarmé, Spire not Apollinaire. But there is a similar perversity of taste in Hulme's preference for Gustave Kahn; and a greater poet than any of them, Rilke, absorbed much from Francis Jammes (another of Pound's favourites) and Paul Fort.

Pound now began his personal act of renovation and at the same time helped to drag English and American poetic taste with him into the twentieth century. Much of the subject material of *Ripostes* is taken from the past, but renovation, for Pound, meant a new approach to the language and form of the poem. Both in language and rhythm it is transitional work. Pound had always experimented with poetic form. Much even of his earlier work, though not free verse by English standards, would be regarded as *vers libre* by the more stringent requirements of French:

> *La Fraisne*
> Once when I was among the young men....
> And they said I was quite strong, among the young men.
> Once there was a woman....
> ....but I forget ... she was ....
> ....I hope she will not come again.
> ....I do not remember....
>
> I think she hurt me once, but...
> That was very long ago.
>
> I do not like to remember things any more.
>
> I like one little band of winds that blow
> In the ash trees here:
> For we are quite alone
> Here 'mid the ash trees.[52]
>
> . . . . .

This poem appeared in the collection *Personae* first published in 1909. The comment of Edward Thomas, older than Pound but himself not yet a poet, is worth remembering. In his review of *Personae* he wrote:

> the rhythms are at one time so free as not to be distinguishable at first from prose ... .[53]

Pound's qualities at this time were summarized by Rupert Brooke, who wrote a criticism of *Personae* for the *Cambridge Review*. Brooke called Pound

> blatant, full of foolish archaisms, obscure through awkward language not subtle thought, and formless; he tastes experience keenly, has an original outlook, flashes into brilliance, occasionally ... . When he passes from stammering to speech, and when he has more clearly recognized the nature of poetry, he may be a great poet.[54]

Brooke's judgment is acute, if not tender. Later, Pound was even more severe about this early work:

A collection of cream puffs ... neither eye nor ear. Ignorance that didn't know the meaning of 'Wardour Street'.[55]

Here is an example of what Pound meant. It is from his 'Villonaud for this Yule':

> Towards the Noel that morte saison
> (*Christ make the shepherds' homage dear!*)
> Then when the grey wolves everychone
> Drink of the winds their chill small-beer
> And lap o' the snows food's gueredon
> Then makyth my heart his yule-tide cheer
> (Skoal! with the dregs if the clear be gone!)
> Wining the ghosts of yester-year.

The difference between this and the poems gathered in *Ripostes* is considerable. The twenty-six poems included in *Ripostes* represent an odd mixture of forms and styles. In 'Apparuit', with its hendecasyllabic lines, Pound thought he was writing sapphics and was unwise enough to say so to Edward Marsh, 'which,' as Marsh recalled, 'implanted in me a lasting suspicion of his artistic seriousness.'[56] It is unfortunate that Pound attempted to meet the classically educated editor of *Georgian Poetry* on his own cultural ground. 'Apparuit', if imperfect as metrical pastiche, is a delicate experiment in rhythms. Only here again the diction is semi-archaic:

> Green the ways, the breath of the fields is thine there,
> open lies the land, yet the steely going
> darkly hast thou dared and the dreaded aether
>                     parted before thee.

The inversions of syntax and the stock use of the second person singular stamp the poem as still in Pound's Victorian manner. In this first stage of his drive towards modernization Pound seems often to be talking about, rather than achieving, modernity. Criticism has tended to fasten on Δώρια and 'The Return' as evidence of Pound's change of direction. Yet the short poem 'The Picture', in which Pound is working in blank, not free, verse, is a more effective example of his art at this period:

> The eyes of this dead lady speak to me,
> For here was love, was not to be drowned out,
> And here desire, not to be kissed away.
> The eyes of this dead lady speak to me.

74

Δώρια and 'The Return' are among the better poems in *Ripostes*. Of the two 'The Return' is the more interesting.[57] It is probably the first poem in which a certain flavour, characteristic of Pound's maturity, can be detected. Δώρια, by comparison, whatever its rhythmic subtleties, is a reworking of well-worn elements of language. 'The Return' is more enigmatic. There has been a good deal of critical discussion about its meaning. Current opinion seems to have settled for the view that it is a poem about poetry. This can almost be compared with Anthony Burgess hearing a lecture in North Carolina which built its argument on the discovery that the name of his first hero R. Ennis was *sinner* spelt backwards. Burgess said he was shocked to realize that, in fifteen years, he had not recognized this. The fact remains, whichever way you look at it, 'The Return' is ambiguous, a quality hardly corresponding with the Imagiste rules shortly to be proclaimed by Pound. Here, surely, Yeats' criticism is applicable—his remark that Pound seemed always to write as if he were 'a brilliant improvisator translating at sight from an unknown Greek masterpiece.'[58]

> See, they return; ah, see the tentative
> Movements, and the slow feet,
> The trouble in the pace and the uncertain
> Wavering!
>
> See, they return, one, and by one,
> With fear, as half-awakened;
> As if the snow should hesitate
> And murmur in the wind,
>              and half turn back;
>
> These were the 'Wing'd-with Awe,'
>              Inviolable.
>
> Gods of the wingèd shoe!
> With them the silver hounds,
>              sniffing the trace of air!
>
> Haie! Haie!
>              These were the swift to harry;
> These the keen-scented;
> These were the souls of blood.
>
> Slow on the leash,
>              pallid the leash-men!

The pace of Pound's development after 1912 suggests that *Ripostes* is not so much the beginning of his mature work as the end of his pupilage.

The first announcement of Imagisme was a proclamation of readiness for new departures. The impulse to change, naturally enough, preceded the ability to change. When 1912 opened Pound was a more reactionary poet than H.D. or even Aldington; a less accurate scholar than Flint; and a man curiously unaware of much that was happening in European literature. Gautier's *Émaux et Camées*, first published in Paris in 1852, was a revelation to Pound in 1912.[59] Pound's early education had been one-sided. His M.A. programme at the University of Pennsylvania shows that he had been a thorough-going medievalist.[60] Only in the study of Spanish drama had his reading got as far as the sixteenth century.

From the autumn of 1912 the tempo of Pound's development intensified. The first sign of his new manner was the sequence of poems called 'Contemporania', originally published in *Poetry* in the spring of 1913.[61] With the various moods and techniques of these poems Pound's Imagiste manner announced itself. In the following year he added the doctrine of Vorticism and, in curious counterpoint, the more delicate lyricism of *Cathay*. The important post-Imagist development summarized in *Mauberley* followed in 1919-20, *after* he had begun work on the *Cantos*.

In 1913 a new dynamism is evident in some of Pound's poems. (The quotations that follow are from 'Contemporania'.)

> *Tenzone*
> I beg you, my friendly critics,
> Do not set about to procure me an audience.
>
> I mate with my free kind upon the crags;
>     the hidden recesses
> Have heard the echo of my heels,
>     in the cool light,
>     in the darkness.

Perhaps the finest poem of the sequence is 'The Garden':

> Like a skein of loose silk blown against a wall
> She walks by the railing of a path in Kensington Gardens,
> And she is dying piece-meal
>     of a sort of emotional anaemia.
>
> And round about there is a rabble
> Of the filthy, sturdy, unkillable infants of the very poor.
> They shall inherit the earth.

In her is the end of breeding.
Her boredom is exquisite and excessive.
She would like some one to speak to her,
And is almost afraid that I
        will commit that indiscretion.

Mixed with this more reflective vein are the squibs or epigrams with
which Pound appeared as a ferocious commentator on the age. In the
autumn of 1913 Pound published another batch of poems in *Poetry*.[62]
Among these there are short lyrical pieces like 'April', which rely for
much of their effectiveness on the device of superposition in the final line:

> Three spirits came to me
> And drew me apart
> To where the olive boughs
> Lay stripped upon the ground:
> Pale carnage beneath bright mist.

There is also 'A Song of the Degrees', which suggests the beginnings of
a complex synaesthesia that points towards Vorticism:

> I
> Rest with me Chinese colours,
> For I think the glass is evil.
>
> II
> The wind moves above the wheat—
> With a silver crashing,
> A thin war of metal.
> I have known the golden disc,
> I have seen it melting above me.
> I have known the stone-bright place,
>         The hall of clear colours.
>         . . . .

In 'Les Millwin' (first published as 'Lustra, II') there appears a note of
more ribald comment by which Pound was beginning to tell London
artistic society what he thought of it.

> The little Millwins attend the Russian Ballet,
> The mauve and greenish souls of the little
>         Millwins

Were seen lying along the upper seats
Like so many unused boas.

The turbulent and undisciplined host of art
    students—
The rigorous deputation from 'Slade'—
Was before them.

With arms exalted, with fore-arms
Crossed in great futuristic X's, the art students
Exulted, they beheld the splendours of *Cleopatra*.

And the little Millwins beheld these things;
With their large and anaemic eyes they looked
    out upon this configuration.

Let us therefore mention the fact,
For it seems to us worthy of record.

This tone of acerbity was to become stronger. Poems like 'Les Millwin'
or the numerous sly vignettes that occur in *Lustra* have little in common
with 'The Return', or indeed with the prescriptions of Imagisme. The
Greek calm is broken; musical subtlety is replaced by a more abrupt
energy. These poems suggest not so much Imagisme in its original sense
as the angry observation and disturbing beauty that characterized
European modernism.

Latin literature, particularly the work of Martial and Juvenal, gives
many instances of such ferocious social commentary, and Pound's
epigrams of this period suggest a general debt to the Roman satirists.
Today, in an age where both tabus and standards are relaxed, such
squibs as 'Phyllidula' or 'The Patterns' no longer shock:

Phyllidula is scrawny but amorous,
Thus have the gods awarded her,
That in pleasure she receives more than she can give;
If she does not count this blessed
Let her change her religion.

### The Patterns

Erinna is a model parent,
Her children have never discovered her adulteries.

Lalage is also a model parent,
Her offspring are fat and happy.

78

English is not well adapted to the lapidary severity of Martial or Petronius. What is weighted and distanced in Latin can become coarse or strident in English, a language where vernacular and literary elements tend to merge into one another easily but not always elegantly.

Pound's lyrical talent served him better than satire. Poems like 'April' or the couplet 'Alba' show a pictorial actualization of the Imagiste formula:

> As cool as the pale wet leaves
> of lily-of-the-valley
> She lay beside me in the dawn.

Here, as in 'Shop Girl', Pound swerves from Imagist dogma by the unnecessary use of simile. Yet Pound's work in those years shows a wider range than that of his colleagues. This applies whether he is remembering a child:

> *Post Mortem Conspectu*
> A brown, fat babe sitting in the lotus,
> And you were glad and laughing
> With a laughter not of this world.

Or celebrating a half-erotic moment, as in 'Shop Girl':

> For a moment she rested against me
> Like a swallow half blown to the wall,
> And they talk of Swinburne's women,
> And the shepherdess meeting with Guido.
> And the harlots of Baudelaire.

It is found equally in his moments of satire. The poem that follows, 'The Temperaments', was presumably too outspoken to find periodical publication. It was issued with, though not published in, the 'unexpurgated' first edition of *Lustra* in 1916. Its first general publication was in *Personae* (New York, 1926).

> Nine adulteries, 12 liaisons, 64 fornications
> and something approaching a rape
> Rest nightly upon the soul of our delicate friend
> Florialis,
> And yet the man is so quiet and reserved in demeanour
> That he passes for both bloodless and sexless.

79

D

Bestidides, on the contrary, who both talks and writes
   of nothing save copulation,
Has become the father of twins,
But he accomplished this feat at some cost;
He had to be four times cuckold.

In the late months of 1913 he found new inspiration in the Classical
literature of China, through obtaining the papers of Ernest Fenollosa
from Fenollosa's widow.

> *Lament of the Frontier Guard*
> By the North Gate, the wind blows full of sand,
> Lonely from the beginning of time until now!
> Trees fall, the grass goes yellow with autumn.
> I climb the towers and towers
>    to watch out the barbarous land:
> Desolate castle, the sky, the wide desert.
> There is no wall left to this village.
> Bones white with a thousand frosts,
> High heaps, covered with trees and grass;
> Who brought this to pass?

The quality of this work has not secured Pound's reputation among
sinologues. It is perhaps even lower in this area than it is among scholars
of Anglo-Saxon who have read his version of *The Seafarer*. (Though a
recent and capable translator of Anglo-Saxon into English verse, Michael
Alexander, praises Pound's rendering.)[63] T. S. Eliot, in a characteristically
double-edged sentence praised Pound as 'the inventor of Chinese poetry
for our time.'[64] The argument about Pound's Chinese scholarship was
settled by Pound himself, when he included his Chinese versions among
his original poems. They have even less relationship to classical Chinese
verse than his Morris-inspired medievalism had to the European Middle
Ages. As poems in English they are perhaps the culmination of the whole
Imagiste enterprise.[65] Pound resorted also to the mediocre rhyming
versions of Chinese poetry by the English scholar H. A. Giles.[66] Whatever
his sources Pound used them to make work out that is altogether his own.
He could write with great delicacy and insight about childhood:

> *The River-Merchant's Wife: A Letter*
> While my hair was still cut straight across my forehead
> I played about the front gate, pulling flowers.
> You came by on bamboo stilts, playing horse,

80

You walked about my seat, playing with blue plums.
And we went on living in the village of Chokan:
Two small people, without dislike or suspicion.

and was equally skilful in establishing an atmosphere of loneliness and claustrophobia. Here is 'The Beautiful Toilet':

> Blue, blue is the grass about the river
> And the willows have overfilled the close garden.
> And within, the mistress, in the midmost of her youth,
> White, white of face, hesitates, passing the door.
> Slender, she puts forth a slender hand;
>
> And she was a courtezan in the old days,
> And she has married a sot,
> Who now goes drunkenly out
> And leaves her too much alone.

One advantage of the Chinese convention was that it enabled Pound to indulge in a certain mandarin fineness, even preciosity.

In *Cathay* Pound got the best of two worlds. While freed from the strait-jacket of literal translation he was able to take many ideas from Fenollosa's drafts. For someone as unconfident in his own ideas as Pound (however undeservedly) this was a useful bonus.

Early in 1914 Pound attached himself to Vorticism. He continued to hold to Imagism (with or without its terminal 'e') until well into 1915, but he labelled himself 'Vorticist' on his first appearance in *Who's Who* (London) in 1915 and kept this description until he became 'Poet' in the 1919 volume. The poems written in the name of the new movement were few, but no doubt Pound regarded all his work of this period as a manifestation of Vorticism. 'The Game of Chess' suggests the kind of prismatic effect Pound was searching for through Vorticism.

*Dogmatic Statement Concerning The Game of Chess:*
*Theme for a Series of Pictures*

> Red knights, brown bishops, bright queens,
> Striking the board, falling in strong 'L's of colour,
> Reaching and striking in angles,
>     holding lines in one colour,
> This board is alive with light;
>     these pieces are living in form,

Their moves break and reform the pattern:
    Luminous green from the rooks,
Clashing with 'X's of queens,
    looped with the knight-leaps.

'Y' pawns, cleaving, embanking!
Whirl! Centripetal! Mate! King down in the vortex,
Clash, leaping of bands, straight strips of hard colour,
Blocked lights working in. Escapes. Renewal of contest.

In the late summer of 1914 Pound's command over the Imagistes was overthrown. The shock of his rejection was no doubt diminished by his adherence to Vorticism. Pound's *Catholic Anthology*, which introduced Eliot's work to English readers, had only limited success. Yet through all the difficulties and disappointments, and against the terrible background of the war, Pound's own development continued. By 1916 Imagism was a dirty word for him. In his 'Status Rerum—the Second' he wrote that Imagisme had gone off 'into froth'.[67] Some of the work that appeared in Amy Lowell's anthologies proves his point. By 1917 he was calling for a return to strict form, though the first draft of the *Cantos* published in 1917 and 1918 show renewed dependence on Browning's blank verse.[68] (This display of dependence is largely eliminated in the revisions and rhythmical reworkings of the definitive text of the *Cantos*.)

In 1919 he published *Quia Pauper Amavi*, which includes *Homage to Sextus Propertius* (written in 1917), a poem in Roman dress incorporating vivid social criticism. In it Pound showed a profound and prophetic awareness of the inner decay of the British Imperial system. *Mauberley*, his 'farewell to London', followed in 1920. For some of his readers, F. R. Leavis among them, this was the peak of his achievement. By Christmas 1920 Pound had left England, moving first to Paris and then in 1924 to Rapallo. He spent the rest of his long life in Italy, apart from the tragic years of his captivity in America from 1945-58:

### Canto LXXXIII
No man who has passed a month in the death cells
believes in cages for beasts.

For over forty years the *Cantos* remained his chief creative interest. In them he applied Imagist-Vorticist method to a poem of major dimensions. The result, though there are superb passages in the *Cantos*, was a heroic failure. Pound himself in his old age thought so and it is difficult to disagree with him:

It's a botch ... I picked out this thing and that thing that interested me, and then jumbled them into a bag. But that's not the way to make ... a *work of art*.[69]

It is hard to say what went wrong. Certainly, Imagist methods are unsuitable to a long poem. Ambition caused Pound to deviate from his own canons and to replace condensation by extensity. His poetic work after *Mauberley* was based on a mammoth self-contradiction. 'This thing and that thing' too often belong in notebooks rather than a finished poem. Maybe Pound, despite his considerable surface confidence, did not believe sufficiently in himself except as a technician. His ideas, most of them acquired in his London years, were borrowed then kept with a tenacity that became obsessional. As Orage had predicted, in the end they proved his ruin. Yet through all his vicissitudes his lyric gift remained:

### Canto XIII
The blossoms of the apricot blow from the east to the west,
And I have tried to keep them from falling.

Suffering, as a prisoner of his country's army, brought a return to more direct feeling. He could see

### Canto LXXIV
The enormous tragedy of the dream in the peasant's bent shoulders.

But his work after the *Pisan Cantos* was frustrated by the long years of imprisonment in Washington when he was in a madhouse (and President Eisenhower occupied the White House).

### The River Song
And I have moped in the Emperor's garden, awaiting an order-to-write!

he had written in earlier and happier times. The order never came. When he was at last freed to return to Italy, something had broken in him and it was too late.

\*　　\*　　\*

With Pound the list of the poets of *Imagisme* ends. The next wave of Imagist writers were, to a large extent, Pound's disciples. There were also other writers who, while not calling themselves Imagists, had close ties with the movement during its crucial years.

One of them, Ford Madox Hueffer, had much influence on Pound and was himself considerably affected by Imagism. Born in 1873, he had already had a long career as a novelist, essayist and poet. Hueffer was never in any formal sense an Imagiste, but his propaganda for the new movement was generous,[70] and he was recognized among its sponsors as early as 1913. Between 1893 and 1912 he had published six books of verse, most of which were included in his *Collected Poems* in 1913. But until the formation of the Imagiste group Hueffer's attitude to poetry had been that of a negligent and rather patronizing amateur. In 1909, as the busy editor of *The English Review*, he had taken no part in the Tour d'Eiffel meetings. Under Hueffer's editorship *The English Review* had a section called 'Modern Poetry', but many of the poems appearing in it were indifferent. During 1909 Pound and Flint contributed poems to *The English Review*, but these were examples of their early and more retrograde work. Up to 1913 there is little to indicate that Hueffer was regarded with much seriousness as a poet, by himself or anyone else. Pound reviewed his pamphlet *High Germany* in Harold Monro's *Poetry Review*,[71] and praised Hueffer for making a 'serious' experiment and for the quality of his 'cadence'. But he noted a lack of intensity in the language and summed up:

> His flaw is the flaw of impressionism, impressionism, that is, carried out of its due medium. Impressionism belongs in paint, it is of the eye .... Poetry is in some odd way concerned with the specific gravity of things, with their nature ....
> ... the *conception* of poetry is a process more intense than the *reception* of an impression. And no impression, however carefully articulated, can, recorded, convey that feeling of sudden light which the work of art should and must convey.[72]

Later Pound was to regard Hueffer more highly. At the end of 1913 Hueffer's name was linked with the Imagistes in an essay on the movement that appeared in the first and only issue of a review called *The Cerebralist*.

> The Grand-father of the movement is Mr Ford Madox Hueffer. He is an Impressionist. They respect his views on prose, and read his later volumes of poetry with interest and kindliness. Mr Hueffer is not an Imagiste, but he had done some pioneer work for which they are grateful.[73]

Having proffered Hueffer as the grandfather of Imagisme, the article proceeded to deflate him. The author quoted at length from 'To All the Dead', then added:

> Of course an Imagiste would scarcely want to print that, but then Mr. Hueffer is essentially a prose writer. He does not believe in vers libre,

which is practised by most of the Imagistes. He thinks blank verse is enough....[74]

This suggests lack of knowledge of Hueffer's verse, much of which is composed in a jogging poulter's measure of free verse with interspersed rhyming. Hueffer had freed himself from traditional form, but he had done so less by art than accident. It is as if he got his form from half-conscious reminiscences of Christina Rossetti's *Goblin Market*. He was a consistent admirer of her work.[75] The colloquial or conversational tone that characterizes his poems even in the nineties[76] seems to be due rather to absence of literary pretensions than to any deliberate theory. Hueffer's poetic work up to 1913 is closer to light verse than to poetry as a pre-meditated art. He recognized this when he wrote:

> ... the writing of verse hardly appears to me to be a matter of work: it is a process, as far as I am concerned, too uncontrollable. From time to time words in verse have come into my head and I have written them down, quite powerlessly and without much interest, under the stress of certain emotions.[77]

This statement comes from the Preface to his *Collected Poems*.

By the beginning of 1914 signs of a literary equivalent of market operations were becoming suspiciously apparent in Imagist activity. Hueffer, already mentioned from time to time as an Impressionist in *Poetry* during 1913, was now linked with the Imagistes. His work was treated with increased respect by Pound, who reviewed the *Collected Poems* in flattering terms in *Poetry*, under the title 'Mr. Hueffer and the Prose Tradition in Verse'.[78] In other quarters the book received little attention.[79] This might be regarded as a comment on the haphazard state of poetry reviewing, then as today, in England. In general, however, Hueffer's poetic output by the age of forty was unimpressive. So far, he was most effective in light or satiric verse. The refrain of 'The Three-Ten' mocks a whole tradition of literary pretensions:

> But see, but see! The clock strikes three above
> the Kilburn Station,
> Those maids, thank God, are 'neath the sod and all
> their generation.[80]

In his more serious poems there is often a reminiscence of Browning:

> *Finchley Road*
> You should be a queen or a duchess rather,
> Reigning, instead of a warlike father,

85

> In peaceful times o'er a tiny town,
> Where all the roads wind up and down
> From your little palace—a small old place
> Where every soul should know your face
> And bless your coming.

In most of his verse there is an uncertainty of tone. He wanders between formal and familiar and seems often to be rather petulantly shouting at the reader. Sometimes, though, he reached a more impressive cadence:

> Images, simulacra, towns of dreams
> That never march upon each other's borders,
> And bring no comfort to each other's hearts!

Even in Hueffer's early work there are moments of spontaneity which must have offered encouragement to Pound in his attempts to escape from the long tradition of nineteenth-century convention:

> All within is warm,
>     Here without it's very cold,
>     Now the year is grown so old
> And the dead leaves swarm.

Almost the most interesting part of the *Collected Poems* is the Preface, in which Hueffer declares his literary doctrine and asserts his own preferences. He acknowledges that

> most of the verses here printed are rather derivative, and too much governed by the passing sanctions of the moment. But I simply cannot tell; is not one of the functions of verse to register passing emotions?[81]

Above all he emphasizes the importance to the poet of contemporary life:

> I may really say that for a quarter of a century I have kept before me one unflinching aim—to register my own times in terms of my own time, and still more to urge those who are better poets and better prose-writers than myself to have the same aim. I suppose I have been pretty well ignored: I find no signs of my being taken seriously.[82]

For Hueffer the 'Crowd', and the individuals who compose it, 'are the real stuff of poetry of our day.'

This emphasis on contemporaneity and urban life suggests something of what he gave to Pound. On reading Hueffer's poems a certain gap

86

becomes apparent between intentions and performance. 'On Heaven' is not an easy poem to read today. It is sometimes garrulous:

> For God is a good man, God is a kind man,
> And God's a good brother, and God is no blind man,
> And God is our father.

though there is always the possibility that here again he is engaged in complex self-mockery. Lines like the following are hard to reconcile with his involved and increasingly uncomfortable relations with Violet Hunt:

> And so I said to my dear one: 'That is our Lady!'
> And my dear one sat in the shadows; very softly she wept:

> Such joy is in Heaven,
> In the cool of the even,
> After the burden and toil of the days,
> After the heat and haze
> In the vine-hills; or in the shady
> Whispering groves in high passes up in the Alpilles,
> Guarding the castle of God.

There is more energy in some of the descriptive passages. For example, this evocation of olive-trees on the slopes below the mountains:

> They whisper; they whisper that none of the living prevail;
> They whirl in the great mistral over the white, dry sods,
> Like hair blown back from white foreheads in the enormous gale
> Up to the castle walls of God . . . .

Pound's admiration for Hueffer seems by this time to have had few limits. To Harriet Monroe he wrote:

> The Hueffer good? rather! It is the most important poem in the modern manner. The most important single poem that is.[83]

Pound was always ready to acknowledge what he got from Hueffer: 'Fordie knew more about writing than any of "them" or of "us".'[84] But the traffic went two ways. Hueffer's style as a poet changed significantly after 1914. A typical example is *Antwerp*, written to commemorate the Belgian Army's defence of that town in the campaign of 1914. It was first published as a Poetry Bookshop pamphlet with decorations by

Wyndham Lewis. A new fluidity of composition is apparent in lines like these:

> For there is no new thing under the sun,
> Only this uncomely man with a smoking gun
> In the gloom. . . .
> What the devil will he gain by it?
> Digging a hole in the mud and standing all day in the rain by it
> Waiting his doom,
> The sharp blow, the swift outpouring of the blood,
> Till the trench of grey mud
> Is turned to a brown purple drain by it.

There are even lines that read like a faint anticipation of Eliot:

> This is Charing Cross;
> It is midnight;
> There is a great crowd
> And no light.
> . . . .
> She has a dead face;
> She is dressed all in black;
> She wanders to the bookstall and back,
> At the back of the crowd;
> And back again and again back,
> She sways and wanders.
>
> This is Charing Cross;
> It is one o'clock.

Hueffer's horror of melodrama leads here to a surprising decrescendo:

> And it was for this that they endured this gloom;
> This October like November,
> That August like a hundred thousand hours,
> And that September,
> A hundred thousand dragging sunlit days,
> A half October like a thousand years . . . .
> Oh poor dears!

*Antwerp*, like most of Hueffer's verse, is largely forgotten today. Yet T. S. Eliot praised it as 'the only good poem I have met with on the subject of the war.'[85] No doubt Hueffer's sense of the ridiculous, his refusal to be tragic even when most serious, is partly responsible for this. 'The Old Houses of Flanders' is better remembered today. Here Hueffer sheds his mockery but replaces it by a looser tone of self-indulgent whimsy:

And those old eyes,
Very old eyes that have watched the ways of men for generations,
Close for ever.
The high, white shoulders of the gables
Slouch together for a consultation,
Slant drunkenly over in the lea of the flaming cathedrals.

After his own experiences of trench warfare Hueffer adopted the Imagist manner to express his vision of a world that had destroyed itself. In 'When the World Crumbled' he mimics H.D.'s style to produce effects very different from hers:

Once there were purple seas—
Wide, wide ....
And myrtle-groves and cyclamen,
Above the cliff and the stone pines
Where a god watched ....
And thou, oh Lesbian ....
Well, *that's* all done!

After 1918 he wrote less verse. His *Collected Poems*, published in New York in 1936, have not yet been issued in England. In the story of Imagism Hueffer represents an interesting oddity, a writer professionally and passionately involved with the novel, who found himself drawn further into poetry by the links of a brief but intense period of friendships and conversations. With the waning of this group-excitement his interest in poetry dwindled and he returned, renewed, to prose and the business of fiction. It is probable that Hueffer's involvement with the Imagists was important less for the poems that were its immediate result than for the increased impetus to concentration which it gave his prose. By 1923 Ford Madox Ford, as he had become, was at work on *Some Do Not*, the first of the four volumes of *Parade's End*. As a poet he remains undervalued. His late work in particular deserves reconsideration. Hueffer's verse has appealed more to poets such as Eliot, Pound and Robert Lowell than to academic critics. Perhaps because his mockery is closer to life than to literary convention.

Richard Aldington, who greatly admired 'On Heaven' when it was first published, still found parts of the poem worthy of inclusion in his vast anthology *Poetry of the English-Speaking World* more than thirty years later. Perhaps Aldington, with his own bitter memories of 1914-18, had responded also to poems like 'Footsloggers':

> Like a lady's skirt,
> A dim, diaphanous cone of white, the rays
> Of a shaded street lamp, close at hand existed,
> And there was nothing but vileness it could show,
> Vile, pallid faces drifted through, chalk white;
> Vile alcoholic voices in the ear, vile fumes
> From the filthy pavements ... vileness!
> And one thought:
> 'In three days' time we enter the unknown:
> And this is what we die for!'

\* \* \*

Up to 1914 Amy Lowell could have been dismissed as rich, eccentric and an amateur poet. She was forty and had published one book of uninteresting verse in a derivative romantic manner, *A Dome of Many-Coloured Glass* (Boston, 1912). The title from Shelley is in itself a warning. Much of the inspiration of the verse comes from Keats and Alice Meynell. The American critic Louis Untermeyer summed up its qualities at the time of its publication:

> to be brief, in spite of its lifeless classicism, [it] can never rouse one's anger. But to be briefer still, it can not rouse one at all.[86]

The poems signed 'H. D. Imagiste' in *Poetry* in 1913 had a crucial effect on Amy Lowell. She spent June to September of that year in London. There she met Pound and John Gould Fletcher. She returned to Boston an enthusiastic proponent of the new poetry. Her next visit to London in the summer of 1914 resulted in her effective takeover of the Imagist movement.

As a critic and theorist she added nothing to what she had learned from Pound, Flint and even from John Gould Fletcher. Her taste lacked, as Gregory notes, 'the finer discrimination Pound fought for'.[87] As a poet, however derivative, she is more difficult to typify. For three out of the four years of her involvement with Imagism she was in effect editor of *Some Imagist Poets*, the anthology of the survivors from Pound's movement. During those years she published two books of verse, *Sword Blades and Poppy Seed* (New York, 1914) and *Men, Women, and Ghosts* (New York, 1916), as well as two critical studies, *Six French Poets* (New York, 1915) and *Tendencies in Modern American Poetry* (New York, 1917). She was also an active propagandist for the cause of poetry as she understood it. Her attitude in most of her public dealings was that of a missionary rather than a critic. It is easier to place the work of Amy Lowell than to sum it up. She was verbose, prolific, insensitive in many of her experiments, sometimes absurd. Yet she cannot be dismissed. In her verse, as in her life, there is too much adipose. But there is also energy, a degree of talent and the indispensable excitement about language. Even at the beginning of her conversion to Imagism there is a vitality in her townscapes which suggests a more ample energy than that of Flint. These are the opening lines of 'The Captured Goddess':

> Over the housetops,
> Above the rotating chimney-pots,
> I have seen a shiver of amethyst,
> And blue and cinnamon have flickered
> A moment,
> At the far end of a dusty street.[88]

She had also, what most of the Imagists lacked, an ample narrative gift. She often abused this, but was able sometimes to concentrate it to produce a successful poem. The well-known 'Patterns' is a convincing example.

> I walk down the garden paths,
> And all the daffodils
> Are blowing, and the bright blue squills.
> I walk down the patterned garden-paths
> In my stiff, brocaded gown,
> With my powdered hair and jewelled fan,
> I too am a rare
> Pattern. As I wander down
> The garden paths.
> . . . .
> And the plashing of waterdrops
> In the marble fountain
> Comes down the garden-paths.
> The dripping never stops.
> Underneath my stiffened gown
> Is the softness of a woman bathing in a marble basin,
> A basin in the midst of hedges grown
> So thick, she cannot see her lover hiding,
> But she guesses he is near,
> And the sliding of the water
> Seems the stroking of a dear
> Hand upon her.
> What is Summer in a fine brocaded gown!

I should like to see it lying in a heap upon the ground,
All the pink and silver crumpled up on the ground.

Sometimes she found a different note. The short poem 'The Cyclists', founded probably on a memory of her visit to England in 1913, is not entirely successful, but it moves with skill from images to symbols. It carries an ominous hint of prediction:

> Spread on the roadway,
> With open-blown jackets
> Like black, soaring pinions,
> They swoop down the hill-side,
>   The Cyclists.
>
> Seeming dark-plumed
> Birds, after carrion,
> Careening and circling,
> Over the dying
>   Of England.
>
> She lies with her bosom
> Beneath them, no longer
> The dominant Mother,
> The Virile—but rotting
>   Before time.
>
> The smell of her, tainted,
> Has bitten their nostrils,
> Exultant they hover,
> And shadow the sun with
>   Foreboding.

Verbosity remains her salient danger. She used Imagist methods, but too often to fashionable effect rather than from integral conviction. 'The Letter', though a short poem, is long enough to illustrate this tendency:

> Little cramped words scrawling all over the paper
> Like draggled fly's legs,
> What can you tell of the flaring moon
> Through the oak leaves?
> Or of my uncurtained window and the bare floor
> Spattered with moonlight?
> Your silly quirks and twists have nothing in them
> Of blossoming hawthorns,

And this paper is dull, crisp, smooth, virgin of loveliness
Beneath my hand.

I am tired, Beloved, of chasing my heart against
The want of you;
Of squeezing it into little inkdrops,
And posting it.
And I scald alone, here, under the fire
Of the great moon.

This poem is almost a free verse transcript of a nineteenth-century type of lyric. There is much detail but little form. The images of the first stanza have no defined centre. The last six lines could stand alone as an Imagist poem. Her talent is in many ways Victorian; ample and diffuse rather than elegant and concentrated. Often she seems to have adopted the trappings of modernism without penetrating the core of the situation to which it related. But she handled in popularized form many of the problems that Pound and his London colleagues had approached with greater delicacy and insight. Like them her most strenuous attempts were concentrated upon the form of the poem. She turned to free verse: only hers, compared with that of Pound or H.D., is often slapdash or improvised. Much of her work remains closer to traditional metres. Sometimes she falls into a prose flatness, as in 'Afternoon Rain in State Street':

Like a four-sided wedge
The Custom House Tower
Pokes at the low, flat sky,
Pushing it farther and farther up,
Lifting it away from the house-tops,
Lifting it in one piece as though it were a sheet of tin,
With the lever of its apex.

In general there is little rhythmic originality in her work. This may explain some part of her interest in poetic prose. She got her inspiration for this from Paul Fort, one of the group of writers whom she discussed in *Six French Poets*. In collaboration with John Gould Fletcher she experimented with what she called polyphonic prose. This was an unfortunate hybrid, a form of prose which used rhyme and sometimes metre. Paul Fort had handled this in French with a certain dexterity; in English it is hardly viable. To quote the opening of 'The Bombardment' should be sufficient:

Slowly, without force, the rain drops into the city. It stops a moment on the carved head of Saint John, then slides on again, slipping and

trickling over his stone cloak. It splashes from the lead conduit of a gargoyle, and falls from it in turmoil on the stones in the Cathedral Square. Where are the people, and why does the fretted steeple sweep about in the sky? Boom! The sound swings against the rain. Boom, again! After it, only water rushing in the gutters, and the turmoil from the spout of the gargoyle. Silence. Ripples and mutters. Boom!
....

In a few poems she escaped her own affectations and limitations. 'In the Stadium' is not one of her more successful poems, but it has a poignant theme, which is explained in its subtitle, 'Marshal Joffre Reviewing the Harvard Regiment, May 12, 1917':

> They are all like this:
> ....
> Sick old men,
> Driving rapidly before a concourse of people,
> Gay with decorations,
> Crumpled with pain.

And it ends with an image that Pound himself might not have despised:

> Behind the boys
> And the old men,
> Life weeps,
> And sheds her garments
> To the blowing winds.

Her work continued after the final volume of *Some Imagist Poets*. Several more books of poems and a collection of Chinese translations *Fir-Flower Tablets* (1921) appeared before she died in 1925. In *Fir-Flower Tablets* she worked with her friend Florence Ayscough to produce versions of far greater scholarly pretensions than *Cathay*. Here, though, as in too many of her own poems, there was an insufficiency of creative power. It is this failure, coupled with her dangerous and excessive fluency, that has caused her work to suffer a neglect by no means altogether deserved.

* * *

John Gould Fletcher was brought into the Imagist fold as a colleague and friend of Amy Lowell rather than by adherence to the original doctrines of the movement. His position in 1913 is summed up by a letter he wrote to Harriet Monroe. He introduced himself as an American expatriate and expressed his admiration for *Poetry*. He reminded her that

Pound had sent her some of his poems, selected from his *Irradiations*. He added this comment:

> Mr. Pound, as you know, is the great apostle of 'vers libre' and 'Imagisme', and the MSS he sent you were 'vers libre' but not 'Imagist.'

Fletcher continued that he was not 'exclusively' a writer of *vers-libre*. He criticized the possibilities of free verse in English:

> To my mind 'vers libre', as I understand it, can scarcely produce, in the English language, the same effects it has undoubtedly produced in the French. There is a fatal tendency on the part of the language to fall back into an essentially prose rhythm. There is also tendency on the part of the 'vers librists' in English, not to adopt a certain regularity of metre and depart from it occasionally, but to be constantly shifting the rhythm (the direct contrary of the French practice).

> I hope that 'vers libre' will develop. But so far as it has gone, I think it is useful merely in extremely short poems, especially in descriptions of a single brief emotion or small scene, where the play of rhyme would interfere with the full intensity of the color and the words. For long narrative poems, dramatic poems, or a mixture of narrative, descriptive, and dramatic, I am convinced—against my will—that vers libre is at present impotent, and that rhyme and regular metre are essential to give the speed and unity that are required.

And he stated his hostility to Imagism:

> With Mr. Pound's 'school' of 'Imagisme', I am in even greater disagreement. 'Imagisme' is an attitude towards technique, pure and simple. I am unable, and I wish that everyone else were unable, to impose upon myself the pedantic yoke of any particular technique .... I have informed Mr. Pound that I do not intend to hamper myself with his technique and his 'don'ts'.[89]

Later, writing to Amy Lowell, Fletcher stated his dissent from Imagism in still more precise terms:

> I do not believe that a poem should present an 'image,' I believe it should present an emotion. I do not believe in 'clear, hard, and definite presentation.' I believe in a complete, that is to say, shifting and fluid presentation .... I do not believe in cadence, but in rhythm (a different thing altogether). I do not believe altogether in 'externality.' Therefore

I do not accept Imagism. I am a Rhythmist or a Symbolist, but not an Imagist.[90]

It seems surprising that Fletcher managed to associate himself with even the diluted formula of *Some Imagist Poets*. He was an Amygist rather than an Imagist and was presumably persuaded by Amy Lowell. Fletcher is interesting as a lesser poet of his period who moved from romanticism in its nineteenth-century form to an updated method based on free verse and a personal impressionism.

Fletcher's early work is ineffective. He seems to have suffered from an almost pathological lack of humour.[91] The following quatrain must deserve a place in any anthology of bad verse:

> *Song of a Night*
> Last night I lay disgusted, sick at heart,
> Beside a sodden woman of the street:
> Who drowsed, oblivious of the dreadful mart,
> Her outraged body and her blistered feet.[92]

This poem comes from one of the five small books of verse by Fletcher published in the early months of 1913. His predominant mood at this period was autumnal. The melancholy and languor of the nineteenth-century lyric poets seem to have retained an extraordinary fascination for those who succeeded them. These stanzas come from Fletcher's poem 'The Evening Clouds':

> Like long terraces the evening clouds
> Prolong themselves to an infinite grey
> Of distances, as shadows seen in a dream.
>
> Like old parks full of autumnal branches
> Which the winds agitate, slowly to and fro;
> The evening clouds, grey interwoven,
> Sway in a stately measure of old.
> . . . .
> Like colonnades along long terraces
> Prolonged, the colonnades of temples,
> Behind whose bronze gates, never opened,
> Crouch the colossal gods of night.

After this his style changed with surprising speed. He took up free verse. In the process his language and syntax underwent considerable remodelling.[93] Fletcher found his personal style with the sequence called *Irradiations*. This short poem is typical:

*Irradiations VII*
Flickering of incessant rain
On flashing pavements:
Sudden scurry of umbrellas:
Bending, recurved blossoms of the storm.

The winds come clanging and clattering
From long white highroads whipping in ribbons
                       up summits:
They strew upon the city gusty wafts of
                       apple-blossom,
And the rustling of innumerable translucent leaves.

Uneven tinkling, the lazy rain
Dripping from the eaves.

Compared with the work being done by Pound or H.D. one notices the superplusage in Fletcher. Most of his adjectives show more fat than muscle. Fletcher did not stop at Impressionism, however. From *Irradiations* he went on to the series of 'Symphonies' which are his most ambitious work in poetry. Again, this next phase of his development was rapid. 'The Blue Symphony', the first of the series to be published, appeared in *Poetry* in September 1914:[94]

> Old gardens sunken:
> And in the gardens is water.
>
> Sombre wreck—autumnal leaves;
> Shadowy roofs
> In the blue mist,
> And a willow branch that is broken.
> Oh, old pagodas of my soul, how you
>     glittered across green trees!

Here Fletcher is moving from Impressionism to attempts at Symbolism, though in this role he is far from effective:

> *Prologue—The Ghosts of an Old House*
> Doors lead to nowhere:
> Squirrels burrow between the walls.
> Closets in every room hang open,
> Windows are stared into by uncivil ancient trees.

In the middle of the upper hallway
There is a great circular hole
Going up to the attic.
A wooden lid covers it.

All over the house there is a sense of futility;
Of minutes dragging slowly
And repeating
Some worn-out story of broken effort and desire.

Symbolism, no doubt: but there is nothing new in it. It says nothing that
Tennyson had not more subtly expressed in 'Mariana', nearly ninety
years earlier. Fletcher's only original contribution here is his dislocation
of form, a rough but perhaps effective break with the pentameter. Fletcher
was a weak writer; his most effective moments are when he is least
pretentious. His art works best when used to fix responses to sense-
impressions. His work is probably much nearer to what Pound meant by
literary impressionism than that of Flint or Hueffer. 'The Skaters' is an
example:

Black swallows swooping or gliding
In a flurry of entangled loops and curves;
The skaters swim over the frozen river.
And the grinding click of their skates as they
    impinge upon the surface,
Is like the brushing together of thin wing-tips
    of silver.

The technique here is limited and the habitual flatness of Fletcher's
rhythms makes for boredom.

Fletcher's later work shows no particular advance on *Irradiations* or
*Goblins and Pagodas*. *Japanese Prints* (Boston, 1918) reveals him
fashionably following in Pound's traces, but with an insight unequal to
his sometimes considerable erudition. Among Fletcher's more valuable
achievements is the pamphlet *Some Contemporary American Poets*, which
appeared in May 1920 as an issue of Harold Monro's *Chapbook*. This
was the first extended study of twentieth-century American poetry in
England. Here Fletcher appears as a critic of considerable ability. As a
poet he does not deserve to be altogether forgotten, but he wrote too
much and too diffusely. And he did not help his own case by his envious
and—in the end—malicious attitude towards Pound. Fletcher's hostility
intensified with time, as a letter to Harriet Monroe in 1917 confirms:

I am sorry that you are letting Ezra Pound empty his rag-bag mind over your pages. I have nothing against Ezra personally; in fact, I would gladly subscribe to give him a comfortable pension, on condition that he did not write any more. For the first of the Three Cantos is such sorry stuff—what a junk-heap! It is all of the 1910 period—which is as dead now as Queen Anne. You ought to have more respect for your pages, now that paper is so scarce.[95]

No doubt he was sincere in writing this; the first published drafts of the early *Cantos* are unimpressive. But his attitude to Pound is regrettable, particularly as he himself would have done better to be far more careful and selective in what he served up for publication.

After his expatriate years in England Fletcher at last returned to Arkansas where he became involved in Southern agrarian politics, wrote history and biographies and eventually committed suicide.

* * *

The last contributor to *Some Imagist Poets* was a writer of much greater ability than Fletcher or Amy Lowell. D. H. Lawrence did not regard himself as an Imagist. He entered the Imagist record at a late stage and almost by accident. His relations to the movement were tangential. Pound and he were antipathetic. He does not mention Hulme at all. With Flint, Lawrence was on terms of vague amity. He became friendly with Aldington and H.D. and these ties continued and outlasted the Imagist period.[96] Lawrence was on good terms with Amy Lowell, but his letters to her contain no discussions of poetry—not that he was much given to impromptu discussion of literary technique.[97]

His first appearance in a journal of national importance was in November 1909 when Hueffer published five pages of his poems in *The English Review*.[98] At that time Lawrence seems to have had some regard for Hueffer, whom he called 'a fine man' in one of his early letters.[99] A few years later he was more sceptical. At the end of 1913 he wrote to Edward Garnett:

The Hueffer-Pound faction seem inclined to lead me around a little as one of their show dogs.[100]

The comment is indicative both of his detachment from the Imagistes and of the closeness of Pound's relations with Hueffer. On his colleagues of *Some Imagist Poets* Lawrence was even more trenchant in a letter written in 1916:

I send you my copy of the Imagists' anthology from America for the sake of the 'Erinnyes' poem which I hope you will like. I think HD is good: none of the others worth anything. Amy Lowell is James Russell Lowell's daughter. She is not a good poetess, I think. But she is a very good friend.[101]

From this it appears that 'Erinnyes' is an example of what Lawrence liked in his own work at that time:

> There has been so much noise,
> Bleeding and shouting and dying,
> Clamour of death.
>
> There are so many dead,
> Many have died unconsenting,
> Their ghosts are angry, unappeased.
>
> So many ghosts among us,
> Invisible, yet strong,
> Between me and thee, so many ghosts of the slain,
>
> They come back, over the white sea, in the mist,
> Invisible, trooping home, the unassuaged ghosts
> Endlessly returning on the uneasy sea.[102]

By any test this is hardly an Imagist poem. Images are never absent for long in Lawrence's verse, but they tend to be presented from the careless abundance of his descriptive gift:

> Her large brown hand stretched over
> The windows of my mind . . . .

'The Snapdragon', from which this is taken, was included in the first volume of *Georgian Poetry*. Lawrence contributed to four of the five volumes of Edward Marsh's anthology. Up to 1914 his affinities, if anywhere, were with the Georgians. At this period he was dubious about Whitman, who is a major influence on his later free verse poems. In a letter to Henry Savage at the end of 1913 he said of Whitman: 'He is really false as hell.—But he is fine too.'[103] Throughout his career, until he settled on the free verse forms in which most of his more memorable poems were written, Lawrence seems to have wandered in search of a technique. The diction of many of his earlier poems is loaded with embarrassing poeticisms. After 1913 there is a loosening in the form of his verse accompanied, however, by a distinct tautening of its rhythms. He defended these changes in his letters to Marsh at the end of 1913:

If your ear has got stiff and a bit mechanical, *don't* blame my poetry. That's why you like *Golden Journey to Samarkand*—it fits your habituated ear and your feeling crouches subservient and a bit pathetic. 'It satisfies my ear,' you say. Well, I don't write for your ear .... [104]

In the progression that brought him to the poems collected as *Birds, Beasts and Flowers* in 1923, Lawrence worked harder and harder to find his own idiom. In 1913 he flirted for a while with Futurism. But he soon lost interest in Marinetti's movement, aware perhaps of the limitations neatly summarized by an English critic of the period:

The mind sees more than the eye, and is always upbraiding the vassel-organ for its limitations. The mind sees objects and places where the eye, left to itself ... could see only a surface. [105]

At the time of his association with Amy Lowell and her group Lawrence was still searching. 'Green', which appeared in *Some Imagist Poets*, shows where he had got to:

> The dawn was apple-green,
>     The sky was green wine held up in the sun,
> The moon was a golden petal between.
>
> She opened her eyes, and green
>     They shone, clear like flowers undone
> For the first time, now for the first time seen.

In a different mood there is the opening stanza of 'Gloire de Dijon', first published as the second poem in the sequence 'All of Roses' in *Poetry* in 1914:

> When she rises in the morning
> I linger to watch her;
> She spreads the bath-cloth underneath the window
> Glistening white on the shoulders,
> While down her sides the mellow
> Golden shadow glows as
> She stoops to the sponge, and her swung breasts
> Sway like full-blown yellow
> Gloire de Dijon roses.

The metaphor indicates that Lawrence was already on the road to *Lady Chatterley*, but at least it is preferable to Flint's fumbling references to bosoms. These poems by Lawrence give point to Amy Lowell's remark:

> The three issues of *Some Imagist Poets* are all equally important, and they are intended to contain only Imagistic verse. Mr. Lawrence's contributions, however, depart from the type.[106]

Pound's comments also support the view that Lawrence was at no time creatively implicated with the Imagists. Pound appears in an attractive light in his dealings with the English writer. He disliked Lawrence, of whom he said:

> detestable person but needs watching. I think he learned the proper treatment of modern subjects before I did. That was in some poems in *The Eng. Rev.* ... .[107]

The poems Pound especially admired were the early realistic pieces in Nottinghamshire dialect. Despite their stiff-collared metre these do have an energy that is absent from Lawrence's more literary pieces then or for some years afterwards. Nottinghamshire dialect was Lawrence's earliest speech, the language of his feelings. This gives added strength to the splendid poem 'Violets':

> Sister, tha knows while we was on th' planks
>    Aside o' t' grave, an' th' coffin set
> On th' yaller clay, wi' th' white flowers top of it
>    Waitin' ter be buried out o' th' wet?
>
> An' t' parson makin' haste, an' t' black
>    Huddlin' up i' t' rain,
> Did t' 'appen ter notice a bit of a lass way back
>    Hoverin', lookin' poor an' plain?
>
> How should I be lookin' round!
>    An' me standin' there on th' plank,
> An' our Ted's coffin set on th' ground,
>    Waitin' to be sank!
>
> I'd as much as I could do, to think
>    Of im' bein' gone
> That young, an' a' the fault of drink
>    An' carryin's on!—
>
> .   .   .   .   .   .   .

Pound also supported the inclusion in *Poetry* of some of the love poems to Frieda. ('Lawrence, as you know, gives me no particular pleasure. Nevertheless we are lucky to get him.')[108] However, Pound never accepted Lawrence as one of his circle. He wrote to Glenn Hughes, many years later, '... Lawrence was never an Imagist. He was an *Amy*gist.'[109]

It was not until 1920 that Lawrence wrote recognizably modernist poems. 'Mosquito' was composed in April of that year:

When did you start your tricks
Monsieur?

What do you stand on such high legs for?
Why this length of shredded shank
You exaltation?

Is it that you shall lift your centre of gravity upwards
And weigh no more than air as you alight upon me,
Stand upon me weightless, you phantom?

I heard a woman call you the Winged Victory
In sluggish Venice.
You turn your head towards your tail and smile.

How can you put so much devilry
Into that translucent phantom shred
Of a frail corpus?

Queer, with your thin wings and your streaming legs
How you sail like a heron, or a dull clot of air,
A nothingness.

        .    .    .    .    .    .    .    .    .    .

Lawrence is now remembered chiefly for his prose. His short stories are among the best in the language. His poems, however uneven, are at least always professional. Some of them, especially the animal and nature pieces in *Birds, Beasts and Flowers*, are works of remarkable insight and power; but they are a long way from Imagism.

*        *        *

The poems of the Imagists heighten the muddle their theories started. Apart from Lawrence, who never pretended to be part of the movement, it is difficult to find a definite link between the poems of those who called themselves Imagists. Aldington, H.D. and Pound dabbled with Classical

103

themes; Pound, Amy Lowell and Fletcher used Chinese and Japanese stage properties; Flint and Hueffer aspired to be recorders of contemporary London life. Pound and Aldington were satirical; Fletcher melancholy; H.D., intense; Campbell, Irish. Storer never found subjects he could fully concentrate on. Only Hulme was always and unswervingly himself.

If there is a common factor, it is not in their themes or their attitudes to those questionable abstractions image, impression or symbol. It can only be in the use of free verse.

In spite of large differences in talent and achievement, none of these writers deserves to be dismissed out of hand. Even the weakest of them, Storer and Fletcher, show hints of talent frustrated by flaws in their circumstances or personality. Flint and Aldington were writers whose poetic potentialities were largely unfulfilled. Aldington was precocious; Flint slow to develop. Flint stopped just when he seemed to be on the point of realization. Aldington was a hit and miss writer whose work has been neglected except, curiously enough, in Russia where he has continuing popularity. Amy Lowell, though today little regarded, contributed in her way to the upsurge of American poetry that began at this period. Hueffer wrote verse, with casual intentions and variable success, as a means of relaxation from the greater intensity of his prose. No doubt the achievements of Imagist poetic work lie to a great extent with Pound. But Campbell, Lawrence and H.D. all wrote poems that give them a definite place among the writers of their generation. A final word of admiration and regret can be kept for T. E. Hulme. Some of his short poems retain what may well be a permanent power to charm, tease or amaze. His renunciation of poetry, followed by his death in the war, meant the loss of a talent of major importance.

# IV

## The Gossamer Web

Just as physically you are not born that abstract entity, man, but the child of particular parents, so you are in matters of literary judgment. Your opinion is almost entirely of the literary history that came just before you, and you are governed by that whatever you may think.[1]

So it was with the Imagists. It would be fatally easy to treat them in terms of their originality and to forget that they exist in a continuum of poets in English. They may have tried to deny their immediate predecessors; they could not escape being affected by them. Here, though, national differences appear. The American writers were much less burdened by an inherited past than the English. If America had too little past England had too much.

Whether British or American, the Imagist writers looked for their models beyond their own culture. Above all they looked to France. (Though this is not true of all of them; H.D. was largely immune to French poetry.) Imagist theory depends heavily on French critics and theorists. As René Taupin said, American poetry spoke French. The groundwork for this had been laid in England; T. S. Eliot acknowledged:

> I myself owe Mr. Symons a great debt: but for having read his book, I should not, in the year 1908, have heard of Laforgue or Rimbaud; I should probably not have begun to read Verlaine; and but for reading Verlaine, I should not have heard of Corbière.[2]

Arthur Symons was the one critical sensibility to survive from the nineties with something to say to the twentieth century. In 1906 he had edited Coleridge's *Biographia Literaria*, a work Hulme drew on for various of his ideas. (Hulme refers to Symons explicitly in the unpublished fragments of 'Language and Style'.)

This initial subjection to France links the Imagists with their contemporaries on the Continent. Early twentieth-century poetry in every major European language turned for ideas and examples to France, to the work of Baudelaire and the Symbolists, and to critics like Rémy de Gourmont. In spite of Pound's attempt to present his Imagistes as 'ardent Hellenists', for English writers the new links with France brought to an end the dominance of Greek and Latin which had persisted through the nineteenth century, inspired by the Hellenism of Shelley and Keats, and fostered by the revival of Classical studies in English schools and universities. Instead, the Imagists pioneered their own classical tradition by appeal to China and Japan.

Though its time was short, Imagism was not a dwindling tradition like the metaphysical school after Donne and Marvell. Rather, it represented the beginning of a new tradition. Over-anxious in their desire to break with their English predecessors, the Imagists were almost obsessively willing to admit their borrowings from foreign sources. It is never easy to distinguish sources from influences. It seems that for the Imagists sources were influences they could allow themselves to acknowledge.

\*   \*   \*

The Imagists were less bold in experiment than many of their contemporaries on the Continent. So far from denouncing the past with Futurist vehemence they often appealed nervously to it for justification. Their place within the tradition of English poets is far clearer than that of Stramm in German or Marinetti's colleagues in Italian. Certain writers from the past had particular value for them. The powerful intelligence of Coleridge, however wrecked or fragmented by drugs and private melancholy, was invoked by Storer to provide sanction for free verse; and Hulme probably founded some of his terminology on the *Biographia Literaria*. Storer specifically claimed Coleridge among the fathers of *vers libre*:

> As a matter of fact, however, we were using *vers libre* in England without making any fuss about it, long before it rose to the eminence of a movement in France. Sydney Dobell, Alexander Smith—Coleridge even, all used it at times. In a sense, nearly all the English poets have been vers-librists . . . .[3]

This statement gains credence from some passages in Coleridge's *Note-books*:

> He looked at his own Soul
> with a telescope. What seemed
> all irregular, he saw and
> shewed to be beautiful
> Constellations: and he added
> to the Consciousness hidden
> worlds within worlds.

106

Coleridge's rhythms can be compared with those of a beautiful fragment by Hulme:

> Over a large table, smooth, he leaned in ecstasies,
> In a dream.
> He had been to woods, and talked and walked with trees,
> Had left the world
> And brought back round globes and stone images
> Of gems, colours, hard and definite.
> With these he played, in a dream,
> On the smooth table.[4]

Even Hulme's categories of fancy and imagination depend essentially on Coleridge, as does his 'counter language':

> FANCY ... has no other counters to play with, but fixities and definites.[5]

(Hulme got further backing for this view of language from Rémy de Gourmont, whose *chiffre* is probably Coleridge's counter, derived from the English writer by a progressive series of borrowings.)[6]

Coleridge offered support for theory. Practical encouragement in the method of free verse came by example from two very dissimilar sources, the American Whitman and the English writer W. E. Henley. Of the two Henley is less known and far less powerful; but in time he was much nearer to the Imagists and both Hulme and Storer drew from him extensively. Henley had established a technique in free verse (though he did not use the term) in the sequence *In Hospital*, written out of his long period of illness in the Edinburgh Infirmary in the 1870s. Henley's 'rhythms', as he called his free verse, had of course English predecessors in Arnold's 'Rugby Chapel' and his choruses from *Empedocles on Etna*.[7] Hulme, who refers in his 'Lecture' with half-humorous approval to 'a few jerky rhythms of Henley', shows traces of direct derivation from the older man. Here is the opening of Hulme's poem 'At Night':

> At night!
> All the terror's in that.
> Branches of the dead tree ...
> ...On the dead white body of the sky.

Henley had written:

> Trees and the menace of night; ...
> ....Thro' the trees in the strange dead night,

Under the vast dead sky,
Forgetting and forgot, a drift of Dead ...[8]

And Hulme's 'Autumn (II)' with its

Dead memory of summer's passion past ...
...Tears that vanished not, but lay red and brown

can be set against Henley's 'Praeludium':

...Subtle and strong browns, reds
Magnificent with death and the pride of death,
The dead-march of the year, ....

At a lower level of effectiveness, Storer's rather feeble 'Piccadilly Circus'
echoes Henley's hardly superior poem on the same theme:[9]

I am alight with life: the very pavement wears
A purple coat against the magic of the streets.
From the low gutters trickle little airs,
Urchins of cockney melody,
And the far splendour of a café's lights
Glows, a cool diamond, on the City's breast.

I hear trees sway in an unnatural wind,
Barren of cloak and with no form or air
And the faint passions of pale violets' hearts
Scatter their simple wine in long, sweet,
    flickering streams.

      ·   ·   ·   ·   ·   ·   ·   ·   ·

(Hulme also produces echoes of Herrick in some of his unfinished
pieces, a curiosity that can best be left to the academic writer anxious
to sniff out new trails.)[10]

Henley is far from negligible. He was an intermittently good poet, a
brilliant editor and polemicist, and a man who endured much suffering
with great courage. As a poetic force he cannot be compared with
Whitman; but the great American meant little to Hulme's colleagues
with the exception of Joseph Campbell. The rest of them did not reject
Whitman through ignorance. A selection from his work had been published in England as far back as 1868. Indeed, Henley had included four
poems by Whitman in his bloodthirsty anthology for boys *Lyra Heroica*
(1891). As early as 1906 his name occurs in the notebooks of Flint who

108

had read him, as he seems in the end to have read everything. Hulme, though, criticized him severely: 'Whitman went wrong through deficiency of selective process',[11] a comment very much to the point.

Campbell was Irish. Whitman had already been circulated among the writers of the Irish movement by Yeats's friend George Russell (AE). The links of sympathy, cultural as well as political, between America and Irish Nationalism were strong. (At their root lay a common resentment of England.) Campbell's interest in Whitman is hardly surprising. The long undulating lines of Campbell's free verse poems in *The Mountainy Singer* are founded almost entirely on Whitman, though Campbell lacks Whitman's skill and artistry. 'A Thousand Feet Up' is one example. Sometimes there is even a specific presence of the American's diction, as in the line

> To me, a habitan of slums[12]

where Whitman's borrowed French-Canadian lingo with its eighteenth-century spelling is dragged straight into twentieth-century Dublin.

Whitman meant still more to the later Imagists, with the exception of H.D. who does not mention him. (No doubt her kind of refinement would have found him tough to assimilate.) Aldington described himself as 'deep in Whitman' in 1912.[13] Pound also admired him but found it difficult to fit him into his pantheon. 'We don't owe vers libre to Whitman, really we don't,'[14] he had written to Harriet Monroe around the time he was manifestly experimenting with Whitmanesque technique in some of his poems:

> *Salutation (Contemporania)*
> O generation of the thoroughly smug and thoroughly uncomfortable,
> I have seen fishermen picnicking in the sun,
> I have seen them with untidy families,
> I have seen their smiles full of teeth and heard ungainly laughter.

Pound's exasperated admiration emerges in a letter to his father:

> Whitman is a hard nutt. The *Leaves of Grass* is the book. It is impossible to read it without swearing at the author almost continuously.[15]

With all his cultural cosmopolitanism Pound always remained very much an American poet. His discomfort in his origins made it hard for him to come to terms with Whitman. He achieved reconciliation in 'A Pact':

> I am old enough now to make friends.
> It was you that broke the new wood,

Now it is a time for carving.
We have one sap and one root—
Let there be commerce between us.

Whitman may not have been the 'very great scoundrel'[16] Gerard
Manley Hopkins thought him (a nervous decision based on the Englishman's recognition that they had homosexuality if not metrical habits in
common). He remains America's greatest poet, though not so great as
to justify D. H. Lawrence's hysterical plaudits:

Whitman, the great poet, has meant so much to me ... Whitman, the
one pioneer. And only Whitman. No English pioneers, no French. No
European pioneer-poets. In Europe the would-be pioneers are mere
innovators. The same in America. Ahead of Whitman, nothing.[17]

The Imagist writers after 1912 relied less and less on sources in
English. Nineteenth-century poets, except for Henley or Arthur Symons,
meant little to them. Aldington summed up their protest in his own
angry fashion:

... the majority of the poetry of the last century had nothing to do
with life and very little to do with poetry. There was a plague of
prettiness and a plague of pomposity and several other minor diseases
—such as over-much suavity, the cult of decorated adjectives. And
except for Browning and a little of Swinburne there was no energy
which was not bombast, no rendering of life without an Anglican moral,
no aesthetic without aesthetic cant.

All that is quite a commonplace, of course, but it cannot be hammered
in too often. As long as the writers in this country go on in a blind and
almost exclusive worship of the 'great figures' of the Elizabethan and
of the Victorian ages, poetry will get weaker and more tedious, more
feebly echoing what has been echoed *ad nauseam*.[18]

Hulme's group stand as intermediaries between the later Imagists and
the traditions represented by Symons or Henley. Flint and Hulme, and
to lesser extent Storer and Campbell, were themselves sources for a
good deal of the Imagist practice and theory after 1912. Apart from
Aldington and the more marginal figure of Lawrence, the later Imagists
were Americans. All of them except H.D. were devotees of French
literature. The American urge to relate to a poetic tradition other than
that of England became more and more in evidence. The attitude of
American writers to British poetry grew increasingly remote or estranged.

This tendency is already marked in Amy Lowell and John Gould Fletcher. It appears still more vehemently in Pound's work and interests (despite such aberrations as his continuing taste for Browning). Amy Lowell and Fletcher exhibited an enthusiastic and sometimes undiscriminating response to their French sources. Amy Lowell's earlier work, the poems of *A Dome of Many-Coloured Glass*, seems often a recension of her wide and haphazard reading of various nineteenth-century English poets. When she opted for modernization she turned to French poetry. In her less successful moments she showed considerable ability to mimic the style of some of the other Imagists. Fletcher's relationship to his sources shows a not dissimilar pattern.

Richard Aldington and H.D., while not at first sharing Flint and Pound's French interests, replaced them by their involvement with the Classical world of Greece. They had all read Pater, who figures, together with Arthur Symons's *Images of Good and Evil*, in Flint's notebook in 1906. H.D. acknowledged Pater among her early interests.[19] Aldington edited him many years later.[20] The shadows of the nineties lay across their early encounters with literature. By 1912 those shadows were slightly more remote, though Eliot's admission of obligation to Arthur Symons could have been echoed, even at secondhand, by most of them. Hueffer certainly never lost sight of the importance of Symons's work. In 1921 he wrote:

And if you wish to see what I mean by the good writing that distinguished the group that were contemporary with his youth and mine, you have only to consider the work of Mr Symons, to consider the gap that there would be in a whole genre of English if Mr Symons had never written. Mr Symons was undoubtedly the best of them .... .[21]

Symons pointed to France, from which sources and examples for Imagist work principally came.

\* \* \*

It is not surprising that they looked to France. As T. S. Eliot said:

The predominance of Paris was incontestable .... . there was a most exciting variety of ideas.[22]

French poetry at this time was approaching the end of the most fertile period in its history. Baudelaire and his successors had given poetic models to the whole of Europe. Paris meant zest and excitement in the other arts too, notably painting. In Paris even Eliot could remember 'female smells in shuttered rooms', a feeling sadly muffled in his later more pious incarnation. Paris was the arena for Apollinaire and the young Braque and Picasso. It was the centre of Europe for artistic ideas.

When Hulme asserted that

> The founders of the modern *vers libres* movement were Kahn and Laforgue,[23]

he judged correctly. One of the originators of the new European movement was Marinetti who had lived in Paris from 1899 to 1904. He acknowledged Gustave Kahn as 'in certo senso maestro'[24] and took largely from him in poetic technique, as Hulme later did in poetic theory. Marinetti, though an important historical figure, was undistinguished as a poet. What he added to his sources was mostly his own incoherence. Hulme made more of his gleanings from Kahn who, if not a considerable poet, was a lucid and persuasive prose writer. (He had the gift also of relentless self-advertisement.) Writers across Europe looked to Paris; the Imagists were no exception. Imagism, as Herbert Read remarked, emerged 'from the general trend'.[25]

The degree of reliance on French sources fluctuated among the Imagists, both among the individual writers and between the different groups. Members of Hulme's group leaned heavily on France. Not only did Flint become one of the best French scholars of his generation in England; Hulme and Storer also had a wide knowledge of French literature and thought. Only Joseph Campbell seems not to have shared this appetite. Both Richard Aldington and H.D. showed at first much less interest in French literature than either earlier or later Imagists. In 1912 Pound, largely through Flint, began to learn about more recent French writers. He responded to this new enthusiasm with almost religious fervour. Until then he had

> spent about four years puddling about on the edges of modern French poetry without getting anywhere near it.[26]

He recorded his enthusiasm in 'The Approach to Paris', a series of seven articles he contributed to *The New Age* in September and October 1913.[27]

Among the later recruits only D. H. Lawrence remained relatively unaffected by the newer French poetry. John Gould Fletcher was an enthusiastic student of some of the Symbolist poets several years before his brief involvement with Imagism. His *Fool's Gold*, published in 1913, is old-fashioned and derivative, but its dedication includes the names of Corbière, Lautréamont, Rimbaud and Laforgue. Amy Lowell's interest in French poetry coincided with her involvement with Imagism. A direct

112

result was her *Six French Poets* (New York, 1915). The authors she wrote about were Henri de Régnier, Verhaeren, Jammes, Rémy de Gourmont, Paul Fort and Albert Samain. In keeping with her tutelary relationship to the earlier Imagists, Amy Lowell relied greatly on Flint while planning *Six French Poets*. The poets she interested herself in and the use to which she put them combine to suggest her dependence, in this as in other ways, on the taste and scholarship of Flint and Pound. Taupin's judgment on *Six French Poets* is harsh, but not unjust:

Le livre n'avait aucune valeur critique: tout ce qu'A. Lowell disait avait déjà été dit soit en France soit ailleurs; mais il présentait ces auteurs d'une façon assimilable aux plus médiocres esprits.[28]

From Flint's notebooks it is clear that his serious involvement with modern French writers began in 1909. In 1906 he was already reading the philosopher and aesthetician Guyau and in 1907 Rémy de Gourmont. The real loading of his notebooks with French authors starts from May 1909, which suggests the encouragement he received from the meetings at the Tour d'Eiffel. Names included in Flint's reading list of that time are J.-M. de Hérédia, Verlaine, Mallarmé, Kahn, Laforgue, Rémy de Gourmont, Paul Fort, Francis Vielé-Griffin, Edouard Dujardin, Jean Moréas, Henri de Régnier and Francis Jammes (whom he read in bulk, listing four or five volumes). Apart from the Parnassian Hérédia this is a roll-call of some of the leading *Symbolistes*. After Verlaine and Mallarmé the other poets listed worked largely in *vers libre*. Flint's range of reading was obviously an important asset for the discussions in Percy Street, as it was later for Ezra Pound:

... that rotten *Poetry and Drama*, established itself solely by Flint's French number which everybody had to get; it was the first large article on contemporary stuff.[29]

The effect of this mass of reading on Flint's own poetic work is less readily demonstrable. One point is clear. By 1909 Flint had become impatient with rhyme. In his notebook he wrote:

English has so few rhymes that all poetry must somewhat be circum- scribed by their limitation. Argument in favour of free verse: rhymeless if need be.

French with its deflected terminations past parts on other hand need feel only the circumscription of art.

113

He transcribed the arguments for *vers libre* offered by Rémy de Gourmont in *La Culture des Idées* (a book also utilized by T. E. Hulme in the development of his theory of language):

> Au fond, il n'y a qu'un genre: le poème; et peut-être qu'une mode, le vers, car la belle prose doit avoir un rythme qui fera douter si elle n'est que de la prose. Buffon n'a écrit que des poèmes, et Bossuet et Chateaubriand et Flaubert.

This is probably the germ of Flint's theory of unrhymed cadence. The position which Flint took up in 1909 remained with him for the rest of his life. In 1940 he reiterated it, in reference to his Imagist colleagues and himself:

> We did not like rhyme; we thought it an intrusion into the expression of poetry.
>
> ... very few people knew then or know now what poetry is. Poetry is not verse. It would be truer to say that verse is the enemy of poetry.[30]

Two poets who greatly affected Flint's work were Émile Verhaeren and Jean de Bosschère, both Belgians. In *The New Age* he reviewed Verhaeren's *Les Heures Claires*, and praised him as the 'greatest of poets writing French ....'[31] His enthusiasm for Verhaeren continued. Some years later Flint translated his love poems into English prose, and in 1917 he published *The Closed Door*, a book of verse translations from the work of Jean de Bosschère. The latter volume includes some of Flint's more effective work and the translations suggest that Flint's later poems owed much to the Belgian poet. Verhaeren seems to have encouraged Flint's ambition to write a poetry of urban experience, of townscapes and urban love. Verhaeren's vision of man in industrial society was inspired by an impassioned Socialism. Flint seems to have been too crushed for any protest he made to be effective. He adopted Verhaeren's themes and atmospheres without equalling the energy with which the Belgian writer invested them.

Verhaeren had little direct importance for the other Imagist writers. But he was one of the appointed masters of the 'Abbaye' group, the so-called *Unanimistes* who are referred to in Pound's 'Prefatory Note' to Hulme's poems in *Ripostes*. The *Unanimistes*, who reacted against Symbolism in favour of a more concrete approach to social actuality, took as their masters Whitman, Verhaeren and Bergson. Their group included at least one writer of importance, Jules Romains, whom Pound discussed in one of the essays in his 'Approach to Paris' series.[32] In their attitude to the image, the *Unanimistes* were closer to the Imagists than the *Symbolistes* had been to either.[33] Unlike the *Symbolistes*, they favoured a poetry of statement rather than evocation. There are distinct resemblances here between *Unanimiste* and Imagist theory; but their difference in social attitude was large, with the Imagists adopting a far more detached view of society.

Flint found justification for his own approach to free verse largely through French examples and French poetic theory. His personal development as poet and critic after 1909 can be traced almost invariably to his French sources. Chief among these was Rémy de Gourmont, whose theories he adopted as wholeheartedly as did Hulme and Pound. Of all French critical writers de Gourmont had the largest individual share in the formation of Imagist theory.

Hulme was a man with very different interests and personality from Flint. Even where he was working in the same areas and reading the same books he showed marked differences of orientation. Flint was a scholar: Hulme a man of ideas. Hulme was primarily concerned with the ideas behind a work rather than the more specific and limited analysis of the text. He has often been regarded as an original thinker; his originality lies in his poems; his prose writings are in large part the work of a brilliant middleman of ideas.

The supporting material in Hulme's 'Lecture on Modern Poetry' is a mosaic of arguments taken from French writers. It is only the predictions and assertions that are personal. Nonetheless his flair for assimilating and making sense out of the material he put together was by no means a negligible aspect of his talent. In exercising it he often worked hand to mouth from his French exemplars. The lecture is built up on direct borrowing and paraphrase from a number of French writers: Gustave Kahn, Rémy de Gourmont, M. Guyau, Jules de Gaultier, André Beaunier and Théodule Ribot.

Hulme's method of working is one that seems to have been characteristic with him. He proceeds by a mixture of rough translation, paraphrase and allusion. At an early point in the evolution of his literary interests he had read André Beaunier's study *La Poésie Nouvelle*. He mentions this in his review of Tancrède de Visan's *L'Attitude du Lyrisme Contemporain*. Hulme praised de Visan's work, but added:

When I first picked it up I saw that it was a collection of essays on all the poets that one has known about for some time. The names on the cover—Verhaeren, De Regnier, Mockel, Paul Fort, Maeterlinck, and Viele-Griffin seem just the same as those in Beaunier's book, *La Poesie Nouvelle*, that I read some five or six years ago. There were no

115

new names. I found this to be an illustration of one of my favourite theories—that French verse, after a short period of great interest, the most vital that had occurred for centuries, had now arrived at comparative stagnation, and had been succeeded by a period during which French philosophy, also for the first time for centuries, was to dominate Europe.[34]

When Hulme wrote:

The new technique ... consisted in a denial of a regular number of syllables as the basis of versification. The length of the line is long and short ..., and is free rather than regular.[35]

he took more or less directly from Beaunier[36] and also from Kahn. Hulme's method is not without flaws. Sometimes he adapts and compresses the argument of the original with considerable loss of accuracy. In his 'Lecture' when he discusses the Parnassians there are surprising mistakes, such as his reference to the 'natural school' presumably for the Naturalists (*L'École Naturaliste*), or the reference to the 'prominent' name of 'Monde' which must surely be a misspelling of the name of Catulle Mendès, the son-in-law of Théophile Gautier, and a leader of the Parnassian school.

Hulme's discussion of verse forms is based on Kahn's preface to his *Premiers Poèmes* (Paris, 1897), though, in the process, it is shortened and simplified. This is Hulme's rendering:

It must be admitted that verse forms, like manners, and like individuals, develop and die. They evolve from their initial freedom to decay and finally to virtuosity. They disappear before the new man, burdened with the thought more complex and more difficult to express by the old name. After being too much used, their primitive effect is lost.

. . . .

The new technique was first definitely stated by Kahn. It consisted in a denial of a regular number of syllables as the basis of versification. The length of the line is long and short, oscillating with the images used by the poet; it follows the contours of his thoughts and is free rather than regular; to use a rough analogy, it is clothes made to order, rather than ready-made clothes.[37]

Such borrowing seems uncritical, yet Hulme took only what he wished

116

to take. Kahn, in keeping with Symbolist doctrine, makes a specific assertion of musicality as an aspect of poetic function:

> ... Le poète parle et écrit par l'oreille et non pas par les yeux ... .[38]

Hulme deliberately excludes this. The new verse, he says, is to be 'read and not chanted'. It is this stubborn independence of judgment that lifts Hulme's work out of the twin ruts of scholarship and journalism.

Hulme used his other sources in similar fashion but to different purposes. Where he had relied on Kahn to support his theories of verse form he used the other writers to bolster his notion of poetic language.[39] There seems little doubt that his concept of the image derived largely from French sources, notably de Gourmont and Théodule Ribot. As a psychologist Ribot was interested in the problems of perception. His particular contribution to Hulme's thinking was the distinction between 'concrete' and 'symbolic' images.[40] According to Ribot, concrete images are the first which we receive. They are more powerful representations than symbolic images, and they relate to direct perceptions from nature (not limited to the visual), bodily sensations, etc. Symbolic images are secondary; they have only mediate relations with things. For example, if visual, they could be written words; or if auditory, spoken words. Ribot uses this distinction to help explain the operations of the mystical imagination. The mystic, as Ribot sees him, works through concrete images. Ribot's account of those images is very near to Hulme's differentiation of the languages of prose and poetry:

> ... there are, roughly speaking, two methods of communication, a direct, and a conventional language. The direct language is poetry, it is direct because it deals in images. The indirect is prose, because it uses images that have died and become figures of speech.
> ....
> For example, when I say that the hill was clad with trees, it merely conveys the fact to me that it was covered. But the first time that expression was used was by a poet, and to him it was an image recalling to him the distinct visual analogy of a man clad in clothes; but the image has died.[41]

Possibly it was from Ribot also that Hulme gleaned his theory of the visual rather than the auditory properties of poetry. Ribot quoted Gautier, who half a century earlier, had made this judgment:

> ... je crois qu'il faut surtout dans la phrase un rythme *oculaire*. Un livre est fait pour être *lu*, non parlé à haute voix.[42]

117

Hulme's argument was:

> We have thus two distinct arts. The one intended to be chanted, and the other intended to be read in the study.
>
> . . . .
>
> I quite admit that poetry intended to be recited must be written in regular metre, but I contend that this method of recording impressions by visual images in distinct lines does not require the old metric system.[43]

De Gourmont seems to have had a particular importance in the development of Hulme's thinking about language. *Le Problème du Style* leaves its deposits in many parts of 'Language and Style'. De Gourmont was one of the preferred critics of Pound, and through Pound, Aldington. His later influence on the Imagists was broad as well as specific. In *Le Problème du Style* de Gourmont classifies:

> ces deux grandes classes d'hommes, les visuels et les émotifs . . . .[44]

This must have been encouraging for Hulme who, it is evident, regarded himself as a 'visuel'. (As Kate Lechmere recalled: 'He didn't care for music. He didn't dance. He liked only brass bands.')[45] To whatever effect, Hulme's statements in 'Language and Style' carry frequent echoes of de Gourmont:

> Each *word* must be an image *seen*, not a counter.
>
> With perfect style ... each sentence should be a lump, a piece of clay, a vision seen . . . .
>
> A man cannot write without seeing at the same time a visual signification before his eyes. It is this image which precedes the writing . . . .[46]

As with Kahn, Hulme did not always follow de Gourmont's arguments very faithfully, whether by intent or through misunderstanding. Antoine Albalat, a lesser critic of the period, is a prime target of de Gourmont in *Le Problème du Style*. De Gourmont quotes Albalat:

> Il faut étudier les descriptions qui ont été faites sur nature et appliquer ensuite à votre sujet *artificiel* les procédés de facture vraie.

Then comments:

> Sentez-vous la supériorité, je ne dis pas du paysan qui herse son blé,

118

ou du vigneron qui sarcle sa vigne, mais du balayeur qui râcle les ruisseaux, sur le rhétoricien qui construit une catastrophe *artificielle* avec des procédés de facture *vraie*.[47]

Hulme picks this up in 'Language and Style', but in terms that suggest he had either missed the point or disagreed with de Gourmont's scorn:

Literature as entirely the deliberate standing still, looking and thinking oneself into an artificial view, for the moment, and not affecting one's real actions at all. Sunsets no consolation in harvest-field.[48]

Kahn and de Gourmont, even more than Bergson (who became a continuing interest with Hulme as amateur philospher and art critic) provided the basis for Hulme's theories of poetic form and language. Unlike Flint, Hulme did not transmit his knowledge in direct form to his colleagues and successors. What he learned was absorbed in the body of his own work. There seems to be little in his poems that is referable to his readings in French. There are possible hints of Baudelaire[49] and in one or two of his poems there are faint traces of the work of Gustave Kahn. One example is fairly striking. The poem 'Songe', in an early volume by the French poet, has these lines:

> Les haches aux mains de forbans,
> Les torches aux mains de rebelles,
> . . . .
> De tristes fantômes passant . . . .[50]

Hulme's poem 'In the City Square' uses the device, common with Kahn, of a half-repeated refrain. It begins:

> In the city square at night. The meeting of the torches.
> The start of the great march,
> The cries, the cheers, the parting . . . .

Sometimes in Hulme's poems there seem to be echoes from other writers; but on closer examination their sources remain elusive. This contrasts with his prose, where he takes and adapts ideas and statements with often ruthless directness.

Storer's knowledge and understanding of French literature probably exceeded Hulme's, but his creative talent was far smaller. Sadly, his lack of talent or his inability to release it nullified his knowledge and left it largely sterile. Storer's one important statement was his 'Essay'. By 1912

119

that had already been supplanted by the more demanding energy in the critical work of Hulme and Flint.

The Imagistes were a very different case from their predecessors. H.D. and Aldington had at first no knowledge of the work coming out of Paris. Soon enough, in the wake of Pound's gathering enthusiasm, Aldington began to be interested in French literature. In his autobiography he remembered Pound in those years:

> ... he invited my attention to the literature of Europe ... he talked of Arnauld Daniel and Guido Cavalcanti, of Homer and Dante, of Ronsard and El Cid in short, of the European tradition .... He gave me Villon, he gave me Verlaine, he gave me the Symbolistes, he gave me Flaubert, and carelessly threw in the Neo-Latins.[51]

By early 1913, when he was staying in Italy, Aldington describes himself as:

> very much interested in modern French poets and their interesting experiments in form.[52]

and by 1915 he was praising the French Symbolists,

> whose influence still dominates all European poetry.[53]

Unlike Pound, Aldington lacked the energy and capacity to assimilate his new ideas into his poetry. He read widely in French, but the effect on the evolution of his own work was slight. One French poet who had some influence on him was Henri de Régnier. Sometimes this is all too apparent. These lines in de Régnier's poem 'Epigramme Venétienne':

> Une barque de fruits croise sur le canal,
> Une gondole lente et close .... [54]

are copied in one of Aldington's 'Images', which begins:

> Like a gondola of green scented fruits
> Drifting along the dark canals at Venice .... [55]

Aldington was by no means immune to the influence of Rémy de Gourmont, although this came too late to have much effect on the work of his Imagist years. Much later he edited and translated some of de Gourmont's critical writings; and the title of his long poem *A Dream in the Luxembourg* carries an oblique tribute to the Frenchman.

120

H.D.'s indebtedness to French sources was even slighter. In an account of her beginnings as a poet she stated:

> I scribbled later, just before coming 'abroad,' a half-dozen rather free verses that might have been *vers libre*, but I had never heard of *vers libre* till I was 'discovered' later by Ezra Pound. [56]

In a much later letter she discusses her reading:

> ... some of de Regnier, Gautier, etc. with Richard Aldington in the early 'Madrigal' days in Paris and London. [57]

There are few obvious traces of French literature in any of her poems. Her total lack of interest in theoretical wranglings left her with no need for the critical delving indulged in by her more contentious colleagues.

Ezra Pound began to study the French writers around the time of his first commitment to Imagisme. Brigit Patmore tells how he fell upon the poems of Théophile Gautier:

> Ezra often came to have tea with me .... One afternoon he picked up a book that was lying on the table: it was Gautier's *Emaux et Camées*. For a quarter of an hour he turned over the pages in silence, then said: 'Why don't I know about this! May I take it with me?' And left immediately. [58]

Gautier became and remained one of Pound's chief admirations among the French poets. His influence is omnipresent in *Mauberley*; [59] he is frequently praised and cited in Pound's later criticism; [60] he appears or is quoted in two of the poems of *Lustra*. One of these, 'Albatre', first appeared in *Poetry and Drama* in March 1914. It is a study in whiteness:

> This lady in the white bath-robe which she calls a peignoir,
> Is, for the time being, the mistress of my friend,
> And the delicate white feet of her little white dog
> Are not more delicate than she is,
> Nor would Gautier himself have despised their contrasts
>     in whiteness
> As she sits in the great chair
> Between the two indolent candles.

In 'The Approach to Paris' Pound discussed some recent French poets. Among them were Rémy de Gourmont, Jules Romains, Charles Vildrac, Laurent Tailhade, Henri de Régnier, Tristan Corbière, Francis Jammes,

Rimbaud, Paul Fort and André Spire. He summarized his findings in the article 'Paris', published in *Poetry* in October 1913:

> I think if our American bards would study Rémy de Gourmont for rhythm, Laurent Tailhade for delineation, Henri de Régnier for simplicity of syntactical construction, Francis Jammes for humanity, and the faculty of rendering one's own time; and if they would get some idea of intensity from Tristan Corbière (since they will not take their Villon in the original), there might be some hope for American poetry.
>
> If our writers would keep their eye on Paris instead of on London— the London of today or of yesterday—there might be some chance of their doing work that would not be *démodé* before it gets to the press. Practically the whole development of the English verse-art has been achieved by steals from the French, from Chaucer's time to our own, and the French are always twenty to sixty years in advance.[61]

Four years earlier he had judged otherwise. In 1909 he had written to William Carlos Williams:

> There is no town like London to make one feel the vanity of all art except the highest. To make one disbelieve in all but the most careful and conservative presentation of one's stuff.[62]

In a letter written around September 1913 he remarked to Harriet Monroe:

> ... you are dead right when you say that American knowledge of French stops with Hugo. And—dieu le sait—there are few enough people on this stupid little island who know anything beyond Verlaine and Beaudelaire—neither of whom is the least use, pedagogically, I mean. They beget imitation and one can learn nothing from them. Whereas Gautier and de Gourmont carry forward the art itself, and the only way one can imitate them is by making more profound your knowledge of the very marrow of art.[63]

During the years 1912 to 1917 Pound contributed two hundred and eighty-five items to periodicals, edited two anthologies, and published seven books, three of them poetry. French literature gave him a set of influences and represented an imaginative stimulus. But it gave also the sources of much that became more valuable and more personal in his own poetry. As Pound himself observed, there are two ways of being influenced by a work of art. The way he prefers is that of the writer who

122

saturates himself in the work and who ends by using it to achieve some new mastery of his own.[64] This, at his best, was his method.

If Pound owed his introduction to modern French poetry to Flint, he went well beyond his mentor in the creative excitement with which he responded to it. During the Imagiste years he also developed an increasing interest in some of the French novelists, above all Stendhal and Flaubert and, to a lesser extent, Maupassant. As these were among Hueffer's favourite writers (he had a particular passion for Flaubert), it is probable that the encouragement to read them came from him. 'Poetry must be *as well written as prose*,' Pound wrote to Harriet Monroe in 1915. And he added:

It must be as simple as De Maupassant's best prose, and as hard as Stendhal's.[65]

In a letter to Iris Barry he amplified this enthusiasm:

... I suppose Flaubert's *Trois Contes*, especially 'Coeur Simple,' contain all that anyone knows *about* writing. Certainly one ought to read the opening of the *Chartreuse de Parme*, and the first half or a more than half of the *Rouge et Noir*. Shifting from Stendhal to Flaubert suddenly you will see how much better Flaubert writes. AND YET there is a lot in Stendhal, a sort of solidity which Flaubert hasn't. A trust in the thing more than the word. Which is the solid basis, i.e. the thing is the basis.

. . . .

And English poetry ? ? ? ? Ugh. Perhaps one shouldn't read it at all.[66]

The French writers who, even more than Flaubert, gave something substantial to Pound's work were Gautier and de Gourmont. 'My generation needed Rémy de Gourmont,'[67] he later remarked. De Gourmont began as one of Pound's enthusiasms and remained always among his loyalties. Pound translated his *Natural Philosophy of Love*, and made him the subject of numerous critical articles. He is referred to with unfailing respect throughout Pound's long career. (It is probable that Pound's interest in medieval Latin poetry was encouraged by reading de Gourmont's study *Le Latin Mystique*.) When Pound first became interested in de Gourmont he praised him as a master craftsman and connoisseur of verse technique.[68] This, like many of Pound's first rushes of enthusiasm, was over-stated. His poetic work owes little to de Gourmont, but his critical work after 1913 forms many of its procedures on models supplied by the French writer. One example is the concept of super-position apparently introduced into English by Pound in 1914. In his essay on Vorticism he defined it as follows:

> The 'one image poem' is a form of super-position, that is to say it is one idea set on top of another.[69]

This seems to be taken from de Gourmont, who in *Le Problème de Style* had written:

> Homère décrit un fait: puis il le compare à un autre fait analogue; les deux images restent toujours distinctes, quoique grossièrement superposables.[70]

When de Gourmont, who had been for many years a recluse and the victim of a kind of leprosy, died in 1915, Pound wrote:

> ... De Gourmont is dead and the world's light is darkened.[71]

To Gautier Pound's loyalty was unfailing. Writing to René Taupin in 1928, he was offhand about most of the poets whom fifteen years earlier he had praised in 'The Approach to Paris', but of Gautier he said:

> j'ai étudié et je le révère.[72]

He did not even mention Duhamel and Vildrac, whose *Notes sur la Technique Poétique* had a distinct influence on his attitudes to the theory of free verse during his Imagiste phase. Gautier outlasted Pound's first involvement with Vorticism and became a major source of technique in the recall to order that he announced with 'Status Rerum the Second' in 1916.[73] In his memorial notice of Harold Monro in 1932 Pound explained how this came about:

> He [T. S. Eliot] also participated in a movement to which no name has ever been given.
>
> That is to say, at a particular date in a particular room, two authors, neither engaged in picking the other's pocket, decided that the dilutation of *vers libre*, Amygism, Lee Masterism, general floppiness had gone too far and that some counter-current must be set going. Parallel situation centuries ago in China. Remedy prescribed *Emaux et Camées* (or the Bay State Hymn Book). Rhyme and regular strophes.
>
> Results: Poems in Mr Eliot's *second* volume, not contained in his first ('Prufrock', *Egoist*, 1917), also H. S. Mauberley.[74]

124

Gautier's poems are exercises in economy of form. They provided, as Pound saw, an invaluable corrective to the looseness that can be a dangerous hazard in free verse.

Pound was not unique in his discovery of Gautier. He seems to have rediscovered for himself someone admired as a master by the aesthetes and decadents of twenty or thirty years earlier. Lionel Johnson had quoted what he called the 'famous lines' of the opening stanza of Gautier's 'L'Art' in his obituary of Walter Pater in 1894.[75] There is a lineage of admiration for Gautier in England that runs from Swinburne and Pater through Wilde to Johnson and Arthur Symons. In his own country Gautier has been less admired. But there are indications of his influence on some of the French writers esteemed by the English Imagists. At least one poem by Henri de Régnier is almost a replica of a poem by Gautier.[76] And Gautier's terminology of *mélopée* and *logopée*, from which Pound seems to have got his melopoeia and logopoeia, is picked up by Gustave Kahn in the titling of some of his poems.[77]

In turning to France the Imagists were responding to an impulse of the age. A contemporary of T. S. Eliot at Harvard remembered that he first heard of the *vers libre* movement and of such writers as Paul Fort and Francis Jammes from Eliot around 1910. Eliot, it was understood, was

> to go over to the Sorbonne for study and to assess these literary influences . . . .[78]

James Joyce, who had read Arthur Symons's *The Symbolist Movement in Literature* when an undergraduate in Dublin, owed much to French Symbolism. He was one of the few English writers of his generation with the capability to understand and assimilate Mallarmé. Each of them made something personal of his French sources. Joyce wrote *Ulysses*, a novel of unfathomable richness and complexity; Eliot succumbed to Laforgue, whose work stamped and dominated his own poems for nearly a decade; Pound adopted French standards and critical methods as well as poetic forms and attitudes. The Imagists took piecemeal from French writers; the important point is that they took at all. The ignorance, among established critics in England, of what was happening abroad was remarkable. John C. Bailey, a regular contributor to the *Times Literary Supplement*, writing in 1907, saw the period that ended with Hérédia (who had died in 1905) as one of retraction. Poetry, he remarked of the Symbolists,

> escapes again not into the crowd or the streets but into the clouds, into the idea, into music.[79]

125

This is, as nearly as possible, the opposite of Imagist doctrine. That Bailey chose to end his study with Hérédia, a so-called Parnassian sonnet-writer (and, incidentally, the father-in-law of Henri de Régnier), is itself significant. A similar time-bar on taste was shown by Lytton Strachey, whose *Landmarks in French Literature*, published in 1912, concludes with Verlaine, who had died in 1896. There is a sad contrast in the little-known work of Jethro Bithell. Bithell equalled Flint in learning and outdid him in taste. From 1908 onwards he compiled a series of critical anthologies of contemporary European poetry. His verse translations, which included fine versions of Kahn and Laforgue, gained all too little recognition. Flint reviewed the first of these, *Contemporary German Poetry* (1909), in *The New Age*.[80] One of Bithell's translations from Else Lasker-Schüler seems to have provided the opening lines of Flint's poem 'Eau-Forte'.[81] Bithell followed this anthology with *Contemporary Belgian Poetry* (1911) and *Contemporary French Poetry* (1912). Whether these volumes were known to any of the Imagists remains uncertain. What is sure is that Bithell showed an awareness of European developments exceptional in England at that time.[82]

Undeniably the French poets gave some of the Imagists invaluable encouragement for their own work. As a movement Imagism benefited vitally from French sources. For the theory and practice of free verse came both justifications and examples. From the concept of the image as employed by French critics and philosophers, Hulme and Pound got ideas, however garbled or confused, which were of crucial value in their advocacy of a poetry founded on perception rather than literature. From the French critics the Imagists got standards and methods of a finer quality than prevailed in England or America. Most important of all, they gained a canon of taste to which some at least of them were able generously to respond.

\* \* \*

In his review of *Ripostes* in 1913 Flint regretted

> that Mr Hulme ever learned German, and read philosophy, and abandoned the making of little Japanese pictures in verse.[83]

How far Hulme's poems can be regarded as Japonesque is doubtful; but Flint's remark is a reminder of a source whose effects on Imagist poetry deserve at least some notice. Too much should not be made of this. The Italian poet Giuseppe Ungaretti was credited with Japanese influences at a time when he knew nothing about Japanese poetry. 'It was in the air', he said in casual explanation more than half a century later.[84] If Flint's

'History' can be taken at face value, Japanese poetry was regarded very seriously as a model by the members of Hulme's group:

> We proposed at various times to replace it by pure *vers libre*; by the Japanese *tanka* and *haikai*; we all wrote dozens of the latter as an amusement....[85]

The problem of access to Japanese poetry was complicated by the fact that none of the Imagist writers had any knowledge of Japanese. In the early years of the twentieth century Japanese literature was almost unknown in Europe. As with China, the visual art of Japan was known in the west before other aspects of Japanese culture. After the adoption of Japanese prints and painting by the Impressionists, Japan inspired a decorative rage exploited by interior designers as well as artists like Whistler and Beardsley. For too many people, though, Japan still meant Gilbert and Sullivan's appalling *Mikado* or the artificial cream of Puccini's *Madame Butterfly*.

Awareness of Japanese art reached Europe later than that of the Chinese. Until the mid-nineteenth century the arts of these two oriental civilizations were hardly differentiated in the European mind. Knowledge came slowly; first to Britain and France, the principal trading and imperial powers of the period, and the countries which had the strongest links with the Far East. Baudelaire, as a letter he wrote to Arsène Houssaye in 1861 confirms, was an admirer of Japanese colour-prints and one of the first among European writers to recognize their merits. In 1885 Judith Gautier, daughter of Théophile, published her *Poèmes de la Libellule*. This, one of the most handsomely produced books of its period, is a sequence of eighty-five tanka based on literal prose versions by Kimmochi Saionji. Judith Gautier, though she had earlier learned some Chinese, had no knowledge of Japanese and her versions make no attempt to imitate the form of the tanka. She adopted a system of rhyming cinquains. In Japanese the tanka, which is unrhymed, consists of five units (the concept of the line is not employed) of five, seven, five, seven and seven syllables respectively. The haiku is an abbreviated form of seventeen syllables, in which the last two units of the tanka are suppressed.

*Poèmes de la Libellule* found only a restricted market and there is no evidence that they had any impact on the Imagist writers:

> The *Poèmes de la libellule* have not had sufficient circulation to become important .... However, Gabriele d'Annunzio's 'Outa Occidentale' 1886, perhaps the first European attempt to write verse in a Japanese metre, were suggested by these translations.[86]

The first serious descriptive study of Japanese poetry in a European language had appeared in English in 1880, five years before the publication of Judith Gautier's translations. This was *The Classical Poetry of the Japanese* by Basil Hall Chamberlain, an Englishman living in Japan. (His brother Houston Stewart Chamberlain settled in Germany, wrote in German a series of works on pan-Teutonic themes of mythology and propaganda, and can be regarded as one of the forerunners of Nazi ideology.) The importance of Chamberlain's study lies in its introduction. The verse translations that follow are poor and unremarkable rhymed jingles. His summary of the nature of Japanese poetry is noteworthy. It implies a kind of sensibility with which most of the Imagist writers could identify:

> There are no soundings of the depths of the human heart: that would be philosophy, and not poetry.... What we find is the expression, in natural language, of the simple feelings common to all mankind, love, regret, loyalty, attachment to old traditions, and, in the place of religion and of moralising, nothing but that hopeless sense of the transitoriness of life, which precedes, as it survives, all culture and all philosophy.[87]

More than twenty years later, in 1902, Chamberlain published in periodical form a long essay, 'Basho and the Japanese Poetical Epigram', on the haiku.[88] (The seventeenth-century poet Bashō is regarded in Japan as one of the great masters of the form.) In 1911 this was incorporated in a revised and enlarged edition of his original work.[89]

Chamberlain's attitude to the haiku is oddly apologetic. He compares Bashō unfavourably with Wordsworth:

> Bashō was not born under the same lucky star as Wordsworth. He inherited a language incomparably inferior as a vehicle for poetry, and was restricted to a single form of verse, and that the poorest.[90]

But he notes the instantaneity and emphasis on perception that characterize Japanese poetry, and sums up his argument in terms that again seem pertinent to Imagism:

> If [the European critic] cannot here discover intact that mirror reflecting the universe of which the Japanese commentators speak, he does find thousands of fragments of shattered glass, among which some of shattered crystal, each reflecting at a different angle some minute corner of a scene, a brief note of some fact in nature, or maybe an indication of some sentiment or fancy. The Japanese epigram at its

best is a loop-hole opened for an instant on some little natural fact, some incident of daily life. It is a momentary flash ... .[91]

Chamberlain's later attempts on the haiku are undistinguished. But they are a considerable advance on his earlier work. In the Preface he claims that he has 'gone over to ... the literalists.'[92] The form he chooses for these literal renderings is an unrhymed octosyllabic couplet. Here is one example, which will show both the quality of the perception and also the inversion of Japanese syntax that Chamberlain, at least on this occasion, practises. It is a haiku by Nishiyama Sōin (1605-1682):

> Oranda no
> Moji ga yokotau
> Ama tsu kari.

In Chamberlain's rendering this becomes:

> The wild-geese in the firmament,—
> These are Dutch letters sideways stretching.[93]

Chamberlain's essay on the haiku had been read with appreciation by Paul-Louis Couchoud, a young French doctor. (He was the medical adviser and friend of Anatole France.) He had also studied Charles Maître's review of Chamberlain.[94] Couchoud spent some time in Japan (and was there during the Russo-Japanese war). He learned something of Japanese literature and became an enthusiastic admirer of the haiku. Back in France in 1905, Couchoud and two of his friends started to write haiku:

on French subjects without any rules of prosody, in imitation, not of the Japanese originals, but of haikai in French prose translations.[95]

Next year, in *Les Lettres*, Couchoud published a study of the haiku, supported by about a hundred illustrative translations.[96] In 1908 F. S. Flint, in his first poetry review in *The New Age*, offered translations of two haiku (or, as he called them, haikai). Flint's versions, in which he adopts the three-line formation that is now common for haiku in English are literal renderings from two of Couchoud's translations. The first is from Buson:

| Alone in a room | Seule, dans la chambre |
| Deserted— | Où il n'y a plus personne, |
| A peony. | Une pivoine. |

The other is a famous haiku by Moritake:

A fallen petal                    Un pétale tombé
Flies back to its branch:         Remonte à sa branche:
Ah! a butterfly!                  Ah! c'est un papillon![97]

In the second example, even Flint's punctuation is identical with that of the French version.

Flint's poems attain little of the condensation of Japanese work. Storer's 'Image' in *Mirrors of Illusion*, which must have been written before Flint's haiku appeared in *The New Age*, shares only its triplet form with Japanese poetry. Campbell's asyntactical experiments, such as 'The Dawn Whiteness' in *The Mountainy Singer*, were probably in proof before he first came to the Tour d'Eiffel. A few of Hulme's poems, however, do suggest, in rhythm or phrase, possible affinities with some of Couchoud's versions. For example, this haiku by Bashō:

Les herbes de l'été!
De tous ces guerriers morts,
Voilà ce qui reste de leurs rêves![98]

can be compared with these lines from Hulme's 'In the City Square':

On the cold hill
The cheers of the warrior dead
(For the first time re-seen)....

At best a thin parallel. At most it would seem that the atmosphere of Couchoud's work enters some of Hulme's poems.

Couchoud's discussion of the properties of the haiku matches well with the theory of poetry that Hulme and Flint were working towards. He differed from Chamberlain in his insistence that the haiku was not an epigram. The 'bite' of European epigrams is 'almost always in the play of words .... They are strokes of language.' Whereas:

Le haïkaï est un coup d'oeil. Il ne dépasse pas la vision pure et simple. Il n'est pas une caricature, parce que la caricature suppose une idée interposée entre l'oeil et l'objet aperçu.

Du poème japonais surtout le discursif, l'explicatif sont extirpés. La bizarre fleur se détache unique sur la neige. Le bouquet est interdit. Le poème prend à sa source la sensation lyrique jaillissante, instantanée, avant que le mouvement de la pensée ou de la passion l'ait orientée et utilisée. À la prose est laissée la liaison logique des sensations ....[99]

130

Between the meetings of the Tour d'Eiffel group and the Imagistes lay the re-publication of Chamberlain's essay in 1911 and in the same year the appearance in Paris of Michel Revon's authoritative *Anthologie de la littérature japonaise des origines au XXe siècle*. Once again, the Imagistes had an advantage over the earlier group. H.D. showed little interest in Japanese literature and claimed that her work was unaffected by Pound's orientalism. Yet 'Oread' can be read almost as a transcript of a Japanese colour-engraving:

> Whirl up, sea—
> whirl your pointed pines,
> splash your great pines
> on our rocks,
> hurl your green over us,
> cover us with your pools of fir.

Her husband Richard Aldington acknowledged the effect of Japanese colour-prints on some of his poems of that time. In a letter to Earl Miner he said that the poem which follows

was written in the B.M. Print Room on a couple of Japanese colour prints. The landscape was certainly Hokusai's. The second one I don't remember, obviously a girl, perhaps an Outamaro, perhaps a Toyokuni.[100]

### The River

I have drifted along this river
Until I moored my boat
By these crossed trunks.

Here the mist moves
Over fragile leaves and rushes,
Colourless waters and brown, fading hills.

You have come from beneath the trees
And move within the mist,
A floating leaf.

O blue flower of the evening,
You have touched my face
With your leaves of silver.

Love me, for I must depart.

Japanese poetry seems to have meant less to Aldington than Japanese painting. He showed some interest in the haiku, or what he understood the haiku to be. He refers to haiku, which, following Pound, he calls hokku, both in poems and letters. However, a Japanese scholar friendly with Aldington stated:

> There is no reference to the Japanese *Haiku* poems in his letters to me, but that he has had some knowledge of them is indisputable. We may sense in some of his earlier poems the influence of the *Haiku*. I do not think, however, that Japanese art and literature influenced him much.[101]

Among the Imagistes the one figure to show a more active interest in Japanese poetry was Ezra Pound. Towards the end of 1913 Pound came into possession of Fenollosa's manuscripts. *Cathay* is often thought of as the prime result of that stewardship. But Pound published Noh plays and critical material on the Japanese classical theatre before the appearance of any of the poems that make up *Cathay*.[102] There is no mention of Japanese poetry in his writings in the first phase of Imagisme. China was Pound's chief oriental source. Fenollosa had spent more time in Japan than in China, and in his work on Chinese poetry he was helped by two Japanese scholars, Mori and Ariga. Pound published *Cathay* with the note:

> For the most part from the Chinese of Rihaku.[103]

He used the Japanese form of the name of the Chinese poet Li-Po. Chinese literature came to Pound mediated through English translations and Japanese sensibility. Even so, he always considered it far more important for his work than the literature of Japan:

> China is fundamental, Japan is not. Japan is a special interest, like Provence, or 12-13th Century Italy (apart from Dante). I don't mean to say there aren't interesting things in Fenollosa's Japanese stuff . . . . But China is solid.[104]

Pound's interest in what he called the hokku preceded his possession of Fenollosa's manuscripts. His choice of terminology may be significant. In Japanese three forms of the word exist: haiku, hokku and haikai, with different shades of meaning. The term *haiku* is generally used now in England and America. Flint, following French usage, always referred to the haikai. Pound's term 'hokku' was adopted by Richard Aldington and is used in the preface to the second volume of *Some Imagist Poets*.[105]

This is interesting, because hokku had been Chamberlain's choice also. In his essay Chamberlain stated the three forms of the word, but in a manner that gave more weight to the first variant:

Their native name is *Hokku* (also *Haiku* and *Haikai*), which in default of a better equivalent, I venture to translate by 'Epigram' . . . .[106]

This would suggest that Pound had read Chamberlain. He makes several references to 'hokku' in his essay on Vorticism.[107] The three examples he gives there are all arranged in two lines. This may reflect Pound's familiarity with Chamberlain's use of the unrhymed couplet in his English versions. It could account also for an otherwise puzzling comment in Pound's essay 'How I Began', when he mentions Japan:

where sixteen syllables are counted enough for a poem if you arrange and punctuate them properly . . . .[108]

The date of publication of this essay (June 1913) confirms that Pound's interest in Japan had developed during his period of Imagisme. Of equal significance is the chain of evidence which leads to Chamberlain as one of his sources. It is possible that he knew Flint's work too. On one occasion he misquotes the haiku by Moritake which Flint had translated. This was not among the poems translated by Chamberlain:

The fallen blossom flies back to its branch:
A butterfly.[109]

As Chamberlain had stated that the haiku operates 'within the limits of seventeen syllables', Pound's reading of him seems not to have been very accurate. Perhaps he was encouraged to read *Japanese Poetry*, which appears to have attracted little general attention, by John Gould Fletcher. Pound and Fletcher were on friendly terms at this time, and Pound often made use of Fletcher's extensive collection of French poets.

Most of Pound's references to Japanese poetry derive from his Vorticist period. This may have been linked with his developing interest in visual art, encouraged by his friendships with Gaudier-Brzeska and Wyndham Lewis. In his article on Edward Wadsworth as a Vorticist, Pound wrote:

I trust the gentle reader is accustomed to take pleasure in 'Whistler and the Japanese.'
From Whistler and the Japanese, or Chinese the 'world,' that is to say, the fragment of the English-speaking world that spreads itself into print, learned to enjoy 'arrangements' of colours and masses.[110]

From this it would seem that Pound, like Aldington, was affected by Japanese visual art as well as poetry. At the most Japanese painting or engraving acted to give Pound sources for his theorizing. There is no exploitation of Japanese themes in his poems. Japanese poetry (or what he learned of its theory) operated to encourage Pound's unrelenting drive in his Imagist years to compression and concentration.

In their interest in Japanese literature, Amy Lowell and Fletcher again followed in Pound's tracks. Amy Lowell, however, had already shown interest in Japanese visual art in her pre-Imagist days. It supplied themes for two of her early poems in *A Dome of Many-Coloured Glass*—'A Japanese Wood-Carving' and 'A Coloured Print by Shokei'—at a time when she probably knew virtually nothing about Japanese literature. Her interest in Japanese and Chinese poetry intensified in the later years of her career. 'Lacquer Prints', the first poems in which she uses Japanese literature as a starting-point, appeared as part of her collection *Pictures of the Floating World* (New York, 1919). In her Foreword to this volume she said that she had followed the haiku pattern, but added:

> I have made no attempt to observe the syllabic rules which are an integral part of all Japanese poetry. I have endeavoured only to keep the brevity and suggestion of the *hokku*, and to preserve it within its natural sphere.[111]

In *What's O'Clock*, published in the last year of her life, there is a sequence of 'Twenty-four Hokku on a Modern Theme'. In this collection she even attempts a tanka.[112] In all these poems she adopts a strict syllabic count. But these experiments, which appear to owe something of their inspiration to the *Japanese Prints* (1918) of her friend John Gould Fletcher, though accomplished, lack vitality.

Like Amy Lowell, Fletcher had a considerable interest in Japanese culture. His knowledge of Japanese literature and philosophy exceeded and probably preceded hers. His main interest in Japan seems to have been at its peak during his period of contiguity with the Imagists. Earl Miner alludes to a letter from Fletcher, who

> remembered reading two English, one French, and two German translations of Japanese poetry and these at a time when he was deeply interested in the Japano-English poet Yone Noguchi .... [113]

It is likely that Chamberlain's work and Revon's *Anthologie* were included among Fletcher's reading. Revon's anthology was the only major collection of Japanese poetry then available in any European language. Fletcher had also read Fenollosa's study *Epochs of Chinese and Japanese Art*, edited by Fenollosa's widow and published in Britain in 1912.[114] From this Fletcher learned about the Zen Buddhist doctrines which are discussed in the preface to his *Goblins and Pagodas* in 1916.[115] But this collection seems to have benefited more from the visual art of Japan than from its philosophy or literature. His specific interest in the haiku crystallized a little later in his *Japanese Prints*. In a preface Fletcher explains the 'main object' of the haiku:

Its object was some universalized emotion derived from a natural fact. Its achievement was the expression of that emotion in the fewest possible terms. It is therefore necessary, if poetry in the English tongue is ever to attain again to the vitality and strength of its beginnings, that we sit once more at the feet of the Orient and learn from it how little words can express, how sparingly they should be used, and how much is contained in the meanest natural object.[116]

Again, unfortunately, Fletcher's talent prevented him from living up to his own critical standards.

In the Imagist approaches to Japan, as in much other Imagist work, we find the problem of pioneer discoveries and insights not equally matched with creative capability. Their relative failure in this area has been discussed by an American critic:

It is this turn on an image in the solution of a philosophical dilemma (the essence of haiku) that makes the American imagists, who imitated the Japanese, appear so shallow by comparison. Amy Lowell tried for images and images alone, as did Ezra Pound in

> On the Station of the Metro
> The apparition of these faces in the crowd;
> Petals on a wet, black bough.

The image is good, but it is not haiku because 'petals' does not emerge from the essential picture and resolve a dilemma; rather, it is a lucky similitude that hangs in space. John Gould Fletcher's dedication of *Japanese Prints* (1918) to his wife:

> Granted this dew-drop world be but a dew-drop world,
> This granted, yet——

is B. H. Chamberlain's translation from the Japanese poet Buson without quotation marks. Fletcher's own work contains no poem that can compare with his dedication ... .[117]

The value of most of the Imagist borrowings lay not in exactitude of scholarship but in what they offered to the imagination. Japanese poetry, the haiku, and Japanese visual art (sometimes mediated through Whistler's Impressionism) offered such incentives. In the discovery of Japan visual art preceded poetry; in the realization of that discovery America was to outmarch England. In their Japanese interests, as with their French sources, the Imagists responded to the spirit of the age. For, as Herbert Read remarked:

> ... imagism relates more or less directly to Art Nouveau and Jugendstil. Beardsley's drawings are 'precise images', and of course it all connects up with Japanese art—the haiku etc. followed in the wake of the Japanese print.[118]

\* \* \*

*Cathay* is one of Pound's more formidable achievements. With these poems he reached what is perhaps the high-point of his Imagist period:

> *Leave-taking Near Shoku*
> They say the roads of Sanso are steep,
> Sheer as the mountains.
> The walls rise in a man's face,
> Clouds grow out of the hill
>     at his horse's bridle.
> Sweet trees are on the paved way of the Shin,
> Their trunks burst through the paving,
> And freshets are bursting their ice
>     in the midst of Shoku, a proud city.
>
> Men's fates are already set,
> There is no need of asking diviners.

They belong, however, to Pound's own progress rather than to the general history of Imagism. He was the only Imagist for whom China became important. Amy Lowell's *Fir-Flower Tablets* emerge from a later phase of her work and show her again trailing in imitation of Pound.

Pound got much from his readings in Chinese poetry. He acquired a mistaken justification for free verse; an oriental atmosphere heavy with exoticism; and a brilliant array of masks to speak through. The China of Pound's imagining was in the standard European tradition of Chinoiserie. It reflected in more cultured form the same impulse that drew audiences of weary soldiers to *Chu Chin Chow*. Chinese literature, while it had almost no influence on the other Imagists, had through Pound a defining effect on Imagism.

During the Imagist years Pound knew no Chinese (he later learned a few characters). He was never in China. Nevertheless the T'ang world had a profound effect on his imagination. His later work was saturated in its history and philosophy. Whatever coherence the *Cantos* possess derives from Pound's view of Confucian China as representing a cultural and political norm, and in all respects a true classical civilization.

In the late months of 1913 Fenollosa's widow sent Pound her husband's manuscripts, apparently on the strength of 'Contemporania'.[119] These manuscripts are the foundation, but not the only source, of most of Pound's Sino-Japanese work. In 1914 Pound published six poems in *Des Imagistes*; four were on Chinese themes: 'After Ch'u Yuan', 'Liu Ch'e', 'Fan-piece for Her Imperial Lord' and 'Ts'ai Chi'h'. The manuscript of *Des Imagistes* was originally sent to New York by Pound in the summer of 1913, at a time when Fenollosa's papers were not yet in his possession.[120] There is plausible evidence to link at least three of the four poems with Pound's reading of H. A. Giles. Giles, like Chamberlain, was an indifferent translator, but his work as a historian of Chinese literature gives him a pioneer importance among European sinologues. Pound had probably learned about Giles's work from Allen Upward, a scholar and amateur of linguistics. Upward, who was a friend of both Hulme and Pound, was a man of versatile interests and intelligence limited, perhaps fatally, by an over-riding eccentricity. He appeared in *Des Imagistes* with a series of prose-poems called 'Scented Leaves from a Chinese Jar'. Upward's acquaintance with Chinese literature was founded on Giles's translations, as his verse letter in *The Egoist* confirms:

### The Discarded Imagist
In the year nineteen hundred a poet named Cranmer Byng
brought to my attic in Whitehall Gardens a book of
Chinese Gems by Professor Giles,
Eastern butterflies coming there into my attic beside
the Stygian Thames,
And read me one of them—willows, forsaken young wife,
spring.

Immediately my soul kissed the soul of immemorial China:
I perceived that all we in the West were indeed barbarians
and foreign devils,
And that we knew scarcely nothing about poetry.[121]

Here he refers to Giles's *Gems of Chinese Literature* (London and Shanghai, 1884). The book Pound worked from was Giles's later volume *A History of Chinese Literature* (1901), of which he claimed:

This is the first attempt made in any language, including Chinese, to produce a history of Chinese literature.[122]

Fenollosa's manuscripts included a variety of notes on Japanese as well as Chinese writings. The Chinese material incorporated versions of poems plus notes and drafts of a lecture on the ideogram.[123] Pound's use of Fenollosa, and the skill with which he turned draft versions of dull literalness into the poems of *Cathay*, are by now well known. That his knowledge of Chinese was non-existent in 1913, and that it never became more than 'self-taught, and little', is hardly relevant.[124] What is important, in terms of creative achievement, is the quality of Pound's translations as poems. This is now admitted even by many Chinese scholars.[125] 'Fan-Piece for Her Imperial Lord', condensed from a much longer version by Giles, is a masterly example:

> O fan of white silk,
>     clear as frost on the grass-blade,
> You also are laid aside.

In Pound's version the form of the Chinese original was utterly lost. He never realised that the standard form of T'ang poetry is the strict quatrain with hemistich. He thought that Li-Po (whom he persisted in calling Rihaku) was a writer of free verse. This is one of the more remarkable errors in the history of the reception and translation of a foreign literature. Yet it was a fruitful error: Pound's confusion had creative results. Hueffer obediently followed Pound's misunderstanding. (It was Hueffer who still believed at the very end of his career that Li-Po and Rihaku were different people!

> Let us once more quote Rihaku, not because he was the greatest of the Chinese poets of the era, that glory being accorded by the Chinese themselves to Li-Po.)[126]

Pound's misconception of Fenollosa's theoretical notes was more serious, even though these may themselves have been founded on far from accurate premises.

From Fenollosa's essay *The Chinese Written Character as a Medium for Poetry* Pound got support for his view of the ideogram. His interpretation is vulnerable because of his defective scholarship. Its guiding principle of encouragement to the visual is far less assailable, but Pound made the mistake of trying to justify himself in academically acceptable terms. The essay also offered a theory of the function of transitive verbs in poetry. As he wrote in a letter to Iris Barry in 1916:

138

... you should have a chance to see Fenollosa's big essay on verbs, mostly on verbs. Heaven knows when I shall get it printed. He inveighs against 'IS,' wants transitive verbs. 'Become' is as weak as 'is.' Let the grime *do* something to the leaves. 'All nouns come from verbs.' To primitive man, a thing only IS what it *does*. That is Fenollosa, but I think the theory is a very good one for poets to go by.[127]

This theory, which incidentally coincides with recent speculation in linguistics, is an important codicil to the notion of a poetry of physical objects. Through the Chinese Pound re-learned one of the basic stylistic principles of English, the primacy of the verb, the word of action. This blended harmoniously with what he had already absorbed from Rémy de Gourmont. The reconciliation of musical with pictorial or sculptural elements in poetry, which Pound pleaded for in his study on Vorticism, finds further support in Fenollosa, who stated the problem:

In what sense can verse, written in terms of visible hieroglyphics, be reckoned true poetry? It might seem that poetry, which like music is a *time art*, weaving its unities out of successive impressions of sound, could with difficulty assimilate a verbal medium consisting largely of semi-pictorial appeals to the eye.

then attempted to answer it:

The truth of a painting or a photograph is that, in spite of its concreteness, it drops the element of natural succession . . . .

. . . One superiority of verbal poetry as an art rests in its getting back to the fundamental reality of *time*. Chinese poetry has the unique advantage of combining both elements. It speaks at once with the vividness of painting, and with the mobility of sounds. It is, in some sense, more objective than either, more dramatic. In reading Chinese we do not seem to be juggling mental counters, but to be watching *things* work out their own fate.[128]

This argument seems to represent the culmination of what Pound had been looking for. Pound did not prepare Fenollosa's essay for publication until late in 1916.[129] It did not get into print until 1919.[130] In retrospect, it represents the end of Imagism rather than one of its sources.

Pound may also have read Fenollosa's *Epochs of Chinese and Japanese Art*. The arguments here fit remarkably with much of what Hulme and Pound had to say about poetic theory. As if in anticipation of later American poets, Fenollosa founded his idea on the doctrines of Zen.

139

He alluded to its Chinese form (apparently unaware that in Chinese it is called *Chan*). He focuses many ideas current among the Imagists, but which they never managed to state coherently on paper:

> All real poetry is just this underground perception of organic relation, between which custom classifies as different. The principle lies at the very root of the enlargement of vocabulary in primitive languages. Nature was so plastic and transparent to the eye of early man, that what we call metaphor flashed upon him as a spiritual identity to be embodied at once in language in poetry and in myth. Zen only tried to get back to that primitive *éclaircissement*. A word, like a thing, means as much as you can see into it, and therefore lights up with a thousand chameleon-like shadings, which, of later days, only the poet knows how to use with a hint of the original colour. So in Chinese poetry every character has at least two shades of meaning, its natural and its spiritual, or the image and its metaphorical range. In Chinese poetry we find extreme condensation, for every word is packed with thought.[131]

Imagist and Vorticist doctrine would have been stronger had they been able to incorporate Fenollosa's interpretation of Zen theory.

\* \* \*

> Gilbert Murray has struck at Greek scholarship and done no good to English verse ... HD is a poet.[132]

Such was T. S. Eliot's judgment. In praising H.D.'s translations from Euripides he found reason also to dismiss Gilbert Murray. At the time it was a formidable gesture of irreverence. Now there can be little doubt that Eliot was right. In face of the excessive mystique that still attaches to Classical scholarship in some circles in England, it is worth remembering that many classical scholars have not proved good writers in their native language. The legacy of years spent over Latin verse and Greek prose is often woefully disappointing in terms of English composition.

Among the Imagistes the one classical scholar was Richard Aldington. He had indeed more scholarship than feeling. The effect of his classical interests on his poems was often disastrous. 'In the Via Sestina' can again be quoted:

> O daughter of Isis, ...
> ....
> A manifest harlot.
> Straight and slim art thou
> As a marble phallus; ...

At best his Greek themes were purely ornamental. He based his rationale for free verse on Greek choruses, mainly because they were unrhymed and had lines of varying length and stress. This was hardly sufficient material on which to construct a poetic method.

H.D.'s Hellenism was more genuine. However limited her scholarship, she had a considerable feeling for Greece. During the Imagiste years she was still learning the language; she even tried to persuade Brigit Patmore to join her in her studies.[133]

As a translator H.D. was explicit in defence of her method:

A literal, word-for-word version of so well-known an author as Euripides, would be useless and supererogatory; a rhymed, languidly Swinburnian verse form is an insult and a barbarism. It seemed, therefore, that the rhymeless hard rhythms used in the present version would be most likely to keep the sharp edges and irregular cadence of the original.[134]

Her Greek world was an imagined private one, as personal as Ezra Pound's China, and for her as compelling in its implications. Indeed, Greece proved too compelling. Some years later, after the collapse of her marriage to Aldington, she visited the Greek islands. The experience was too intense, and she suffered a severe emotional breakdown. No doubt H.D.'s attitude to her Hellenism was too private; it became an aesthetic retreat with all the dangers inherent in such a withdrawal.

H.D.'s interests among the Greek poets seem to have been close to those of Aldington. It is likely that her taste was fed by his. During the period of their Imagiste involvement, which coincided with the period of their happiest personal relations, they were in close artistic rapport. At the time H.D. seems to have been interested particularly in Euripides, Sappho, and the short poems of *The Greek Anthology*. Her versions of some of the Choruses from Euripides' *Iphigeneia in Aulis* were published by the Egoist Press in 1915. In a prefatory note to her translations she praised Euripides and claimed for the Choruses:

something of that rocky quality, of that imaged clarity, which are so admirable in the earlier lyric poets.[135]

H.D. took little of her technique from Sappho; but was profoundly influenced in terms of feeling. She undoubtedly identified with the great Greek writer, whose fate and character were so unlike her own. It was the ιδεα of Sappho rather than the latter's work (all too little of which survives) that particularly affected her imagination. To see H.D.'s work in any line of direct descent from that of the Greek poet would be wrong. Sappho was above everything a celebrant of love, of love as passion, physical and emotional. H.D.'s work exists on the borders of discourse. In her poems there is often an intensity disproportionate to the apparent situation. Her interest in the poets of *The Greek Anthology* is self-explanatory.

The poems of Bion and Moschus (whose work had some influence on Pound's *Mauberley*), the lyrics and epigrams of the often anonymous later Greek writers (Alexandrian or Hellenistic), meant something to each of the original Imagiste trio. The short epigrammatic poem, often Greek in inspiration, is a form common in Aldington's earlier work. Many of H.D.'s poems are epigrams in the Greek rather than the Latin connotations of the word:

> *Epigram*
> The golden one is gone from the banquets;
> She, beloved of Atimetus,
> The swallow, the bright Homonoea;
> Gone the dear chatterer.

The earlier and later Imagist writers showed little more than perfunctory interest in Classical Greek. The suggestion that the Imagistes were 'a group of ardent Hellenists' was a product of wishful thinking by Pound. Even he by 1920 was sardonic about H.D.'s 'Alexandrine Greek bunk'.[136] The ardent Hellenists reduce, in the end, to H.D. alone.

\* \* \*

Latin literature also had a place in the diet of the Imagistes. They took as source-material Latin poetry of two widely separated periods, Classical and Renaissance. Pound and Aldington were firm admirers of the Roman satirists; and Pound encouraged H.D. to read Renaissance Latin poetry. The ferocity of some of Pound's epigrams derives from Martial or Juvenal. Catullus is a name that often appears in Imagist conflation. Pound mentions him already in 'A Few Don'ts by an Imagiste', and two years later Aldington declared:

> Imagists seek the qualities that mark Sappho, Catullus, Villon, the French Symbolists ... great.[137]

For the Imagists Catullus was a credential rather than a source. There was nothing revolutionary in their taste for him. The Roman poet had been equally admired in the nineties. Beardsley's translation of the 'Carmen CI', 'By ways remote and distant waters sped', is a graceful traditional rendering. There is however, a fundamental difference of approach between Beardsley's version and the methods of the Imagists.

142

In their dealings with Classic poetry, the Imagist poets abandoned rhyme. Where they did not attempt fidelity to the verse-structure of the original they looked for equivalent cadence and auditory properties in English. They sought to isolate and to respond to the qualities of language and feeling of the text they worked from. Until then most verse translation in English had remained subservient to principles established by Dryden and Pope.[138] When Gilbert Murray needed a method with which to handle Greek tragic drama he could resort only to the rhythms and language of Swinburne and William Morris. The Imagists firmly turned their backs on these out-dated modalities.

Classical Latin was not a large part of their source-material. Of more striking and immediate effect, in particular in the work of H.D., was the Latin of the Renaissance. In a letter to Glenn Hughes she explained how Pound had introduced her to an anthology of Renaissance Latin poets. The effect of this on her work was considerable. As she put it:

Ezra ... was beautiful about my first authentic verses, 'Hermes' and 'Spare Us From Loveliness' and 'Acon' (a transposition from that Renaissance Latin Book) ... .[139]

As yet the particular anthology has not been identified. The Latin original on which 'Acon' is modelled was composed by the sixteenth-century Venetian, Giovanni Battista Amalteo. 'Acon', as published in *Des Imagistes*, carries the ascription 'After the Latin of Joannes Baptiste Amaltheus'. (Later publications dropped this.)

Amalteo, whose 'Acon' was first published in 1550,[140] is now largely forgotten,[141] but in the seventeenth and eighteenth centuries his work had considerable popularity in England.[142] His sixth Eclogue 'Lycidas' may even have provided a model for Milton's great poem.[143] In Italian Amalteo was an accomplished sonnet-writer.[144]

H.D.'s version of 'Acon' is very free. In its casualness of attitude to the original text it anticipates the method that Pound was to use in *Homage to Sextus Propertius*. Amalteo's poem begins with these lines:

O Qui Dictaei statuat me in vertice montis,
Aut fortunatos Erymanthi sistat ad amnes;
Ut saturis panacem calathis, ut molle cyperum,
Dictamnumque legam, et fragrantia germina myrrhae,
Et relevem infirmos artus languentis Hyellae.
Illa quidem vix aegram animam sustentat anhelo
Pectore, et indignis singultibus interrumpit;
Nec vis ulla potest saevum lenire dolorem.
Illam etiam lacrimantem, etiam sua fata querentem ....

143

In H.D.'s version this becomes:

> Bear me to Dictaeus,
> And to the steep slopes;
> To the river Erymanthus.
>
> I choose spray of dittany,
> Cyperum frail of flower,
> Buds of myrrh,
> All-healing herbs,
> Close pressed in calathes.
>
> For she lies panting,
> Drawing sharp breath,
> Broken with harsh sobs,
> She, Hyella,
> Whom no god pitieth.

The sincerity and liveliness which the Imagists brought to their explorations compensate amply for their deficiencies in scholarship. Classical sources gave them material for what became a new approach to translation. The harvest of this appeared a few years later: with Pound's *Homage to Sextus Propertius*; with his interweaving of Classical themes and techniques in *Mauberley*; with H.D.'s version of Euripides; and with the whole undertaking represented by the Poets' Translation Series of the Egoist Press. Though other writers are represented in that series (Flint and Storer also contributed) these classical interests were fostered primarily by the Imagistes. Imagiste practice suggested possibilities for new ways of translation. The rejection of traditional methods is already explicit in H.D.'s preface to her versions of the Greek choruses. The new way, approved and endorsed by Eliot, was to have vital effects on the development of poetic translation, particularly in America, in the middle of the present century. The Imagistes were rediscovering an age-old tradition by which English poetry had renewed itself through translation from foreign sources. As Pound remembered, Chaucer was praised by his contemporaries as 'grant translateur'. Victorian cultural isolation had broken this pattern. Now it reappeared. In the complex web of Imagist sources Greek and Latin poetry have a limited but distinct importance.

\* \* \*

The Bible seems to have been considered a possible source of literary form only since its acceptance as the 'Word of God' has diminished. The

144

efforts of a hundred years of translators combined to make the King James Bible of 1611 one of the great literary achievements in the English language. The Bible has had profound effects on the idiom and imagery of English, written or spoken. Its influence on the form of English poetry has been much slighter. It manifests itself in the eighteenth century in Smart's *Song of David* and Blake's *Prophetic Books*. With Whitman in the nineteenth century it enters American poetry. Flint, in his account of the searchings of his Tour d'Eiffel colleagues, mentioned 'poems in a sacred Hebrew form ...' And he added: 'Joseph Campbell produced two good examples of this, one of which, 'The Dark' is printed in *The Mountainy Singer* ... '[145]

> This is the dark.
> This is the dream that came of the dark.
> This is the dreamer who dreamed the dream that came of the dark.
> This is the look the dreamer looked who dreamed the
>     dream that came of the dark.
> This is the love that followed the look the dreamer looked
>     who dreamed the dream that came of the dark.

*    *    *

Campbell was experimenting with the aggregative principle which has the same place in Hebrew verse that it holds in the composition of some English nursery rhymes, though his experiments do not appear to have had any effect on the Imagist writers. Much later, Ford Madox Hueffer argued that the English Bible provided a sanction for free verse:

> ... most of the Psalms of David, the Books of Job and of Ruth, and some of the prophetic writings ... without reference to the Hebrew original, present an unanswerable case for rhythmic expression of emotions. I do not say that they exclude metrical or rhymed expressions, merely that they present an unanswerable case for the existence of *vers libre* as a form.[146]

(Hueffer and Campbell as Roman Catholics would theoretically be more familiar with the Douai than the Authorized Version; but the differences are not large.)

Behind the *vers libre* of two French poets, Gustave Kahn and Flint's friend André Spire (whom Pound described in 1913 as 'very like an Imagiste'),[147] lay at least some knowledge of classical Hebrew. In roundabout fashion, through the reading of Whitman, the English Bible also had its effect on some of the pioneers of *vers libre*. This was reinforced, if Rémy de Gourmont's judgment is correct, by the German Bible of Luther which had been studied by Gustave Kahn. In his account of foreign influences on French poetry, de Gourmont mentioned above all Whitman, who first reached France through the translations of Laforgue and Vielé-Griffin. De Gourmont suggested that Whitman was a 'son of the Bible' and that *vers libre* is founded on Hebrew verse form[148]

Many of the desiderata of the Imagist poetic are anticipated in Classical Hebrew. Hebrew poetry is accentual, not quantitative. The language has no regular metrical system. Rhyme is rare. The common measure is a long free-verse line. Abstract nouns and ornamental adjectives are avoided; diction is concrete and rooted in the physical.[149] Only the familiar Hebrew device of parallelism would seem out of place in the Imagist context. And even that is hinted in Pound's poem 'Dance Figure':

> I have not found thee in the tents,
> In the broken darkness.
> I have not found thee at the well-head
> Among the women with pitchers.

\*　\*　\*

In their scholarship the Imagists were often muddled and inconsistent. They took ideas and techniques haphazardly, and without much selection, from a wide range of literatures. Hulme in his intellectual borrowings was careless, abrupt, sometimes simplistic to the point of coarseness. Pound, though he had a finer critical sense, jumbled theory with practice far more uncertainly than the Englishman. The others can hardly be treated with the same respect. But all of them were alert to what they could learn beyond the containing walls of English literary culture. Without their readiness to rummage among a variety of sources, they could not have ventured into aesthetics with even the limited success they did achieve.

# V

The Mountain and the Cloud

Without their theories, however misconceived these now appear, the Imagists would have gained far less notice in their own time or today. Though they often disclaimed revolutionary intentions, they were enthusiastic drafters of manifestos. They were fertile also in critical utterance. At the same time Pound, in particular, got himself in difficulties by trying to analyse what areas of consciousness a poem emerged from. Many of their statements had large theoretical implications. In exploring these they often lost themselves in a desert of ideas. The result was sometimes disastrous. Hulme's renunciation of poetry has semantic as well as emotional justification.

All theories about poetry are speculative attempts to analyse the attributes and functions of poetic art. Theories about the origins and imaginative materials of poetry lead into the ontogenetics of art; a sphere of darkness. Philosophers have tried to penetrate this mystery; but none of them, not even Kant, has so far found an answer. In Greece the masters of tragedy came first: Aristotle followed. In poetry, where aims and methods are far less directly comprehensible than those of the theatre, the relation of theory to practice often resembles a two-way mirror. With the Imagists, poetic theory, for the first time in English since Wordsworth and Coleridge, asserted claims to predominance.

## The Question of Free Verse

Demand for change in the form of the poem is the unifying factor in the activities of the Tour d'Eiffel group. Flint's 'History' makes this clear. He remarks that the members of the group were brought together by their 'dissatisfaction with English poetry' as it was then being written:

We proposed at various times to replace it by pure *vers libre*; by the Japanese *tanka* and *haikai*; we all wrote dozens of the latter as an amusement; by poems in a sacred Hebrew form of which 'This is the House that Jack Built' is a perfect model; Joseph Campbell produced two good specimens of this, one of which, 'The Dark', is printed in *The Mountainy Singer*; by rhymeless poems like Hulme's 'Autumn,'

147

and so on. In all this Hulme was the ringleader. He insisted too on absolutely accurate presentation and no verbiage .... [1]

T. S. Eliot wrote:

> The poem comes before the form, in the sense that a form grows out of the attempt of somebody to do something. [2]

For the English poets of the nineteenth century form had tended to become formula. By the latter part of the century forms were sought and utilized for their own sake. The essay 'A Plea for certain Exotic Forms of Verse', published in *The Cornhill* in 1877, pinpoints this attitude. This was a learned analysis of half a dozen forms, all of which had recently been imported into English poetic practice. Their use became a marked feature of the lesser poetic work of the last quarter of the nineteenth century. This emphasis on form is oddly echoed in Hulme's 'Lecture':

> All kinds of reasons are given by the academic critics for the efflorescence of verse at any period. But the true one is very seldom given. It is the invention or introduction of a new verse form .... You will find the burst of poetic activity at the time of Elizabeth put down to the discovery of America. The discovery of America had about as much effect on the Courtier poets at that time as the discovery of a new asteroid would have had on the poetic activity of Swinburne. The real reason was, I take it, that the first opportunity was given for the exercise of verse composition by the introduction of all kinds of new matter and new forms from Italy and France. [3]

Hulme's notions of form were limited. They might at first appear to restrict verse to a species of high-octane conversation. But his theory of metaphor, however insufficient, had the great merit of allowing poetry to operate as the central dynamic force of language. At that early stage of Imagist activity the arguments of both Hulme and Storer were most convincing in their discussion of free verse. Hulme says:

> I want to speak of verse in a plain way as I would of pigs: that is the only honest way.

And he explains why he prefers free verse:

> Regular metre to this impressionist poetry is cramping, jangling, meaningless, and out of place. Into the delicate pattern of images and colour it introduces the heavy, crude pattern of rhetorical verse. It

148

destroys the effect just as a barrel organ does, when it intrudes into the subtle interwoven harmonies of the modern symphony.

. . . .

The criticism is sure to be made that when you have abolished the regular syllabled line as the unit of poetry, you have turned it into prose. Of course this is perfectly true of a great quantity of modern verse. In fact, one of the great blessings of the abolition of regular metre would be that it would at once expose all this sham poetry. [4]

Edward Storer's argument proceeds from different premises and uses different means to reach a remarkably similar conclusion. He asserts that rhyme and what he calls 'rhythm', in which he seems to include formal metrical patterns, are superfluous. (Rhythm and metre are not separated in Greek and Latin poetics.)

Their use for their own sake may safely be left to the music-hall and ballad concert type of poetry. Their employment in serious poetry must only be secondary and subsidiary. So far, it seems to me, that most of the good poetry of the world has been written, as it were, by accident, in spite of colossal self-imposed difficulties and constrictions, such as the employment of forms in which it is practically impossible to write poetry at all except at the rate of about one really fine thought a page, if as much as that. Such difficult and precious forms as the *ballade*, the *triolet*, the *villanelle*, and to a less degree the sonnet— charming as they often are—were originally the work of word-tricksters rather than poets . . . . [5]

In place of these set forms Storer proposes what he calls blank verse 'cut up and spaced'. He argues that this is 'a still more plastic and more natural form' than regular blank verse and he attempts to assimilate it to *vers libre* in French:

This is, of course, only the *vers libre*, supposed to be the invention of M. Gustave Khan, and since then adopted by French poets like Verhaeren, Viele-Griffin, Henri de Regnier, Cte Robert de Montesquiou, etc., and English poets like Henley and Francis Thompson. As a matter of fact, however, we were using *vers libre* in England without making any fuss about it, long before it rose to the eminence of a movement in France. Sydney Dobell, Alexander Smith —Coleridge even, all used it at times. In a sense, nearly all the English poets have been vers-librists, for we never insisted on such rigidity of form as the French did, until their traditions were shaken by the decadents, symbolists and vers-librists of the last twenty or thirty years.[6]

Arthur Symons, who pioneered the study of the French Symbolist poets in England, admitted his inability to understand *vers libre* at the time it was at the height of its early fashion in Paris and Brussels. On balance, Symons decided against the admissibility of *vers libre*:

> 'Le vers libre' in the hands of most of the experimenters becomes merely rhymeless irregular prose; in the hands of Gustave Kahn and Edouard Dujardin it has, it must be admitted, attained a certain beauty of its own .... 
> But M. Dujardin is a poet: 'vers libres' in the hands of a sciolist are the most intolerably easy and annoying of poetical exercises.[7]

*Vers libre* in French cannot be too exactly identified with free verse in the English sense. The differences of tone and rhythm between the two languages preclude exact correspondence. As Storer suggested, it is doubtful whether *vers libre* (the term, incidentally, occurs already in the sixteenth century)[8] does much more than introduce into French liberties that were never long absent from English verse. Since Chaucer most poetic forms in English have been acclimatizations of Continental models. Free verse was to be no exception. Both Hulme and Storer put primary reliance on French exemplars. They were to be followed by Flint.

The pronouncements of the Imagistes of Pound's circle and of the later Imagists differ from these early statements in two important respects. They lay much less emphasis on France as a source of practice, and their attitude to free verse is more cautious and tentative than that of Hulme or Storer. When the Imagistes were first named in *Poetry* Pound, or Harriet Monroe on his behalf, described them as:

> a group of ardent Hellenists who are pursuing interesting experiments in *vers libre*; trying to attain in English certain subtleties of cadence of the kind which Mallarmé and his followers have studied in France.[9]

There was an element of inflation in this announcement. The only good Greek scholar among them was Aldington. The use of Greek choric models for free verse involved the Imagistes in a peculiar act of transference. For Greek lyric poetry, whether choric or monodic, had an obligatory musical accompaniment.[10]

If the Imagiste attitude to free verse was tentative in theory, their practice was not. They virtually abandoned traditional forms. In this

150

they were followed by the later adherents to the movement. Any general statement about free verse must be qualified. Within its boundaries there can exist a vast range of forms and rhythms. Rhyme is by no means excluded. Hulme used it sometimes and with effect as in 'The Embankment':

> Once, in finesse of fiddles found I ecstasy,
> In the flash of gold heels on the hard pavement.
> Now see I
> That warmth's the very stuff of poesy.
> Oh, God, make small
> The old star-eaten blanket of the sky,
> That I may fold it round me and in comfort lie.[11]

But from 1912 onward rhyme largely disappeared from Imagist works, except for its intermittent use in the polyphonic prose indulged in by Amy Lowell and John Gould Fletcher.

Within the usual Imagist pattern of unrhymed free verse the strophe and the organization of the line within the strophe show many variations. Much of their work fulfilled or anticipated T. S. Eliot's requirement that

> the ghost of some simple metre should lurk behind the arras in even the 'freest' verse; ... freedom is only truly freedom when it appears against the background of an artificial limitation.[12]

Eliot's emphasis on the need to maintain a rhythmic structure within the poem was made at a time when Imagist free verse seemed already to be disintegrating. Earlier, Hulme had recognized the difficulty inherent in the adoption of free forms:

> It is a delicate and difficult art, that of evoking an image, of fitting the rhythm to the idea, and one is tempted to fall back to the comforting and easy arms of the old, regular metre, which takes away all the troubles for us.[13]

Free verse, to succeed, requires the accomplishment of that 'difficult' art. Storer, though he foresaw the emergence of new rhythms, did not wholly understand this; Aldington was unable fully to achieve it. Yet it remains that the struggle to break the pentameter was the starting-point of the Imagist attack on the inherited auditory patterns of verse in English. As Pound said: 'to break the pentameter, that was the first heave.'[14]

Free verse can also divagate into very long or very short lines. Of the lines with the long flow preferred by Whitman there are few examples in

Imagist work. Such lines were being handled among their contemporaries by Apollinaire and Claudel in France and, with different emphases of technique, by Carl Sandburg in America. A few instances of the long Whitmanesque line can be found in poems by Joseph Campbell, written around the time of the Tour d'Eiffel meetings:

### A Thousand Feet Up

Westwards, a clump of firtrees silhouetted against
    a bank of blue cumulus cloud;
. . . .

The mountain trail, white and clear where human feet
have worn it, zigzagging higher and higher till it loses
itself in the southern skyline.

There are frequent examples in D. H. Lawrence's later work:

### The Song of a Man who has Come Through

If only, most lovely of all, I yield myself and am borrowed
By the fine, fine wind that takes its course through the
    chaos of the world
Like a fine, an exquisite chisel, a wedge-blade inserted;
. . . .

But these have hardly more than a collateral relationship to Imagism. More characteristic are the short lines favoured by H.D. in much of her earlier work. Such lines had been written by Edward Storer as early as 1907. Here is the end of Storer's poem 'The Poplar':

Slim, straight, mysterious length
Of hissings and of broken whispers,
You are beautiful I know,
And strong and straight,
And by the river's edge you stand:
But more I do not know!

A passage by no means inferior to some of H.D.'s much-praised early work—'Storm', for example:

I

You crash over the trees,
you crack the live branch;

the branch is white,
the green crushed,
each leaf is rent like split wood.

## II

You burden the trees
with black drops,
you swirl and crash:
you have broken off a weighted leaf
in the wind—
it is hurled out,
whirls up and sinks,
a green stone.

H.D.'s economy anticipates the precision if not the spareness achieved a few years later by her friend William Carlos Williams in such poems as 'Iris', 'Metric Figure', and 'The Red Wheelbarrow'. Pound, with greater technical versatility than any of his colleagues, showed himself a master of both short and long lines. This ability reaches a peak of measured complexity in *Cathay*, where both are cunningly interwoven:

*The River Merchant's Wife : A Letter*

At sixteen you departed,
You went into far Ku-to-yen, by the river of swirling eddies,
And you have been gone five months.
The monkeys make sorrowful noise overhead.
You dragged your feet when you went out.
By the gate now, the moss is grown, the different mosses,
Too deep to clear them away!
The leaves fall early this autumn, in wind.
The paired butterflies are already yellow with August
Over the grass in the West garden;
They hurt me. I grow older.

The final concentration of Pound's short line was attained when he returned briefly to rhyme and stanza in the quatrains of *Mauberley*, and in so doing achieved some of his finest work, for example these stanzas from 'Yeux Glauques' with their final throw-away line *à la* Hueffer:

Thin like brook-water,
With a vacant gaze.
The English Rubaiyat was still-born
In those days.

The thin, clear gaze, the same
Still darts out faun-like from the half-ruin'd face,
Questing and passive .....
'Ah, poor Jenny's case' .....

These loosened quatrains would be classified as *vers libre* in French; it is doubtful whether they can be called free verse in English.

An Imagist poem may consist of one brief strophic movement (when it can be reduced to an epigram or a random perception), or it may of course be longer. A free-verse poem which exceeds half a dozen lines will develop its own strophic patterns, though with far greater flexibility than in more formalized verse. A couplet may be a poem, a line a stanza. There are various examples of the couplet-poem in Pound's work. 'Fan-Piece, For Her Imperial Lord', 'Ts'ai Chi'h', 'In a Station of the Metro' and 'Alba' all belong to his Imagiste period, yet in their handling of the couplet they can be sharply differentiated. 'The Return', a poem of slightly earlier date, concludes with a single line which acts as its last stanza:

Slow on the leash,
pallid the leash-men!

If the poem is short enough to be limited to the presentation of a single theme it may end with what Pound called a super-position, a term he probably got from Rémy de Gourmont.[15]

The separation of free verse from prose was a problem that troubled some of the early Imagists. Hueffer claimed that there was no effective difference between them. Objectively, distinctions are hard to find, especially when formal metre and rhyme have been dispensed with. Hulme recognized that the core of the problem was rhythm and saw the poet as someone who could 'trust himself to the obscure world from which rhythm springs.'[16] Here, more nearly than in the assertions of the 'Lecture', he reaches the hidden roots of poetry. Pound, throughout, retained his intense, even finicky, concentration on poetic rhythm. Some of the other Imagist writers were less subtle. Hueffer's prose, especially his later prose, is capable of far stronger poetic effects than his sometimes humdrum verse. The attempt to marry prose and verse in the form of the prose poem seemed often to result in the worst of both worlds. Aldington and Edward Storer experimented with prose poems but had little success. The 'polyphonic prose' favoured by Amy Lowell and John Gould Fletcher is better forgotten. Few writers have attempted the prose poem in English. Fewer still have put into it anything of their talent. In the eighteen-nineties, Ernest Dowson's *Decorations* included several prose poems, but these are among his more feeble productions. (More effective were George Moore's translations of those prose poems by Mallarmé in his *Confessions of a Young Man* in 1888.)[17] It has been left for some recent American writers to bring the prose poem at last to life in English.

## The Language of Poetry

When T. E. Hulme's 'Complete Poetical Works' were reviewed in *The Quest*, they were described as 'scraps'. Within five years T. S. Eliot would quote 'The Embankment' and praise, even over-praise, its beauty.[18] The reduction of the tolerated minimum of poetic dimension is characteristic of our time. Imagist method put increased emphasis on metaphor, even at the expense of other elements in the poem.

Increased reliance on metaphor went hand in glove with a more stripped and functional syntax. Hulme's earlier statements on the language of poetry show his awareness of language as metaphor. He was the only one among the writers of the Tour d'Eiffel group to concern himself with language and with the properties of words. He attempted to distinguish words in prose from the language of poetry. In so doing he reached a functional answer, not very different from that of the nineteenth-century Positivists:

... there are, roughly speaking, two methods of communication, a direct, and a conventional language. The direct language is poetry, it is direct because it deals in images. The indirect language is prose, because it uses images that have died and become figures of speech.[19]

He developed this theme:

In prose as in algebra concrete things are embodied in signs or counters, which are moved about according to rules, without being visualised at all in the process. There are in prose certain type situations and arrangements of words, which move as automatically into certain other arrangements as do functions in algebra .... Poetry, in one aspect at any rate, may be considered as an effort to avoid this characteristic of prose. It is not a counter language but a visual concrete one. It is a compromise for a language of intuition which would hand over sensations bodily. It always endeavours to arrest you and to make you continuously see a physical thing, to prevent you gliding through an abstract process. It chooses fresh epithets and fresh metaphors not so much because they are new and we are tired of the old, but because the old cease to convey a physical thing and become abstract counters.[20]

155

In France the positivist theory of language was adopted to his own uses by Rémy de Gourmont, through whom it had a considerable influence on Hulme and Flint, and later on Pound and Aldington. As Hulme saw it, poetry had to renew language. The essence of this renewal was to be metaphor or analogy. Hulme took the argument for analogy from Bergson, whose study *Les Données Immédiates de la Conscience* had had a profound effect on him when he first read it. In advocating analogy Hulme effected a link between artistic method and late nineteenth-century notions of the scientific method. Bergson's contemporary, the great sociologist Émile Durkheim, had recommended comparison as an operating principle, on the ground of human inability to grasp fact by other means.[21] There is nothing new in the statement that language works by analogy. It is a reminder of the dependence of language on metaphor. The argument that metaphor is the heart of poetry goes back to Aristotle, if not earlier.

From 1912 onward Pound continued the argument, though on somewhat different lines from those of Hulme. Pound's criticism aimed towards a poetry in which the trope or image finds expression through appropriate rhythms without preconceived limitations of form. This is the reality behind the metaphors of his diagnostic statements, embodied in such remarks as poetry getting 'nearer the bone', with fewer 'painted' adjectives, 'austere, direct, free from emotional slither.'[22] In 'A Few Don'ts by an Imagiste' Pound gave some practical hints about the language of poetry:

Use no superfluous word, no adjective, which does not reveal something.

Don't use such an expression as 'dim lands *of peace*.' It dulls the image. It mixes an abstraction with the concrete. It comes from the writer's not realizing that the natural object is always the *adequate* symbol.

Go in fear of abstractions.[23]

The question of metaphor leads inevitably to the problem of diction. With all the Imagist writers the notion of a type of poem seems to have preceded any theory of diction. This was certainly so with Hulme. Storer's 'Essay' says nothing about diction. Flint's principal concern was with poetic rhythms. Aldington's main interest seems to have been the form of his poems. The language of H.D.'s poems is her own discovery: to link it with other people's theories or with the practice of other writers would be by no means easy. Pound, even in his early work, had looked for rhythmic or metrical originality, at a time when his diction was frequently a muddle of archaisms and borrowings. But of all these writers, Pound after 1912 is the only one who attempted to evolve or apply a coherent theory of poetic language. Hulme and Flint had remained content to specify 'concreteness'.

A quarter-century after the Imagist period Flint said that it is 'first of all' language which attracts the reader to a poet:

> One of the chief functions of a poet is to create and recreate his native language, to invent new metaphors and turns of speech, to take dead words and put fresh life into them. But time is ungrateful to him, because his new speech becomes common speech . . . .[24]

Here, as in other respects, Pound went further. What he had to say about language was never modified. His theoretical dicta tended to be written as part of a series of discoveries emerging from his own practice or the development of his attitudes to that practice. The result is a set of complex formulations in which, perhaps following Hulme and Flint, he prescribes verbal concreteness, '*res* not *verba*',[25] a reified not a literary poetry. The use of concrete language solved only part of the problem. There was also the necessity of choice between literary and vernacular idiom. In the preface to *Some Imagist Poets 1915* the group that had ousted Pound stated a number of principles which they modestly claimed as 'the essentials of all great poetry . . . .' (This document seems to have been drafted largely by Aldington and Flint.) The first of their proposals was 'To use the language of common speech, but to employ always the *exact* word . . . .'[26] The fallacy is evident. 'Plain speech,' as Hulme had said, 'is essentially inaccurate.' Unfortunately their flawed logic obscured their true objective, the rejection of nineteenth-century poetic language which had treated Shakespeare and the Bible as current literary English. Pound showed a subtler cognizance of the problem than any of his colleagues. His awareness had been sharpened by his discussions with Ford Madox Hueffer. Hueffer's remedy for the staleness of poetic language was to blend the traditions of prose with the demotic of current speech. In his discussion of poetry he remarked:

> The actual language, the vernacular employed, is a secondary matter. I prefer personally the language of my own day, a language clear enough for certain matters, employing slang where slang is felicitous, and vulgarity where it seems to me that vulgarity is the only weapon against dullness.[27]

This is at some remove from Pound's view of a language for poetry, but Hueffer influenced Pound in other ways. From Hueffer came his increasing emphasis on prose as a source for verse. Hueffer's tastes may have encouraged Pound's recourse to Henry James and Conrad in many poems from 1913 onwards. It would be a mistake to regard this as a poetry of common speech. The later James and Conrad are mannered, even mannerist, writers and their characteristic idioms represent a balance between literary elements and brilliant personal deformations of the vernacular. The combined effect on Pound's work is seen in 'Liu Ch'e', a fine remodelling of one of Giles's Chinese translations:[28]

> The rustling of the silk is discontinued,
> Dust drifts over the court-yard,
> There is no sound of foot-fall, and the leaves
> Scurry into heaps and lie still,
> And she the rejoicer of the heart is beneath them:
>
> A wet leaf that clings to the threshold.

The opening line has more than a hint of the finicky exactitude of James's late style. 'The leaves / scurry into heaps and lie still' could almost be Hueffer's prose in action. The poem attains its cadence by an elaboration of syntax that is another legacy from James or Conrad. This appears to contradict the Imagist tendency to simplify syntax, but Pound was his own law. The consummation of simplicity was reached a little later by some of the writers more marginal to Imagism, for example William Carlos Williams.

This mandarin quality is a useful element in Pound's resources of style. One aspect of his achievement was his ability to write a high or low style with equal felicity. Hulme, in arguing for metaphor, engaged himself in linguistics. The more effective of Pound's formulations had usually a practical emphasis. Pound's practice is itself a commentary on the notion of vernacular idiom, favoured by Hueffer and by many critics since. This is a problem that every generation has to decide for itself. Wordsworth had said:

> It may safely be affirmed that there neither is, nor can be, any *essential* difference between the language of prose and metrical composition.

Most of the comments left by the Imagist writers suggest an inability to recognize one fundamental fact: the language of poetry is symbolic. According to Emerson, 'We are symbols, and inhabit symbols.' A principal exponent, and perhaps victim, of the anti-symbolist theory of language was Hulme. His baffled comments, written in 1914, may help to account for his sudden revulsion from poetry around 1910. He dismissed his own poems as mere descriptive writing:

158

The handicap of the intelligent man who is not a poet is that he cannot trust himself to this obscure world from which rhythm springs. All that he does must remain 'clear' to him as he does it . . . . All that he can do is to mention one by one the elements of the scene and the emotions it calls up. I am moved in a certain way by a dark street at night, say. When I attempt to express this mood, I make an inventory of all the elements which make up that mood.[29]

What is curious is Hulme's continuing insistence on the surface properties of language, his complete failure to recognize the symbolist qualities of poems like 'Mana Aboda' or 'Above the Dock'. This neglect or rejection of symbolism runs all through the Imagist formulations. Edward Storer had had a sounder-based view, though his prose is so muffled that his contemporaries may be forgiven their failure to notice what he was saying:

> . . . good poetry . . . seems to be made up of scattered lines, which are pictures, descriptions or suggestions of something at present incapable of accurate identification, yet nevertheless convincing enough to some one portion of the brain, to be accepted as true by all the rest. Mirages, as it were, for whose essential verity, outside the illusion and circumstances of ordinary, every-day life, we have only the insistent and unexplainable protest of some kind of sixth sense. In a word, symbolism, and symbols, but an unconscious non-arbitrary symbolism for which we have no key, not a crude arbitrary symbolism such as is suggested in Rimbaud's 'Sonnet of the Vowels,' but something infinitely more allusive and subtle than such a silly rebus game as that.[30]

The problem for the Imagist writers was that they leaned on and took largely from the French Symbolists, while at the same time they attempted to dissociate themselves from the cloudiness and vagueness into which the work of the lesser Symbolists had descended. In rejecting flummery they put themselves in danger of rejecting the mystery essential to poetry. The persisting confusion is epitomized in a statement by Ezra Pound:

> I believe that the proper and perfect symbol is the natural object, that if a man uses 'symbols' he must so use them that their symbolic function does not obtrude; so that a sense, and the poetic quality of the passage, is not lost to those who do not understand the symbol as such, to whom, for instance, a hawk is a hawk.[31]

Both Pound and Storer are in different ways and from different directions approaching the distinction set up by de Saussure between *la langue* and

159

*la parole*, between a public language and its current associations. With Pound, in particular, the approach was only partial. He remained trapped in his world of natural objects. His rejection of symbolism allowed him only the escape into abstractions that ruins large tracts of the *Cantos*.[32]

The later Imagists remained tied to the notion of precise description, even if there is little enough of that in their poetry:

> ... we believe that poetry should render particulars exactly and not deal in vague generalities, however magnificent and sonorous. It is for this reason that we oppose the cosmic poet .... [33]

In the later stages of the movement the Imagists got fogged by their own technique. The exact word is only worthwhile if it mirrors the full clarity of the image or metaphor. H.D.'s use of language was at times exact but nonsensical:

### Song

You are as gold
as the half-ripe grain
that merges to gold again,
as white as the white rain
that beats through
the half-opened flowers
of the great flower tufts
thick on the black limbs
of an Illyrian apple bough.

Can honey distill such fragrance
as your bright hair—
for your face is as fair as rain,
yet as rain that lies clear
on white honey-comb,
lends radiance to the white wax,
so your hair on your brow
casts light for a shadow.

This suggests her precise sense of discrimination; but where the core of the image is missing no amount of verbal nicety can create it.

Language is the essential tool of the poet. Brilliant camera work on its own cannot produce an outstanding film; unrelated verbal elegance does not create an effective poem.

'It is better to present one image in a lifetime than to produce voluminous works.'[34] With these words Pound introduced his Image to the public early in 1913. Nearly twenty years later Flint gave credit to Pound for inventing Imagism, but called him 'the most irritating devil in the world' and added:

> Like most inventors, Pound did not create out of the void. The 'image' he took from T. E. Hulme's table talk. The 'ism' was suggested to him by the notes on contemporary French poetry which I wrote for Harold Monro's *Poetry Review*. The collocation of 'image' with 'ism' came to Pound after I had told him about Fernand Divoire's essay on 'Stratégie Littéraire.' Pound devised a 'stratégie littéraire.'[35]

The image seems to have meant different things to different members of the Imagist movement. None of them were very clear in their definition of what they meant by it. Hulme and Pound had most to say, but it is probable that their notions varied considerably. Pound at first was deliberately mysterious:

> They held also a certain 'Doctrine of the Image,' which they had not committed to writing; they said that it did not concern the public, and would provoke useless discussion.[36]

Behind the image lies Plato's Idea, the classical *imago veritatis*. Horace's 'ut pictura poesis' was a Latin commonplace. The image, in its Platonic guise of idea, appears again in the *cinquecento*. As Raphael wrote to Castiglione while painting his Galatea:

> Io mi servo di certa idea che mi viene alla mente.

In the seventeenth century the image appears in the *Leviathan*, used by Hobbes with something close to its more recent connotations.[37] Hobbes believed that imagination, by means of which images were created, was the reflection of visible and only of visible objects.[38] After Hobbes 'imagining' was taken to mean 'seeing', a process by which the content of physical vision was supposed to be brought into verbal form. Dryden said that 'imagining' was 'the very height and life of poetry.' In his defence of Cowley's odes he praised the 'strength' of Cowley's images.[39] From this time on there was a shared epistemology between the image of the philosophers and the image of the writers, or critics, of literature. For Locke knowledge was attained by the reception of impressions 'in the mind'. In his influential *Essay concerning Human Understanding* he asserted the need to interpret 'seeing' literally. Locke allowed man no inner light. His theory of language had no place for metaphor or for symbols. He was corrected by Berkeley, who postulated a 'permanent' self as receptor of impressions and ideas. Berkeley's permanent self was destroyed by David Hume, whose argument is important not for its adequacy but for its role in the shift of emphasis to the primacy of the imagination. In *The Task* Cowper summed up the function of the poet:

> To arrest the fleeting images that fill
> The mirror of the mind, and hold them fast.[40]

In the eighteenth century the image extended from philosophy (more exactly, from the psychology of perception), through aesthetics, into the language of literary criticism. By the Romantic period its use in literary criticism was well-established. Since the seventeenth century there had been an increasing proportion of visual referents in the imagery of English poetry. In the sixteenth century poetry had shown a relatively higher proportion of tactile images. Among recent English poets perhaps the only one to show a predominance of tactile imagery is that oddly timeless figure Robert Graves.

The use of the term 'image' is common in the criticism and theorizing of Wordsworth and Coleridge. From them it was taken up by the second Romantic generation, and then by the Victorians. The capacity to present images was regarded as a cardinal test of poetic ability by the critics of the Romantic period. A terminology of the image was developed, which in time came to be applied to prose as well.[41] In the Victorian period its connotations were broadened. The reason for this seems to lie in the relationship established between philosophy and literary criticism, and the obedience with which literary critics took their notions of perception from the theories of philosophers. Most of the critics of the Romantic epoch had remained tied to the rather limited account of perception offered by the eighteenth-century empiricists. Coleridge and (to an extent) Wordsworth went beyond this. Each had seen the possibility of a unified picture, of a poetry which would do more than present visual images. Above all, the influence of Kant helped to broaden the concept of the image and to freight it with symbolic possibilities. The *misterioso* implications of the high-Victorian notion can be seen in a comment on Tennyson in William Morris's *Oxford and Cambridge Magazine*:

No fitter poem than The Lady of Shalott can be taken for illustrating a faculty very desirable, if not absolutely requisite in poetry—painting in words. There is a mysterious sympathy between the different

162

branches of Art, which binds them all into one closely connected whole.[42]

The following quotation comes from an essay by a distinguished though little-known Victorian critic, George Brimley. Brimley praised Tennyson's 'great power of painting scenery', and noted in his early poems:

> the germ of a principle of landscape painting which Mr. Tennyson has in his later poems brought to great perfection, and largely employed. The principle consists in a combination of landscape and figures in which the landscape is not merely background to the figures, or the figures animated objects in the landscape, but the two are dynamically related .... And thus we get a landscape which is at once ideal and real—a collection of actual images of external nature, grouped and coloured by a dominant idea ....[43]

Here, in all but name, is a symbolist theory of poetry. In a discussion of Sydney Dobell's *England in Time of War* in 1856 his earlier work *The Roman* was praised with this qualification:

> Under the name of a drama it was a long monologue .... The images were strung together like beads upon a thread.[44]

This implied definition of the image seems very close to that of Storer half-a-century later. The image, in the practice of which Storer, according to Flint, 'chiefly' led, was a trope in the traditional nineteenth-century sense. His poem 'Image' is itself confirmation of this:

> Forsaken lovers,
> Burning to a chaste white moon,
> Upon strange pyres of loneliness and drought.

Flint, to judge from his comment on this poem, shared the same notion of the image. Looking back to 1909, he wrote:

> Mr Storer was then in favour of a poetry which I described in reference to his book, as 'a form of expression like the Japanese, in which an image is the resonant heart of an exquisite moment.'[45]

Hulme's interpretation was different. He appears to have regarded the image as a percept rather than a trope. In the Victorian tradition Hulme assimilated image to metaphor. But he gave the primacy to the image, of which the metaphor was conceived as only the reflection in words.

Poetry ... is not a counter language, but a visual concrete one .... It chooses fresh epithets and fresh metaphors, not so much because they are new and we are tired of the old, but because the old cease to convey a physical thing and become abstract counters. Nowadays, when one says the hill is 'clothed' with trees, the word suggests no physical comparison. To get the original visual effect one would have to say 'ruffed,' or use some new metaphor .... Visual meanings can only be transferred by the new bowl of metaphor: prose is an old pot that lets them leak out.[46]

This is explicit enough, but the argument is reinforced in his 'Lecture':

Say that the poet is moved by a certain landscape, he selects that from certain images which, put into juxtaposition in separate lines, serve to suggest and to evoke the state he feels.

... I contend that this method of recording impressions by visual images in distinct lines does not require the old metric system.

... the new visual art ... depends for its effect not on a kind of half sleep produced, but on arresting the attention, so much so that the succession of visual images should exhaust one.[47]

This was the concept of poetry that Hulme abandoned in his recantation of 1914. It seems to be a clear statement of his theoretical position in the days of his involvement with the Tour d'Eiffel group. Perhaps this helps to explain the confusion in which the group appears to have broken up. The gulf between Hulme's position and that of Storer or Flint must have been considerable. If their discussions involved the use of identical words with disparate connotations it is hardly surprising that no intelligible results were attained. Hulme was a visual thinker. The tone of his prose writings and the illustrations he chooses equally confirm this. He had no feeling for music (though he admitted to a taste for military bands). Hulme's readings in French joined with his predilections in fortifying this notion of the image. The effect of poetic developments in France after Baudelaire was to encourage the evolution of a more concentrated lyricism. The image grew to be a more and more important part of the poem. In the end, indeed, it *became* the poem. In the course of these developments the connotations of the image began to change their emphasis. There was an increasing stress on its visual content. Two influences in particular were at work to bring this about. One was the doctrine of the school of psychologists prevailing in France in the late nineteenth and beginning twentieth century. The other was the influence of painting, with the

164

numerous links established in Paris between writers and painters from the Impressionist generation onward.

All these deposits of meaning lie beneath the image pre-empted by Hulme. His self-imposed task, like that of anyone who deals in philosophy, was the clearance of his own lines of communication. But his attitude to complex words was probably a simple or at least a simplifying one. He was also to some extent an ideologue. Pound's aims were different and more practical. For him the predominant commitment was to the poem itself. His was a twofold struggle. He wanted to come nearer to the essence of poetry and all the time he was working to become more efficient in the art of writing. Thus he progressed to Imagisme in 1912, and from Imagisme to the discovery of the image itself in the years that followed. During these years Pound's interpretation of the image underwent several changes. When he abandoned mystification he attempted to define the image in terms very different from those of Hulme:

An 'Image' is that which presents an intellectual and emotional complex in an instant of time. I use the term 'complex' rather in the technical sense employed by the newer psychologists, such as Hart, though we might not agree absolutely in our application.[48]

Here Pound refers to the psychologist Bernard Hart. How far he understood Hart is questionable. In dynamic psychology the complex is a metaphor which serves to represent a cluster of energy in the individual unconscious. Pound seems to be suggesting that such a complex can be actualized by means of the image. If this, indeed, was his position in 1913 it is a long way from Hulme's doctrine of the recording of visual images. Pound's image must be regarded as the standard image of the Romantics, a magical kernel of poetic knowledge communicated in an instantaneity in which phrase and insight join. On this view the image is neither a trope, as it had been for the Victorians, nor a percept, as it was reduced to by Hulme, though its translation into verbal expression would no doubt involve the use of percepts. The image of 1913 seems to be something germinated by the unconscious of the poet, and emerging at last as a phrase of particular insight or illumination. When Pound entered his Vorticist phase his definition underwent further alteration. In 1914 he wrote:

The image is not an idea. It is a radiant node or cluster; it is what I can, and must perforce, call a *Vortex*, from which and through which, and into which, ideas are constantly rushing.[49]

His expansion of this statement a few months later is hardly a clarification:

... the Image is more than an idea. It is a vortex or cluster of fused ideas and is endowed with energy. If it does not fulfil these specifications, it is not what I mean by an Image. [50]

At this point it is difficult to know whether Pound is talking about the image or about the complex from which the image supposedly originated. His added qualification is far from illuminating:

These are bad expressions if they lead you to think of the artist as wholly passive, as a mere receiver of impressions. The good artist is perhaps a good seismograph, but the difference between the man and the machine is that man can in some degree 'start his machinery going.' He can, within limits, not only record but create. [51]

Or, as he wrote in his essay on Vorticism:

The image is itself the speech ... the word beyond formulated language. [52]

But there was also another connotation of the Image. This brought him much nearer to Hulme's interpretation. In the same essay Pound gave this other view:

There is a sort of poetry where music, sheer melody, seems as if it were just bursting into speech.

There is another sort of poetry where painting or sculpture seems as if it were 'just coming over into speech.'

The first sort of poetry has long been called 'lyric' ....

The other sort of poetry is as old as the lyric and as honourable, but, until recently no one had named it. Ibycus and Liu Ch'e presented the 'Image.' [53]

This visual interpretation of the Image seems to have been a secondary part of Pound's intentions. It was not a specific part of his Imagiste formulations before 1914. In that year he analysed it into a separate poetic kind. By 1918 it had become phanopoeia, one of the three categories of poetic means now distinguished by Pound. (The others were melopoeia and logopoeia. Imagism was now known as phanopoeia. He restored its earlier name a number of years later.) [54] On balance it seems that Pound in 1914 was closer to incorporating an aspect of Hulme's theory than he

166

had apparently been in 1912. After the first formulations of the Vortex he divagated again. In the end, Imagism or phanopoeia became merely one of the means of poetry, 'the power to cast images upon the reader's imaginaton.' And Pound, like Hulme, was quick enough to recognize the limits of the visual as arbiter of poetic value. He indicated this in 1923:

> I think Hueffer goes wrong because he bases his criticism on the eye, and almost solely on the eye. Nearly everything he says applies to things *seen*. It is the exact rendering of the visible image, the cabbage field *seen*, France *seen* from the cliffs.[55]

In this welter of statements and definitions it may be that Pound intended to differentiate the image from Imagism. 'From the Image to Imagisme,' he wrote in one of his essays.[56] If so, it is a pity he was not more explicit. As it stands, we seem to be left with two theories of the image, one perceptual (embodying the argument for the visual), the other cognitive. In all the statements made by the Imagists these very different significations seem never to have been clearly separated. Even Hulme expanded the ambit of his image beyond its primary visual associations, though without giving any indication that he knew he was doing so.[57]

The attempt to do without a theory of symbolism contributed largely to this muddle. Recognition of the symbol had been commonplace in the eighteenth century, where it existed side by side with the theory that meaning is derived from images.[58] The merely pictorial or visual function of the image, which had been stressed by the Parnassians (and which Hulme was again to emphasize), was rejected by the *Symbolistes*. Their aim was to utilize images to express a lyrical intuition:

> ... les symbolistes, réfusant de se contenter de l'image plastique, avaient voulu qu'elle fût seulement une sorte d'évocation préparatoire, une sorte de rideau bordé et transparent, s'évanouissant peu à peu devant les transcendances auxquelles il nous permettait d'accéder.[59]

Out of *Symboliste* aesthetics, crossed with the metaphysics of Bergson, came the poetic theory summarized by T. E. Hulme as

> an attempt by means of successive and accumulated images to express and exteriorise such a central lyric intuition.[60]

Pound complained of Hulme diluting his evenings with 'crap like Bergson.' But Pound's image, in its primary sense, seems very near to Bergson's notion that states of mind have a corresponding actualization through images. As a dogmatic statement in the psychology of perception

167

that is probably incorrect, but it is the one common denominator for the image of the Imagist writers.[61] It seems feasible that Pound took the notion of the image from Hulme, but tried to work out the concepts implied in it in his own terms and to his own satisfaction. The lack of clarity in these attempts at formulation is reflected in Flint's sardonic comment of a quarter-century later:

> ... we had a doctrine of the image, which none of us knew anything about. To this day I don't know what the doctrine of the image was, although I was an Imagist.[62]

The importance of the image was that it acted as an incentive to concreteness and physicality of language. 'Die Wahrheit ist konkret' was Brecht's way of putting it. The notion of the concrete leads to a poetry of things. A poetry of things links with a poetry of prose virtues. Pound praised Hueffer in these terms in his review of the *Collected Poems*:

> I find him significant and revolutionary because of his insistence upon clarity and precision, upon the prose tradition; in brief, upon efficient writing—even in verse.[63]

The concept of the image, though philosophically insufficient, was capable of useful practical effects.

Pound's image ended as Hulme's had begun, as a picture-making faculty. The other Imagists had nothing to add. Pound's notion was most effective when closest to traditional Romantic definitions; Hulme's poems are more impressive than his theories.

Pound's conception of the image in visual terms was immensely encouraged by his mythical view of China, in particular the Chinese ideogram and its relation to the Chinese language. His involvement with the ideogram came too late to have any particular effect on the other Imagist writers. But it was not too late to crystallize the aesthetic that developed out of Pound's Imagist and Vorticist years. His notion of the function of the ideogram was almost totally incorrect. The study of even half a dozen Chinese characters will confirm that their original pictorial qualities have long ago been formalized as brushstrokes.[64] Even Classical Egyptian, which is ideographic in a far more exact sense than Chinese, offers little encouragement to Pound's theories.[65] When ideograms are in common use the original pictorial effect is quickly eroded. In Egyptian, the original hieroglyphic writing was in continuous modification into a more cursive hieratic script. This in turn modified into the still more rapid form of hieratic known as demotic.[66] The fallacy of Pound's reasoning was that it separated the pictorial and the auditory functions of language, thus ignoring the fact that if language exists to describe things, it is also and in essence a system that depends on auditory relations. Even in Egyptian the ideogram 'represents words rather than objects or notions connected therewith.'[67] There is no correlated Word/ Picture system in Egyptian; and the possibilities for inferring such a system from Chinese are still more limited.

However wrongheaded it was, the adoption of this theory of the ideogram no doubt stimulated Pound's imagination. The result of its incorporation was to bring the concept of the image, already over-burdened, into further confusion. Pound's phanopoeia ends in advocacy of a language of inbuilt visual images. Ultimately this would reduce the poet's function to a sophisticated form of constructional activity. Pound had hoped by using the ideogram to unify language and picture. He ended by scattering ideograms across the *Cantos* like unrelated pieces of a jigsaw puzzle.

Though the account offered by the Imagists was incoherent, the image remains an important point of focus. Long before, Ibsen had said, 'To be a poet is most of all to see.' He wrote impromptu and about the theatre, but his remark has a wider relevance. However clumsy its terms, the Vorticist mobile image with its 'radiant node or cluster' restored the creative principle of human imagination.

## Ideologies

Entangled in a web of literary ideologies, the Imagists indulged in a series of intellectual buzzings at the mercy of the philosophy spider. They struggled for identity by distinguishing themselves from Impressionists and Symbolists; Pound alighted on a new doctrine among the Vorticists; some critics have even tried to push Imagism into the conceptual trap of Hulme's neo-classicism.

### IMPRESSIONISM

What has found expression in painting as Impressionism will soon find expression in poetry as free verse[68]

wrote T. E. Hulme in his 'Lecture'. Edward Storer, whose *Mirrors of Illusion* were praised at the time for their 'brilliant impressionism',[69] offers in his 'Essay' justification for an Impressionist view of poetry. Both in painting and writing Impressionism evoked very different atmospheres from those sought by the Imagists. Imagist poems aimed to flash images directly onto the mind, to produce what was essentially a surprise effect. Vision or contact are never direct in Impressionist work, which presents broken or analytical images through a filter used as a distancing device. Lionel Johnson had diagnosed Arthur Symons as:

169

... a slave to impressionism, whether the impression be precious or no. A London fog, the blurred, tawny lamplight, the red omnibus, the dreary rain, the depressing mud, the glaring gin-shop, the slatternly shivering women.[70]

The rain falls in Impressionist paintings as it does in the poems of Verlaine.

By the nineties Impressionist jargon was in free use among literary critics. Arthur Symons resorted to it frequently. Ford Madox Hueffer, who had grown up in the nineties, always regarded himself as an Impressionist. In his memoir of Joseph Conrad he wrote:

... we saw that Life did not narrate but made impressions on our brain. We, in turn, if we wished to produce on you an effect of life, must not narrate but render ... impressions.[71]

During the Imagiste years he had been even more explicit:

I would give almost anything to have written almost any modern German lyric, or some of the ballads of my friend Levin Schücking. . . . These fellows, you know ... they sit at their high windows in German lodgings; they lean out; it is raining steadily. Opposite them is a shop where herring salad, onions and oranges are sold. A woman with a red petticoat and a black and grey check shawl goes into the shop and buys three onions, four oranges and half a kilo of herring salad . . . . And there is a poem![72]

An attractive formula, though in fact Hueffer was much closer to Impressionism in his prose than in his poems.

The Imagists got into a complicated situation in relation to Impressionism. Their efforts at differentiation led to statements like this by Pound:

Impressionism belongs in paint, it is of the eye . . . . Poetry is in some odd way concerned with the specific gravity of things, with their nature. . . .
The *conception* of poetry is a process more intense than the *reception* of an impression. And no impression, however carefully articulated, can, recorded, convey that feeling of sudden light which the work of art should and must convey.[73]

Pound saw his movement as a reaction against the supposed vagueness of the Impressionists:

170

Also chance for crit of FMH—Impressionism—probably closest accord with your own attitude—really in opposition to my constant hammering on vortex, concentration, condensation, hardness. [74]

Flint, to whom he wrote that, was regarded as an Imagist by Hueffer, an Impressionist by Pound and both Imagist and Impressionist by Aldington:

> I think many people prefer Mr. Flint because he is an Impressionist. I don't say that he isn't an Imagist. He is, and the whole theory and practice of Imagism owe a great deal to him. [75]

Often, as his work developed, Flint seemed to grow closer to Impressionist methods than to any definition of Imagism. This is evident in poems like 'Cones' or 'Terror':

### Terror

Eyes are tired;
the lamp burns,
and in its circle of light
papers and books lie
where chance and life
have placed them.

Silence sings all around me;
my head is bound with a band;
outside in the street a few footsteps;
a clock strikes the hour.

I gaze, and my eyes close,
slowly:

I doze; but the moment before sleep,
a voice calls my name
in my ear,
and the shock jolts my heart:
but when I open my eyes,
and look, first left, and then right ...

no one is there.

A finer example of what Impressionism could mean in poetry is Harold Monro's 'Overheard on a Saltmarsh' (*Georgian Poetry 1913–1915*, p. 181):

Nymph, nymph, what are your beads?
Green glass, goblin. Why do you stare at them?
Give them me.

No.

Give them me. Give them me.

No.

Then I will howl all night in the reeds,
Lie in the mud and howl for them.

Goblin, why do you love them so?

They are better than stars or water,
Better than voices of wind that sing,
Better than any man's fair daughter,
Your green glass beads on a silver ring.

Hush, I stole them out of the moon.

Give me your beads, I want them.

No.

I will howl in a deep lagoon
For your green glass beads, I love them so.
Give them me. Give them.

No.

Monro was not by conscious intent an Impressionist, but this poem (one of his best) offers strong contrast to the typical short pieces of the Imagist canon, 'Oread' or 'In a Station of the Metro':

The apparition of these faces in the crowd;
Petals on a wet, black bough.

In Monro's poem the core experience is reached through a filter. 'Overheard on a Saltmarsh' is pervaded by a sense of abstract mystery. The paradox is that this apparent randomness is less vague than the Imagist clarity and compression.

172

It is always easier to judge in retrospect. In their time none of the Imagist writers saw the essential differences between the two doctrines. They argued in a circle of confusion and ended in a void.

*　*　*

## Symbolism

The boundaries set up between Imagism and Symbolism are all too like those European frontiers which can never be settled because they have never been agreed. The Imagists were trying to separate themselves not so much from symbolism as from the legacy of the *Symbolistes* in France. Much nonsense has been written about the *Symbolistes* (and a good deal was uttered by them). The important French poets often called Symbolist in England did not belong to the *Symboliste* groups; they preceded them. Baudelaire, Verlaine, Mallarmé, Rimbaud, Laforgue and Corbière—all of them except Mallarmé had done their best work before the first promulgation of *Symbolisme* by Jean Moréas in 1886. (Baudelaire and Corbière were long dead, Laforgue was mortally ill, Rimbaud in self-imposed exile with barely five years to live.)

The attitude of the Imagists to Symbolism as a doctrine and to the *Symbolistes* as a group was founded on negation. They regarded themselves as expressing values antithetical to those of Symbolism. Their hunt for differentiation was self-defeating. The first stages of *Symbolisme* were bound up with the struggle for *vers libre*, and Imagist theory took much of its justification for free verse from France. Though the Imagists' assertions were altogether too strident, they were trying to stress one essential difference. They condemned the vagueness and cloudiness of much *Symboliste* work. It is possible to attribute these qualities to *Symboliste* doctrines. It is more to the point to relate them to the frequent mediocrity of the *Symbolistes* as poets. The *Symbolistes* had rejected a literature of ideas, with all the stringent conceptual limitations that this implied in the rational Cartesian tradition of French literary theory. They committed themselves to notions of indefiniteness and musicality and aimed at an art of suggestion. They represent a renewal of Romantic artistic aims, and they often looked to English poets for the qualities they sought and admired. The extent to which they took their doctrines from Poe's half-formed theories (themselves heavily dependent on Coleridge) is well known. There is also a direct link between the English Romantics and the *Symbolistes*, via Tennyson and the Pre-Raphaelites.[76] In England the Romantic lesson had been only too thoroughly learned. Much Victorian poetry had suffered from the conscious striving for musicality, with a concomitant blurring of the outlines of experience. The aspect of Symbolist doctrine that paralleled this was rejected by the Imagists. In its place they opted for a heightened precision of statement and reference.

173

The American critic Edmund Wilson has epitomized Symbolism as follows:

> All symbols are metaphors that stand for things; and what symbolism did was merely to cut the metaphors loose from their moorings.[77]

The Imagists tried to tie their metaphors up again. This attempt to identify word with object gave a powerful stimulus to the notion of a poetry of things. It also involved a denial of the basis of symbolism on which any poetic idiom must depend. This no doubt helps to explain the flatness, even prosiness, of much Imagist work. It also accounts for much of its restraint. The Imagist formula had a restrictive effect. By relying on the photographic properties of the perceptual image they were farther from an accurate account of perception than the Symbolists had been:

> Lately ... the perceptual image ... has been broken up by scientific investigation so that the original naive experience of it as a direct photographic image of the object no longer holds.

> It has been discovered that the stimulated neurones in the brain form patterns on the cortex unlike the shape of the object under observation. This is almost all that the body is known to contribute to the apparently true conscious image of the external object.

> This image is called symbolic by neurophysiologists because it represents the external object closely enough for its existence to be established by inference.[78]

Of all the Imagists Ezra Pound was particularly vehement in attacking Symbolism. The pragmatic dogmatism of his thinking was responsible for much of the coolness the Imagists of 1912 and after showed to *Symboliste* theory. Even Flint recanted his enthusiasm of 1912: two years later he wrote disparagingly of the 'dreamy emptiness' of Symbolism.[79] The Imagists' failure to see the full possibilities in Symbolism severely limited their own work and deprived them of an opportunity to align English poetry with the richness of the European writers who came after the Symbolists. Only Yeats continued, relying on translation and on his memories of Arthur Symons's teachings in the nineties, to bring his own work to a new splendour and exactitude of symbolist expression and, in so doing, to remind us of the possibility the Imagists threw away.

### Neo-Classicism

By 1912 T. E. Hulme was experimenting with a fresh theory. This was to be a revived Classicism, a notion that has been seized and utilized

174

since his death by various of his admirers. T. S. Eliot's assertion of classicist sympathies is well-known and it is unlikely that he would have been so definite without the example of Hulme's paper 'Romanticism and Classicism'.[80]

Hulme's argument for classicism is predictive. It begins:

I want to maintain that after a hundred years of romanticism, we are in for a classical revival, and that the particular weapon of this new classical spirit, when it works in verse, will be fancy.

and he continues,

I think that there is an increasing proportion of people who simply can't stand Swinburne . . . . I prophesy that a period of dry, hard, classical verse is coming.[81]

Hulme acknowledged that his position derived from 'Maurras, Lasserre and all the group connected with *L'Action Française*'.[82] In the later eighteen-nineties Charles Maurras had developed a theory with political implications. He claimed to be an empiricist, called himself classical and announced that romanticism was non-French. With classicism went monarchism. Maurras reached a doctrine of what he called integral nationalism which he evolved from an *a priori* system of cultural values. He attacked 'unFrench' elements in French culture in a manner that points to Nazi *Blut und Boden*.

Hulme's definition of classicism is clear enough. It underlines his rejection of Romantic voyages into the unreal:

What I mean by classical in verse, then, is this. That even in the most imaginative flights there is always a holding back, a reservation. The classical poet never forgets this finiteness, this limit of man. He remembers always that he is mixed up with earth. He may jump, but he always returns back; he never flies away into the circumambient gas.[83]

The arguments with which he supports this are vague or self-justifying; the examples he gives are few and unconvincing. As Classical writers he mentions Racine and Shakespeare: as Romantics, Hugo and Swinburne. He also drags in Pope and Horace.

Hulme's reasoning here is hard to disentangle. He was correct, even belated, in announcing the end of the Romantic movement, but the new art he welcomed was, whether in painting or poetry, a further development within the romantic tradition. What he says is more intelligible

G

if understood as an attack on the *fin de siècle* slops of romanticism. But with characteristic pugnacity he went beyond the limits of his brief and denounced romanticism at large. The arguments and the authorities he depends on are largely self-contradictory. Maurras's doctrines were essentially national and *völkisch* in their origins. The European and comparatist bases essential to the classical were almost totally lacking. There are other weaknesses in Hulme's argument. He tries to locate classical sanity in the dogma of original sin. He seems, not unusually for him, to have been writing against the clock, so that his examples are sometimes muddled or perfunctory. Yet it is hard not to feel that his paper has been judged too ponderously. Hulme's arguments are forcefully directed against lacrymose romantic dregs. They have usually been evaluated as a positive plea for a kind of neo-classicism that could never have existed. The case for fancy is typical of Hulme's position:

> ... I can get on to the end of my paper in this way: That where you get this quality exhibited in the realm of the emotions you get imagination, and that where you get this quality exhibited in the contemplation of finite things you get fancy.[84]

Hulme is using the term 'fancy' (in its dichotomy with imagination one of the less fortunate legacies of the great intelligence of Coleridge) in a peculiar and personal connotation. What he says, though, makes sense. The important point is not Hulme's vagaries of terminology but the message he is trying to convey. His 'finite things' reappear in different dress in a comment by Pound:

> a work of art is the honest reproduction of a concrete image. Imagination is the faculty which finds out all about this image ....[85]

Pound's imagination has exactly the same function as Hulme's fancy. In literature the Romantic movement had grown out of the exhaustion as well as the limitations of eighteenth-century classicism. The exhaustion, in turn, of romanticism could not be the signal for a return to the old-style classicism of Pope or Dryden. As Hulme recognized: 'Although it will be classical it will be different because it has passed through a romantic period.'[86] An eclectic revivalism can be incorporated into the technique of an artist. An ideology founded on revivalism is almost certain to be sterile. Hulme's classicism is thoroughly romantic in its intellectual vagueness, its restlessness, and the longing for what is not. The subsequent use of neo-classicism for other and different purposes is not among the direct effects of the Imagist development. Its share in the ethos of the Imagist movement must be regarded as negligible.

176

'Romanticism and Classicism' has been unfortunate in its history. Drafted probably in 1912 it remained unpublished until 1924. It has been treated as an essay and accorded the solemn respect of literary analysis. It was more likely a lecture, written extempore and intended to provoke, interest, and shock an audience. The lessons derived from it by T. S. Eliot and others can be largely discarded. Hulme's neo-classicism was at best a brilliant speculative youthful play of ideas.

## Vorticism

The origins of Vorticism are by no means as uncertain as those of Imagism. The movement was the creation of Wyndham Lewis, who organized and edited its review *Blast*. Its name was suggested by Ezra Pound. ('Invented the term Vorticism,' wrote Pound laconically in 1930.)[87] It was Pound who worked most strenuously to provide it with adequate theoretical foundations. But Wyndham Lewis's retrospective claim seems justified:

> Vorticism, in fact, was what I, personally, did, and said, at a certain period. This may be expanded into a certain theory regarding visual art: and (much less theoretically) a view of what was excellent in literary art. *The Enemy of the Stars* and the first version of the novel *Tarr* exemplified the latter of these two intellectual novelties .... [88]

At first Wyndham Lewis used Vorticism as a theoretical backing for his painting. *Blast* was 'intended to be' a periodical. As such, it

> was the verbal expression of a movement in visual art whose vivacious span, 1913 and 1914, was wedged in between the outbreak of war and its initial impulse in the autumn of 1912.[89]

The model for *Blast* appears to have been Apollinaire's manifesto 'L'Anti-tradition Futuriste' with its ferocious apothegms and bold explosions of typography.[90] And the problem of delimiting Vorticism from Futurism must have required some ingenuity. Futurism had been known in England since early in its development.[91] There was a large-scale exhibition of Italian Futurist painters at the Sackville Gallery in March 1912.[92] By the summer of 1914 there had been three or four Futurist showings in London.[93]

Though *Blast* had been in contemplation since the autumn of 1913, Wyndham Lewis had not managed to differentiate his own group from the Futurists. Indeed, in June 1914, only a week or two before *Blast* made its debut, Marinetti and his one English disciple of any consequence,

177

the talented painter C. R. W. Nevinson, had produced a Futurist manifesto called 'Vital English Art'. In this Wyndham Lewis, Epstein, Wadsworth and Bomberg are listed, together with other painters and sculptors later grouped as Vorticist, as 'the great Futurist painters or pioneers . . . .'[94] So far, poetry had not been brought into the campaign. Marinetti gave histrionic readings of his own verses in London in 1914; but Futurism in poetry had little impact on the phlegmatic English culture. The literary manifestations of Futurism had been given extensive and generous treatment in Harold Monro's review *Poetry and Drama* in September 1913, but this support was withdrawn, without explanation, in the following issue.[95] There is no evidence that it attracted any serious attention to Futurist poetry. The way was clear to introduce a movement in imitative dissent from Futurism. The painters were joined by Ezra Pound who, like them, suddenly discovered he was a Vorticist.

Though Vorticism was primarily a movement in painting, its theories were based on the theory of poetry stated in Pound's article 'Vorticism' in *The Fortnightly Review*.[96] Pound, seeing himself suddenly abandoned by the other Imagists, looked hungrily for a new cause. He found it, changed the title of his latest, and published it as a statement about Vorticism. A few weeks before it appeared he had written to Harriet Monroe:

> My article on Imagisme has been stoked into the Fortnightly Review, under an altered title. Vorticism being the generic term now used on all branches of the new art, sculpture, painting, poetry.[97]

Pound attempted to extend the aesthetic principles of Imagisme into the other arts—and into the visual arts in particular. At the same time he tried to apply to poetry principles taken from sculpture and painting. Ironically, this was Pound's final and most ambitious attempt to make a coherent statement out of the Imagist aesthetic.

Pound's notion of Vorticism, hastily transferred from Imagisme, could hardly coincide with Wyndham Lewis's picture of Vorticism taken from painting. Although Wyndham Lewis was an important writer, he was interested in Vorticism mainly for its possibilities in the visual arts. If anything he wrote can be regarded as Vorticist work it is his play *The Enemy of the Stars* first published in *Blast*. His notion of Vorticism drew some of its methods and something of its ideology directly from Futurism. Like Futurism it was national, even nationalist, in its assertions, though, of the original Vorticist triumvirate, Pound, Wyndham Lewis and Henri Gaudier-Brzeska, only Lewis was an Englishman (and he had American family connexions). There are common attitudes to the handling of line and shape in the painting styles of the Cubists, Futurists and the German

Expressionists. Vorticist pictorial art has affinities with each of these developments. And Wyndham Lewis used the terms Vorticist, Cubist and Futurist as virtually interchangeable.[98] The best of the Vorticist painters had already exhibited in 1914 as members of the London Group, which had formed through the amalgamation of the Camden Town Group and the English Cubists.[99] Lewis began to show a more precise sense of differentiation as the Vorticist movement developed. The war and the break-up of the group which had formed around him frustrated what might have been a significant development in English painting.[100]

Not untypically, Pound's Vorticist theories were preceded by the poems they were supposed to justify. 'Heather', first published in *Poetry and Drama* in March 1914, is referred to in the essay as an example of what he was now trying to do:

> The black panther treads at my side,
> And above my fingers
> There float the petal-like flames.
>
> The milk-white girls
> Unbend from the holly-trees,
> And their snow-white leopard
> Watches to follow our trace.

Pound defended this poem on the ground of its impersonality and cited it as an example of 'absolute metaphor'. He quoted the following anecdote:

> A Russian correspondent, after having called it a symbolist poem, and having been convinced that it was not symbolism, said slowly: 'I see, you wish to give people new eyes, not to make them see some new particular thing.'[101]

Pound's later summing-up was as follows:

> ... vorticism from my angle was a renewal of the sense of construction ... was an attempt to revive the sense of form.[102]

He was not slow to react against the frequent indiscipline and sloppiness produced in the name of free verse by self-styled Imagist and other writers. Meanwhile, he argued for a more strenuous precision of form, using as examples his friends and colleagues among the Vorticist sculptors and painters—Lewis, Edward Wadsworth, Gaudier-Brzeska and Epstein.

He even brought music into the argument, in terms that suggest some vague intention to link Vorticism with Hulme's neo-classicism:

> Music was vorticist in the Bach-Mozart period, before it went off into romance and sentiment and description.[103]

Maybe the most significant long-term effect of Pound's Vorticism was that it restored mobility to the image. In so doing it became feasible for writers in the Imagist tradition to break away from the method of 'lyrical pictures'[104] to which so many of their earlier poems seemed committed. At the end of the Vorticism essay Pound answered another question:

> I am often asked whether there can be a long imagiste or vorticist poem. The Japanese, who evolved the hokku, evolved also the Noh plays. In the best 'Noh' the whole play may consist of one image. I mean it is gathered about one image. Its unity consists in one image, enforced by movement and music. I see nothing against a long vorticist poem.

> On the other hand, no artist can possibly get a vortex into every poem or picture he does. One would like to do so, but it is beyond one ... a vorticist or imagiste writer may be justified in presenting a certain amount of work which is not vorticism or imagisme, just as he might be justified in printing a purely didactic prose article.[105]

Here, already, is the rationale of the *Cantos*.

The misfortune of the Vorticists was that they launched their propaganda only a few weeks before the outbreak of the European War in 1914. There seems no doubt that the war prevented them, not from gaining popular acceptance (of that there was little danger), but from injecting their work with their full imaginative energy. Wyndham Lewis was the best British painter of his generation; he was also a writer of potentially major ability. He returned soured and embittered from the war. Much of his later work is impressive, but the emotional damage he suffered while an artillery officer on the Western Front dulled his spontaneity.[106] Gaudier-Brzeska did not return.

At the end of the war Pound, having written *Mauberley*, left England. His career as a writer continued, but as a man he became increasingly isolated. His subsequent history might have been different if he had continued to have colleagues with the qualities of Lewis and Gaudier-Brzeska.

The war ensured the failure even of the Vorticist review *Blast*. This had been planned in the later months of 1913, but the first number did not appear until July 1914.[107] *Blast* was a formidable publication, and in

180

several respects almost revolutionary. It is outstanding among the magazines of the period for its physical aspect, with bold typography and rich magenta paper cover. It is equally notable in its contents, a splendid mélange of gaiety, irreverence, intelligence and talent in verse, prose and visual art. It is surprising that such a perceptive commentator as Wallace Martin should call it 'a coterie magazine without a coterie'.[108]

A central concern of Vorticism was to establish bridges between literature and the visual arts. *Blast* attempted to provide a platform for this on a basis of organic interrelation between the arts. It was the first magazine in Britain in the twentieth century to try to do so. Its only predecessors, at a long remove of time, were *The Germ* and *The Savoy*. *The Germ* is only historically important: in itself it was a feeble production. *The Savoy* was above everything a showcase for the talents of Beardsley and Arthur Symons. *Blast* spoke to the future, perhaps to a future that has not yet arrived.

*　　*　　*

The best *Ars Poetica* comes comparatively late in the history of the movement it helps to define,[109]

wrote an early commentator on Futurism. Perhaps Imagism did not continue long enough to reach full awareness of its own intentions. From the preliminary statements by Hulme and Edward Storer, the development of its aesthetic moved with curious gaps and hesitations to Pound's grander and sometimes more cryptic utterances a few years later. Attitudes and opinions from Hueffer and F. S. Flint were incorporated on the way, and the doctrine received its most elaborate statement in the announcements of Pound's Vorticist period. The Prefaces to *Some Imagist Poets* issued in 1915 and 1916 had all the disadvantages of committee work. Pound's contempt, whatever personal hurt or anger it covered, was justified. In aesthetic statement as in poetry, the Amygists represented a dilution.

Through rejecting Symbolism the Imagists lost themselves in cloud before they could reach the top of their mountain. Symbols are inescapable in poetry. Even the conceits of the seventeenth-century metaphysical writers Donne and Crashaw are images which carry symbolic implications. The words dance out their play; and the dance is prototype of a symbolic language.

Pound demonstrates this dilemma in his attempt to claim 'The Magi' as an Imagist poem. Of course Yeats's lyric embodies a visual image, but it is an image seen 'in the mind's eye' as Yeats, with a confident resort

181

to cliché, explicitly tells us. The poem is symbolist, the secretive restatement of a religious problem in the poet's own elliptical terms. In a review of Yeats, Pound quoted the opening lines of the poem, saying that they constituted 'a passage of *imagisme*':

> Now as at all times I can see in the mind's eye
> In their stiff painted clothes, the pale unsatisfied ones
> Appear and disappear in the blue depths of the sky
> With all their ancient faces like rain-beaten stones,
> And all their helms of silver hovering side by side...[110]

He acknowledged that Yeats was a Symbolist, but claimed he had written 'des Images', an assertion which hardly increases the clarity of what he intended his readers to understand by Imagism. The denial of symbolism accompanied a failure to recognize the essential ambiguities of both poetry and its theory:

> Theories, if they are to be synoptic in any way, however limited, must incorporate an element of poetic ambiguity.[111]

The Imagists failed to understand or reconcile the opposing directions in which their working aims led them. One direction was toward the strictness of a new artistic order: the other led to enhanced, even anarchic, freedom.

There was another dichotomy between the Imagists' concern with the musical rhythms of their work and the sculptural intensity they gave to it. They were contemporary with remarkable developments in European sculpture as well as painting. Hulme's friendship with Jacob Epstein is paralleled by Pound's admiration for Henri Gaudier. (Pound too was an admirer of Epstein and later developed a strong taste for the work of Brancusi.) As Hulme had said, 'This new verse resembles sculpture rather than music'. The best free verse of the period has a marble clarity that justifies the metaphor of hardness which the Imagists were so fond of invoking. Both arts after a few brilliant years of innovation partially succumbed to the temptation of novelty in place of originality.

'All ancient vision was definite and precise', asserted Yeats.[112] The Imagists sought and admired but rarely achieved the sculptor's precision. They lingered sometimes in the chambers of the sea, too often only in its ante-chambers.

Any attempt to sum up the Imagist aesthetic leaves one floundering in a quagmire. The adequacy of the theory can finally be tested only by its subsequent effects: above all, by the poems it supported, and sometimes contradicted. At the time it might well have seemed to the Imagists that the fate of their theories was entombed in Edward Storer's gloomy comment:

> ... to do a thing without saying anything about it, and to do it, make a principle of it, and defend it, are two different things in England. You can do almost anything you like in this country, provided it is not against the law, so long as you do not propound any reason, any philosophy for doing it.[113]

# VI

## The Punished Ground

It is the history of yesterday, and it seems already at the distance of half a century. Then, what brave petulant outbursts of poets and artists, what comic rivalries and reluctances of publishers, what droll conflicts of art and morality, what thunders of the trumpets of the press! The press is silent now, or admiring; the publishers have changed places, and all rivalries are handsomely buried, with laudatory inscriptions on their tombstones.[1]

The fine drifting cadences of Symons's prose were an epitaph for more than Decadence. They are a reminder of the brevity of all such movements and moments, but the Imagists had one essential difference from their predecessors. Where the nineties had conferred an attitude, Imagism offered a technique.

After it was all over Ford Madox Hueffer decided:

> ... it would be of immense service to humanity if the Anglo-Saxon world could agree that all creative literature is Poetry; that prose is a form as well adapted for the utterance of poetry as verse ... .[2]

This view is by no means far-fetched. *Ulysses* is a great poem: maybe the greatest twentieth-century poem of the English language. Extended works in verse like the *Cantos* or Carlos Williams's *Paterson* look pallid beside Joyce's epic. Prose and verse, in a kind of artistic unisex, have been drawing closer.

> Over the broken chair
> and out
> through the tool-house window
>
> whitewash whipping in a cold spring wind
>
> on a limestone cliff over the river
> piece of moon smoke hangs in china blue sky

Motel motel motel
broken neon arabesque
loneliness moans across the continent
like foghorns over still
oily water of tidal rivers.

The river is served sir

Dead leaves fill the fountain
and geraniums run
wild with mint.[3]

As printed here a creditable imagistic poem, though it is in fact taken from William Burroughs' remarkable novel *The Naked Lunch*. In ironic counterpoint much free verse has subsided to the level of prose. Even Pound could nod:

Mr Hecatomb Styrax, the owner of a large estate and
of large muscles, a blue and a climber of mountains,
has married at the age of twenty-eight, being at that
age a virgin, the term virgo being male in medieval
latinity. His ineptitudes have driven his wife from
one excess to another. She has abandoned the vicar
for he was lacking in vehemence; she is now the high-
priestess of a modern and ethical cult, and even now
Mr Styrax does not believe in aesthetics.

Hulme had hoped free verse would get rid of sham poetry. Unfortunately, it seems nothing can guarantee that.

A more positive result is that verse and prose have been brought into something closer to equilibrium. At last the prose poem emerges in English as a distinct form of its own. Even prose in fiction has benefited from the Imagists. There is a marked imagistic quality in Hemingway's early work, especially some of the vignettes of *In Our Time*, written before his own manner had overtaken him:

They shot the six cabinet ministers at half-past six in the morning against the wall of a hospital. There were pools of water in the court-yard. There were wet dead leaves on the paving of the courtyard. It rained hard. All the shutters of the hospital were nailed shut. One of the ministers was sick with typhoid. Two soldiers carried him down-stairs and out into the rain. They tried to hold him up against the wall but he sat down in a puddle of water. The other five stood very quietly

185

against the wall. Finally the officer told the soldiers it was no good trying to make him stand up. When they fired the first volley he was sitting down in the water with his head on his knees.[4]

A passage that shows up the feebleness of Imagist prose poems, particularly those by Fletcher and Amy Lowell. In contrast to their shambling attempts here is a finer example by the San Francisco writer Michael Palmer:

*Prose 12*
The sunlight was the same as the plant life but longer and darker. It was the darkness of a great forest the size of a five-legged chair. The ferns had always been there before the paintings on the wall. They had been there before the numbers and the ladders. There were hanged men in bogs and on cards. The rain came down inside and outside and the people walk by with wet faces and green thumbs.

The liberation of form sought so humbly and patiently by those first pioneers in London has at last found fruition.

Yet it was not all plain sailing. While good poems have resulted from the Imagists' assault on conventional form, some of them scented danger and went back on their own beliefs. Flint and Aldington after 1920 enacted something of what Hulme and Storer had gone through a decade earlier. Aldington was characteristically turbulent. 'Why should you feel annoyed at my denouncing free verse?' he asked Flint, then continued with this fine rush of invective:

... man alive, how can a mere form 'create a fresh point of view' for poetry, especially free verse which is at least Anglo-Saxon? And, when one sees the kind of person who uses vers libre, one sees pretty clearly that it is done to disparage the traditional culture of Europe. I am sure there are a few people who use the form purely as artists, people like H.D., Spire, Dujardin, yourself, but, o my God, Frank, what a set most of 'em are. Romains, a doctrinaire of the dullest type; Duhamel, a snivelling philanthropist; Durtain, a social revolutionary now copying Proust ad majoram plebis gloriam; Vildrac, Jouve, snivellers and slimers; and then Cendrars, le nègre juif; Cocteau, the bugger of the boulevards; Jacob, the jester of Notre Dame; Apollinaire, le juif fumiste; finally Dada ou les cochons savants .... I am sick of this faux avant-garde.[5]

Perhaps D. H. and T. E. Lawrence got fairly moderate treatment from Aldington after all. His revulsion from free verse is hardly rational, on

186

a par with the taste that lumps the splendid talent of Apollinaire with the mocking word-games of Dada. In his anger Aldington seems to be denouncing the whole notion of organic form adopted by Pound. Yet it is true there is much that Imagist method did not find room for:

> *The Hand that Signed the Paper*
> The hand that signed the paper felled a city;
> Five sovereign fingers taxed the breath,
> Doubled the globe of dead and halved a country;
> Those five kings did a king to death.
>
> The mighty hand leads to a sloping shoulder,
> The finger joints are cramped with chalk;
> A goose's quill has put an end to murder
> That put an end to talk.
>
> The hand that signed the treaty bred a fever,
> And famine grew, and locusts came;
> Great is the hand that holds dominion over
> Man by a scribbled name.
>
> The five kings count the dead but do not soften
> The crusted wound nor stroke the brow;
> A hand rules pity as a hand rules heaven;
> Hands have no tears to flow.

Imagism has had a large share in the development of American poetry and its influence even spread to Russia; but it never took full root in England. English writers, as the Welsh novelist Emyr Humphreys pointed out, took other and more parochial directions:

> Without Joyce, Eliot and Pound the atmosphere of English literature today would be that of the bar of a suburban golf club.[6]

There can be no doubt that the effects of Imagism involve the fortunes of Ezra Pound as much as those of the movement itself. He was a powerful critical force and entrepreneur as well as a poet. Apart from Hulme, who was dead, the English Imagists did not prove very effectual. Imagism in England seems often to have led to free verse denuded of images. It is as if writers, misunderstanding Pound and certain aspects of Eliot, latched onto the intellectual side of the movement without grasping its possibilities for the expression of feeling and imagination. Americans have sometimes almost hysterically encouraged the flow of imagination and feeling without a balancing regard for the intellect. In both countries the development, not so much from Imagism as from Pound himself, has often been an unfortunate mixing of supposed cleverness with mechanical recourse to free verse.

In contrast the Russian followers of Imagism seem to have known very well what they wanted from the London movement, which interested them for its focus on the image rather than its experiments with form. These Imaginists, as they called themselves, included some of the brilliant new generation that appeared around 1914 in St Petersburg and Moscow. Outstanding among them was the lyric poet Sergei Esenin. Imagism, together with Futurism, also influenced the earlier work of Boris Pasternak.

There are Imagist traces in English poetry since 1918, but on the whole these are slight. Aldous Huxley, a representative *Kulturmensch* of his time, was acerbic about *The Egoist*:

> horrid little paper ... which is filled by Aldington and his fellow what you may-callem-ists ... .[7]

After Imagism failed in London the old-style gentry culture made its comeback. English culture was settled, even contracting, where that of America was wide open. Form was again at a premium for English poets, as shown in the tight quatrains of Graves and the carefully worked stanzas of Auden and Dylan Thomas. By the nineteen-fifties form had become formalism, a phenomenon hardly worth pursuing. There were odd exceptions like Herbert Read, who could say, almost at the end of his life, 'I have always regarded myself as an Imagist'; but they do not alter the general balance. Read's earlier work was an uneasy collage of Imagism with more traditional turns of style:

*Cranach*

But once upon a time
the oakleaves and the wild boars
Antonio Antonio
The old wound is bleeding.

We are in Silvertown
we have come here with a modest ambition
to know a little bit about the river
eating cheese and pickled onions on a terrace by the Thames.

Sweet Thames! the ferry glides across your bosom
like Leda's swan.

The factories ah slender graces
sly naked damsels nodding their downy plumes.

He was to do better later, notably in his longer poem 'The End of a War'.

There is oblique evidence of Imagist influence on one of the few recent English poets of any stature, Keith Douglas, who was killed in Normandy in 1944, having found his fulfilment in the war. His prose book *Alamein to Zem Zem* quotes from only one poem in English, 'The Embankment' by T. E. Hulme. Douglas's poems are rich in both image and statement but his verse forms were those of the English thirties, with occasional reversions to greater freedom:

### Aristocrats

'I think I am becoming a God'

The noble horse with courage in his eye
clean in the bone, looks up at a shellburst:
away fly the images of the shires
but he puts the pipe back in his mouth.

Peter was unfortunately killed by an 88:
it took his leg away, he died in the ambulance.
I saw him crawling on the sand; he said
It's most unfair, they've shot my foot off.

How can I live among this gentle
obsolescent breed of heroes, and not weep?
Unicorns almost,
for they are falling into two legends
in which their stupidity and chivalry
are celebrated. Each, fool and hero, will be an
    immortal.

The plains were their cricket pitch
and in the mountains the tremendous drop fences
brought down some of the runners. Here then
under the stones and earth they dispose themselves,
I think with their famous unconcern.
It is not gunfire I hear but a hunting horn.

For American writers, Imagism became part of something much larger,

189

a movement with other pivots: the Chicago of *Poetry*; T. S. Eliot's poems; Amy Lowell's popularizings; the work in the twenties of writers as various as William Carlos Williams, Robinson Jeffers, E. E. Cummings and John Peale Bishop. The list of American poets who can be related to Imagism extends from these and many others through the generation of Ginsberg and Ferlinghetti to such recent writers as John Wieners and Michael Palmer.

In this process of development American poets had many advantages. The 'stark directness' that D. H. Lawrence called for was easier for them to attain, though luckily no one went quite as far as Kenneth Rexroth, who wanted an American poetry purified of English influences, based on French Symbolist and Imagist models. Presumably this ideal American poetry would be written in Choctaw. As early as 1921 a review of Robert Nichols's *Aurelia and Other Poems* carried a statement of Anglo-American differences, by no means inapposite today:

> ... the poet in this book has returned frankly to pre-war psychology and subject-matter. The book as a whole ..., has assumed in manner, emotion and subject the conventional limitations of the finely wrought but minor poetry of academic England.
>
> ....
>
> It is unfortunate that Robert Nichols should have only the poised and static culture of his particular English group to support him.[8]

The line of American poets in the Imagist tradition seemed to weaken in the nineteen-thirties and forties but has reasserted itself strongly since. Here again Pound's importance is evident. The fact that he was an American is probably the main reason why Imagism in America has attained a significance it never began to reach in England. After his political vicissitudes in the thirties and during the war Pound's name became anathema to many people in America, above all to the type of 'intellectual' who sees Communism as respectable, Fascism merely a term of abuse. But Pound's unpopularity was only a temporary reaction; since his death his place in an American Pantheon begins to look fairly secure.

To gain his niche he went the long way round; first an expatriate, then a prisoner, and finally in old age an exile. The sadness of his destiny should not cloud its meaning. In however muddled a fashion, Pound bore witness the only way he could. He began to re-emerge as a force for younger American writers during his long imprisonment in St Elizabeth's Hospital. The American hunger for fixed points for an American culture, quite as much as any sense of outrage and justice, helped to encourage his revival. Pound became a founding father for the leaders of the Black

Mountain group, in particular Charles Olson and Robert Duncan. This developed out of a context more familiar in America than elsewhere, in which a college or university provides both a forum and a platform for artistic undertaking. The platform was the *Black Mountain Review*, edited by Olson's colleague Robert Creeley from 1954-57.

Pound's life as well as his art helped to reconcile younger writers to him. The Black Mountaineers were essentially drops-out within the walls of academe. Pound, who had rejected society and was in turn mistreated by it, represented an archetypal anti-establishment figure. It is likely that many of his later admirers saw only this and not that most of what he stood for was antithetical to their avowed ideals. For Americans rebellion and revolution are not always clearly differentiated. Allen Ginsburg, an amusing, if mildly archaic, poetic radical (of academic critics he said, '. . . the trouble with these creeps is they wouldn't know Poetry if it came up and buggered them in broad daylight') was billed in America as a revolutionary. By the late fifties, in some circles, anyone who brushed against the establishment was liable to achieve instant godhead. Unlike England, where similar postures became only, and most damningly, symptoms of 'bad taste'.

These recent movements in American poetry tend, not untypically for American writers, to have strong regional affiliations. Black Mountain College was located in a remote part of North Carolina. Since then the main centres of poetic activity have shifted to New York and, above all, San Francisco. The poems that emerge from this tradition are uneven. Sometimes they are too close to a primitive Imagism to be effective or flattering:

### The Willow

> My neighbor's willow sways its frail
> Branches, graceful as a girl of
> Fifteen. I am sad because this
> Morning the violent
> Wind broke its longest bough.

> *Tu Fu*

Other writers, though, have refined Imagism into a method of subtle implication. An elegant example is 'Vaquero' by Edward Dorn, who had been a student at Black Mountain College:

> The cowboy stands beneath
> a brick-orange moon. The top

of his oblong head is blue, the sheath
of his hips
is too.

In the dark brown night
your delicate cowboy stands quite still.
His plain hands are crossed.
His wrists are embossed white.

In the background night is a house,
has a blue chimney top,
Yi Yi, the cowboy's eyes
are blue. The top of the sky
is too.

In the end, of course, too much must not be made of divisions into schools. Laura Riding, one of the better American poets of this century, stands outside all facile classification. But Laura Riding, apart from her profound influence on Robert Graves, represents only herself.

The future of free verse is uncertain. A new order will come into the language only when the linearity of early free verse has been reconciled with the more complex harmonies of traditional forms. The image itself has gained greatly in importance, largely through the growth and development of visual media like cinema and television. Today, most selling techniques are geared to the visual with its direct shock of assault. In this there are evident dangers. Pictures can corrupt more swiftly than words. The visual emphases of recent sub-culture have been underlined by such hallucinogenic experiments as the acid 'trip'. Alcohol, the traditional drug of European man, blurs images: hallucinogens activate them. But all that is a long way from the austere predications of Imagism.

Poetry in English had got into an impasse from which the Imagists attempted to rescue it. Even now it is too early to say how far they succeeded. Their achievement was blurred or waylaid, but the doctrine and some of their poems survive as examples or reminders. Since their time the fragmentation of our civilization has proceeded with increasing momentum. Today's culture is a maze of superficialities. All is trend: a doctrine of instantaneity triumphs. Yet underneath the superficiality lurks an inevitable dissatisfaction. The ways of expressing it are often desperate. It is not easy now for writers to be celebrators. Jim Morrison of 'The Doors' was both a creature and a creator of the trends of the moment. He was also a serious poet. Perhaps, at one level, this poem is a comment on the frenzied idol-worship he and his colleagues had to endure. However one chooses to interpret it, it remains a striking Imagist work:

Fall down.
Strange gods arrive in fast enemy poses.
Their shirts are soft marrying
        cloth and hair together.
All along their arms ornaments
        conceal veins bluer than blood
        pretending welcome.
Soft lizard eyes connect.
Their soft drained insect cries erect
        new fear, where fears reign.
The rustling of sex against their skin.
The wind withdraws all sound.
Stamp your witness on the punished ground. [9]

# Notes

I THE DEAD ART

1 Arthur Symons, 'Ernest Dowson', *The Fortnightly Review*, LXVII N.S. 402 N.S. (1 June 1900), 948.
2 Ford Madox Hueffer, 'Thus to Revisit', vii, *The English Review*, 32 (March 1921), 220.
3 *Ibid.*, 221.
4 See for example, E.W.G., 'A Plea for Certain Exotic Forms of Verse', *The Cornhill Magazine*, XXXVI (July 1877), 53–71.
5 William Morris to Georgiana Burne-Jones. Letter quoted by William Gaunt, *The Pre-Raphaelite Tragedy* (London, 1942), 200.
6 Leonard Woolf, *Sowing: An Autobiography of the Years 1880–1904* (London, 1960), 169.
7 Ezra Pound to Harriet Monroe, 13 August, 1913. *The Letters of Ezra Pound 1907–1941*. Edited by D. D. Paige. With a Preface by Mark Van Doren (New York, 1950; London, 1971 [as *The Selected Letters of Ezra Pound 1907–1941*]), 21 letter 21.
8 Ford Madox Hueffer, 'Impressionism—Some Speculations. II', *Poetry*, II.6 (September 1913), 220.
9 John C. Bailey, *The Claims of French Poetry: Nine Studies in the Greater French Poets* (London, 1907), 286.
10 Henry Newbolt, 'Futurism and Form in Poetry', *The Fortnightly Review*, XCV N.S. 569 (1 May 1914), 804–18.
11 Letter of 31 December 1917. Quoted in Edmund Blunden's 'Memoir' in *The Collected Poems of Wilfred Owen* (New York, 1964), 171.
12 Richard Aldington, *Life for Life's Sake: A Book of Reminiscences* (London, 1968 edition), 100.
13 John Drinkwater, 'Of Greatham (*To those who live there*)', *Georgian Poetry 1913–1915* (London, 1915), 90–91.
14 Ezra Pound, 'National Culture: A Manifesto—1938', in *Impact: Essays on Ignorance and the Decline of American Civilization*, edited and with an Introduction by Noel Stock (Chicago, 1960), 3.
15 Allen Tate, 'Emily Dickinson', in his *Collected Essays* (Denver, 1932). Reprinted in *Emily Dickinson: A Collection of Critical Essays*, edited by Richard B. Sewell (Englewood Cliffs, New Jersey, 1963), 17–18.

16 Fred Lewis Pattee, *A History of American Literature Since 1870* (New York, 1915; reprinted 1968), 271.

17 See Alain Bosquet, *Emily Dickinson*, Poètes d'aujourd'hui, 57 (Paris, 1957), 48–49.

18 On this see Yvor Winters, 'Emily Dickinson and the Limits of Judgment', *In Defense of Reason* (Denver, 1947), 283.

19 Pattee, *op. cit.*, 340–41.

20 See his list of writers who began to publish between 1870 and 1889, *ibid.*, 321–22.

21 Hovey's work is discussed by René Taupin, *L'Influence du Symbolisme Français sur la Poésie Américaine de 1910 à 1920* (Paris, 1929), 45–52. See also William Archer, *Poets of the Younger Generation* (London and New York, 1902), 206–19.

22 See Larzer Ziff, *The American 1890's. Life and Times of a Lost Generation* (New York, 1966; London, 1967). America specializes in lost generations. For a very different attitude to culture in America, see Daniel J. Boorstin, *The Americans*: Vol. 2. *The National Experience* (New York, 1965; London, 1966).

23 First published Venice, 1908. Reprinted as *A Lume Spento and Other Early Poems*, with preface by Ezra Pound (London and New York, 1965).

24 Kenneth Rexroth, 'The Influence of French Poetry on America', *Assays* (Norfolk, Conn., 1961), 153.

25 Louise Bogan, *Achievement in American Poetry, 1900–1950* (Chicago, 1951), 17.

26 John Berryman, *Stephen Crane* (Cleveland and New York, 1962 edn.), 274–75.

27 James Whitcomb Riley to Madison Cawein, July 1890. In James Whitcomb Riley, *Letters*, edited by William Lyon Phelps (Indianapolis, Ind., 1930), 102.

28 G. K. Chesterton, 'The Political Poetry of Mr. William Watson', *The Fortnightly Review*, LXXX, N.S. LXXIV. (2 November 1903), 762–66. J. D. Beresford, 'Anger and Dismay', *The Blue Review*, I (June 1913); 88. Lascelles Abercrombie, 'Poetry' *ibid.*, 121. Letter of Robert Graves to Robert Ross, 24 November, 1916, quoted in *Robert Ross, Friend of Friends*, edited Margery Ross (London, 1952), 296.

29 W. H. Auden. 'Letter to Lord Byron', Part IV, *Letters from Iceland* (London, 1937), 209.

II THE AGE DEMANDED

1 F. S. Flint, 'The Appreciation of Poetry'. [Unpub. lecture given in

Southport, 1940], 2. Typescript in the Collection of the Humanities Research Center, University of Texas, Austin.

2 Ezra Pound to James Vogel, 21 November, 1928. *Letters of Ezra Pound 1907–1941*, 219–20; letter 231.

3 See *The Letters of Maurice Hewlett*, ed. Laurence Binyon (London, 1926), 108; and Gilbert Frankau's Preface to Simpson's poems, *Lauds and Loves* (London, 1930), 9. Simpson's lack of poetic ability can be seen in any collection of his work.

4 Donald Gallup, *A Bibliography of Ezra Pound* (London, 1969), 133.

5 Ebenezer Cunningham to author. Unpublished letter, 22 April, 1965.

6 'A Mock Funeral / An Undergrad "Sent Down",' *The Tatler* XI, 144 (30 March 1904), 513.

7 Alun R. Jones, *The Life and Opinions of T. E. Hulme* (London, 1960), 151, mentions a hotel bill dated 26 May 1908 with a draft of Hulme's poem 'Sunset' on the back.

8 Jones (*ibid.*, 31). Jones does not indicate the source of this comment. Simpson's papers, if intact, would be worth investigation.

9 See, for example, Stanley K. Coffman, Jr., *Imagism: A Chapter for the History of Modern Poetry*, 1951, 5; Geoffrey Wagner, *Wyndham Lewis: A Portrait of the Artist as the Enemy* (London, 1957), 130 & 144; William Pratt (ed.), *The Imagist Poem* (New York, 1963), 14; J. P. Sullivan (ed.) *Ezra Pound: A Critical Anthology* (Harmondsworth, 1970), 399.

10 F. S. Flint, 'The History of Imagism', *The Egoist*, II.5 (1 May 1915), 70.

11 F. S. Flint, 'Book of the Week: Recent Verse', *The New Age*, IV.16 (11 February 1909), 327.

12 *The New Age*, IV.5 (26 November 1908), 95–97.

13 Flint, *The New Age* (11 February 1909), 327–28.

14 21 May 1909. *Letters of Ezra Pound*, 8, letter 4.

15 Hulme's poems can be found in Alun R. Jones, *The Life and Opinions of T. E. Hulme*, Part II: 'The Poetical Work of T. E. Hulme', 155–82.

16 *The New Age*, IV.17 (18 February 1909), 350.

17 *Ibid.* (11 February 1909), 327–28.

18 *The Times* (Tuesday, 20 October 1908), 11 a/b; (Thursday, 17 June 1909), 12d; (Wednesday, 10 November 1909), 2e.

19 Hulme to Flint. Unpublished letter, 24 March 1909. Humanities Research Center, University of Texas, Austin.

20 F. S. Flint, *The Egoist* (1 May 1915), 70–71.

21 *The Tyro*, 2 (1922), vi.

22 *Everyman Remembers* (London, 1931), 251–56. Rhys refers to a meeting at which Yeats, Pound, D. H. Lawrence and Hueffer were present. This must have been during 1909.

23 From 'A Morning Round', *Poems* (London and Edinburgh, 1907), N.P.

24 Flint, 'History of Imagism', *loc. cit.*

25 Florence Farr, *The Solemnization of Jacklin* (London, 1912), 158.

26 E.g., 'Affirmations ... I. Arnold Dolmetsch', *The New Age*, XVI.10 (7 January 1915), 246–47; 'Vers libre and Arnold Dolmetsch', *The Egoist*, IV.6 (July 1917), 90–91. Both these were reprinted in Pound's *Pavannes and Divisions* (New York, 1918).

27 T. E. Hulme, 'A Lecture on Modern Poetry'. In Michael Roberts, *T. E. Hulme* (London, 1938), 266–67.

28 An example is 'The Earth and We', *The Second Book of the Poets' Club* (London, 1911), 39–40.

29 Quoted by Brigit Patmore, *My Friends When Young: The Memoirs of Brigit Patmore*, edited with an Introduction by Derek Patmore (London, 1968), 81.

30 F. S. Flint, 'The Appreciation of Poetry', (Southport, 1940), 7.

31 In Herbert Hughes's *Songs of Uladh*. See Frank O'Connor, 'A Gambler's Throw', *The Listener*, LXXV, 1925 (17 February 1966), 238. See also the *Irish Folk-Song Society Journal*, I.1 and I.2 (April and July 1904) for some Celtic-crepuscular verse and prose by Campbell.

32 *The Rushlight*, 64.

33 Yeats to Katharine Tynan, letter probably written September 1906. *The Letters of W. B. Yeats*, edited by Allan Wade (London, 1954), 585.

34 Campbell's poems are to be found in *The Poems of Joseph Campbell*. Edited with an Introduction by Austin Clarke (Dublin 1963).

35 Unpublished letter of T. E. Hulme to F. S. Flint. Undated, but written in the summer of 1909. In the Collection of the University of Texas.

36 Arthur Symons, 'The Decadent Movement in Literature', *Harper's Monthly Magazine*, XXVI (European edn.) LXXXVII (American edn.), 522 (November 1893), 858–67.

37 F. S. Flint, 'Recent Verse', *The New Age*, IV.5 (26 November 1908), 95.

38 Edward Storer, 'An Essay', *Mirrors of Illusion* (London, 1908] 102.

39 *Ibid.*, 106–7.

40 Ezra Pound, 'Prologomena: Credo', *Poetry Review*, I.2 (February 1912, 73.

41 Pound, 'Affirmations, IV. As for Imagisme', *The New Age*, XVI.13 (28 January 1915), 349–50.

42 Edward Storer, *op. cit.*, 113–14.

43 T. S. Eliot, 'Reflections on Vers Libre', *New Statesman*, VIII.204 (3 March 1917), 518–19. Reprinted in *To Criticize the Critic* (1965), 183–89.

44 'Searchers after Reality, II: Haldane', *The New Age*, V.17 (19 August 1909), 315–16; review of Tancrède de Visan, *L'Attitude du Lyrisme Contemporain*, *The New Age*, IX.17 (24 August 1911), 400.

45 'Notes on Language and Style', *The Criterion*, III.12 (July 1925), 485–97; Michael Roberts, *T. E. Hulme* (London, 1938), Appendix III, 271–303.

46 Roberts, *T. E. Hulme* (London, 1938), Appendix II, 258–70.

47 Roberts, *op. cit.*, 'A Lecture', 264.

48 *Ibid.*, 267.

49 *Ibid.*, 269.

50 *Ibid.*, 285–86.

51 Flint, 'History', *loc. cit.*

52 A useful recent study of Pound's early work and its background is Thomas H. Jackson, *The Early Poetry of Ezra Pound* (Cambridge, Mass., 1968).

53 See Christopher Middleton, 'Documents on Imagism from the Papers of F. S. Flint', *The Review*, 15 (April 1965), 33 & 51.

54 Padraic Colum, 'The Beggar's Child', *Wild Earth and Other Poems* (Dublin, 1916), 18.

55 Flint, *loc. cit.*

56 T. E. Hulme, *Speculations*. Edited by Herbert Read (London, 1924), 133.

57 *The New Age*, VI.10 (6 January 1910), 233–34.

58 *The Tramp*, II (November 1910), 183.

59 Edward Storer, 'Caravan', *Terra Italica* (London, 1920), 3.

60 Hulme to Flint. Unpublished letter, 8 August 1913. Collection of University of Texas.

61 Ezra Pound to Michael Roberts, July 1937. *Letters of Ezra Pound*, 296; letter 329.

62 Pound to F. S. Flint, 7 July 1915. Collection of University of Texas.

63 Pound to Flint, 30 January 1921. University of Texas Collection.

64 *Ibid.*

65 *Ibid.*

66 Daniel Cory, 'Ezra Pound', *Encounter*, XXX.5 (May 1968), 38.

67 Unpublished letter Ezra Pound to Isabel W. Pound, 12 February 1912. Original in Yale University Library.

68 Ezra Pound, 'This Hulme Business', *The Townsman*, II.5 (January, 1939), 15.

69 Ezra Pound, 'Ford Madox (Hueffer) Ford: Obit', *Nineteenth Century and After*, CXXVI.750 (August 1939), 178–81.

70 See Violet Hunt, *The Flurried Years* (London, 1926), 179.

71 Herbert N. Schneidau, 'Pound and Yeats: The Question of Symbolism', *ELH*, XXXII.2 (June 1965), 224. Schneidau (*loc. cit.*) is

wrong to say that Pound resisted Hueffer's modernism for about a year.

72 *My Friends When Young*, 64.
73 Gallup, *A Bibliography of Ezra Pound* (1969 edn.), 199–201. *Patria Mia* was republished in book form (Chicago, 1950; London, 1962).
74 *Des Imagistes* had first appeared as an issue of *The Glebe* (New York), I.5 (February 1914), 1–63. The bound version was published in New York by A. & C. Boni (2 March 1914), and in England by the Poetry Bookshop (April 1914).
75 See Alfred Kreymborg's autobiography, *Troubadour* (New York, 1925), 204–5.
76 Undated letters from the Harriet Monroe Collection, University of Chicago Library. Harriet Monroe notes that the second of these was answered 24 October 1913. H.D.'s second letter refers to her 'Acon', published in *Poetry*.
77 Richard Aldington, *Life for Life's Sake* (1968 edn.), 101.
78 Aldington, *ibid.*, 123.
79 F. S. Flint to Leroy C. Breunig. Quoted in Leroy C. Breunig, 'F. S. Flint, Imagism's "Maître d'Ecole" ', *Comparative Literature*, IV.2 (Spring 1952), 134.
80 Pound to Patricia Hutchins, 17 November 1957. Quoted in Patricia Hutchins, *Ezra Pound's Kensington* (London, 1965), 128.
81 Pound to Carlo Izzo, 23 August 1935, quoted Carlo Izzo, 'Lettere inedite di Ezra Pound', *Nuova Corrente*, 5–6 (January–June 1956), 134.
82 *Life for Life's Sake* (1968), 127.
83 Charles Norman, *Ezra Pound* (New York, 1960; London, 1969), 152.
84 Ezra Pound to Amy Lowell. *Letters of Ezra Pound*, 38; letter 47.
85 Quoted Charles Norman, *Ezra Pound*, 154.
86 Ezra Pound, *Profile: An Anthology Collected in MCMXXXI* (Milan, 1932), recto of first leaf.
87 Ford Madox Ford, 'Those Were The Days', Foreword to *Imagist Anthology 1930* (1930), ix.
   'So that but for mightier thunders and invasions who knows
   what London might not have been today . . . .'
88 Pound to William Carlos Williams, 19 December 1913. *Letters of Ezra Pound*, 28, letter 31.
89 Wyndham Lewis, 'Note for Catalogue', *Vorticist Exhibition: Catalogue* (1915), 3. The names listed in 1915 recur, with a few additions and deletions, in *Wyndham Lewis and Vorticism*. Tate Gallery Catalogue (1956).
90 Ezra Pound, 'Vorticism', *The Fortnightly Review*, XCVI (N.S.) 573. (1 September 1914), 461–70; reprinted in *Gaudier-Brzeska: a Memoir* (New York, 1970), 81–94.
91 *The Tyro*, 2 (1922), vi.

1 'Modern Poetry and the Imagists', *The Egoist* I.11 (1 June 1914), 202.

2 Pound to Flint, 7 July 1915, unpublished letter. University of Texas Collection.

3 Flint to Pound, 3 July 1915, unpublished. University of Texas Collection.

4 Pound to Flint, *ibid*.

5 *Some Imagist Poets 1916* (London, Boston and New York, 1916), Preface, v–viii, x, xii.

6 Ford Madox Hueffer, 'A Jubilee' (Review of *Some Imagist Poets* [1915]), *The Outlook*, XXXVI (10 July 1955), 46–48.

7 Storer's poems can be found in *Inclinations* [1907] and *Mirrors of Illusion* [1908].

8 Unpublished letter, 2 July 1915, University of Texas Collection. The remark is referred to by Christopher Middleton, 'Documents on Imagism from the papers of F. S. Flint', *The Review* (April 1965), 41.

9 These examples come from another sequence-poem, 'Ghost Pictures', *Inclinations*, 14–19.

10 E. Storer, 'Grotesques of Pirandello', *Forum* (October 1921), 271–81.

11 Letter dated 12 January 1910.

12 See Campbell's 'Three Poems', *The Nation*, XVIII.21 (19 February 1916), 731. For subsequent publication of poems by Campbell see *The Nation* (1 April 1916), 18; (24 June 1916), 378; (16 Sept. 1916), 760.

13 'Short Reviews', *The Egoist*, IV.11 (December 1917), 172.

14 Communication from Fordham University, New York, 3 May 1965.

15 In Part II of his critical and biographical study *The Life and Opinions of T. E. Hulme*. Jones's editorial work has some inaccuracies; but it is the nearest approximation to an adequate text so far.

16 F. S. Flint, 'Book of the Week: Recent Verse', *The New Age* (11 February 1909), 327.

17 Anon., review of *Ripostes*, *The Quest*, IV.4 (July 1913), 784.

18 That is Eliot's later opinion. But he had praised the 'beauty' of Hulme's 'The Embankment' in his 'Reflections on Vers Libre', *New Statesman* (3 March 1917), 518–19; reprinted in *To Criticize the Critic*, 185–86.

19 R. D. Laing, *The Divided Self: A Study of Sanity and Madness* (Harmondsworth, 1960), 187.

20 T. E. Hulme, 'A Lecture on Modern Poetry'. Roberts, *T. E. Hulme*, 266.

21 Letter Ebenezer Cunningham to J. B. Harmer, *loc. cit*.

22 Jones, *op. cit*., 151.

23 'German Chronicle', *Poetry and Drama*, II.6 (June 1914), 228.

24 T. E. Hulme to Edward Marsh, 24 September (1916). Unpublished, in Keele University Library.

25 Conversation Kate Lechmere—J. B. Harmer, 1965.

26 Ezra Pound, 'This Hulme Business', *The Townsman* (January 1939), 15.

27 Hulme, *Speculations*, 229.

28 *Ibid.*, 225.

29 *Ibid.*, 245.

30 Hueffer and Wyndham Lewis were among the contributors to this uneven but not uninteresting periodical.

31 F. S. Flint, *The Tramp* (November 1910), 183.

32 Unless otherwise stated Flint's poems are quoted from *Cadences* (1915) and *Otherworld* (1920).

33 Pound to F. S. Flint, 7 July 1915. Unpublished. University of Texas Collection.

34 Unpublished letter Pound to William Carlos Williams, 24 January 1937. Original in Lockwood Memorial Library, State University of New York, Buffalo.

35 Letter of 7 July 1915, *loc. cit.*

36 Hueffer, 'A Jubilee', *The Outlook* (10 July 1915), 46–48.

37 Edward Storer, *The British Review* II.3 (September 1915), 472. Hueffer's praise is to be found in 'A Jubilee', *loc. cit.*, 47.

38 These letters, probably written in 1913, are undated and unpublished. The originals of both are in the Modern Poetry Library of the University of Chicago.

39 H.D.'s poems will be found in her *Collected Poems* (New York, 1925; 6th printing, 1940).

40 H.D., *The Usual Star* (London and Dijon, 1930), 86.

41 *The Egoist*, III.12 (December 1916), 183–84.

42 Aldington's poems are taken from *The Complete Poems* (London, 1948).

43 See *Life for Life's Sake* (1968), 133–34.

44 Written in January 1915. *Letters of Ezra Pound*, 49; letter 60.

45 Read's comments will be found in *Richard Aldington: An Intimate Portrait*. Edited by Alister Kershaw and Frédéric-Jacques Temple (Carbondale and Edwardsville, 1965), 131–32.

46 Among them Roy Campbell and C. P. Snow. Quoted in *Richard Aldington: An Intimate Portrait*, 4–11 & 134–40.

47 Letter Aldington to Amy Lowell, 20 November 1917. Quoted Charles Norman, *Ezra Pound*, 89. Original in Harvard University Library.

48 Written in 1924. Quoted in *Richard Aldington: An Intimate Portrait*, 125.
49 'Introduction', *The Poems of Richard Aldington* (Garden City, N.Y., 1934), xiii & xiv.
50 This had its appeal for some people, among them Robert Bridges and Henry Newbolt. See the letter from Newbolt to Pound, written *c*. 1920, and quoted in Noel Stock (ed.), *Ezra Pound: Perspectives* (Chicago, 1965), 120–21.
51 See *passim* the poems of *A Lume Spento* (Venice, 1908).
52 Pound's poems are collected in *Personae* (New York, 1956 edn.) [in England as *Collected Shorter Poems* (2nd edn. London 1968)] and *The Cantos* (London, 1964).
53 Edward Thomas, 'Two Poets', *The English Review*, II.3 (June 1909), 627. The other book reviewed was Maurice Hewlett's *Artemision*. (This, like *Personae*, was published by Elkin Mathews.)
54 Quoted in Christopher Hassall, *Rupert Brooke: A Biography* (London, 1964), 210.
55 From his 'Foreword', dated 19 August 1964, to the reprint of *A Lume Spento and Other Early Poems* (London and New York, 1965), 7.
56 Edward Marsh, *A Number of People: A Book of Reminiscences* (London, 1939), 328.
57 It is noteworthy that Aldington chose these poems to represent Pound in his *Poetry of the English-Speaking World* (London, 1947), 876–77. This says more about Aldington's taste than about Pound's development.
58 W. B. Yeats, 'Introduction'. *The Oxford Book of Modern Verse 1892–1935* (Oxford, 1936), xxvi.
59 As told by Brigit Patmore, 'Ezra Pound in England'. *Texas Quarterly*, VII.3 (Autumn 1964), 72. There is another version of this story in *My Friends When Young: The Memoirs of Brigit Patmore*, 64.
60 The emphases of his formal education can be learned from the courses he took for his M.A. in Romanics at the University of Pennsylvania, 1905–7. See *E.P. to L.U.: Nine Letters* (1963), 33–34.
61 *Poetry*, II.1 (April 1913), 1–12. Seven of these twelve poems were reprinted as 'The Contemporania of Ezra Pound' in *The New Freewoman*, I.5 (15 August 1913), 87–88. Eleven appear in *Lustra* (1916). 'Pax Saturni' was never reprinted.
62 'Poems', *Poetry*, III.2 (November 1913), 53–60. Thirteen poems, of which ten are in *Lustra*. Two were not reprinted in book form; 'The Choice' is in Harriet Monroe and Alice Corbin Henderson's anthology *The New Poetry* (New York, 1917), 257 ff.
63 See *The Earliest English Poems*. Translated and introduced by

Michael Alexander (Harmondsworth, 1966), 23. 'I was fired by the example of Ezra Pound's version of *The Seafarer* (which gives far and away the most concentrated impression of Anglo-Saxon poetry) . . . .' I cannot endorse this opinion.

64 T. S. Eliot, 'Introduction', *Ezra Pound: Selected Poems* (1928), xvi.

65 Pound's Chinese scholarship is discussed by Michael Reck in *Ezra Pound: A Close-up* (New York, 1967, London, 1968), 166–75. This confirms that Pound worked mostly from Fenollosa's draft versions. In the process, the form of the Chinese, which is a strict pattern of quatrains, was utterly lost.

66 I had thought this my discovery, until I read A. C. Graham's *Poems of the Late T'ang* (Harmondsworth, 1965), 33–35. Though see *Ezra Pound: Perspectives*, 177–79, 'The Fenollosa Papers'. For a still more direct comparison between Pound and Giles see 'The Beautiful Toilet', which Pound in *Cathay* ascribed to Mei Sheng, 140 B.C., and compare it with the untitled version printed by Giles over the name 'Mei Sheng (d. B.C. 140)'. (H. A. Giles, *A History of Chinese Literature* (London, 1901), pp. 97–98).

67 *Poetry*, VIII.1 (April 1916), 38–43.

68 'Three Cantos'. *Poetry*, X.3–5 (June, July & August 1917), 113–21; 180–88; 248–54. Excerpts from these were reprinted in *Future*, II.3–5 (February, March & April 1918), 63 & 121.

69 Daniel Cory, 'Ezra Pound', *Encounter* (May 1968), 38.

70 Hueffer's comments on the Imagists can be studied in several of his journalistic pieces. See his 'Literary Portraits—XXXV: Les Jeunes and "Des Imagistes",' *The Outlook*, XXXIII (9 & 16 May 1914), 636 & 653, 682–83; 'A Jubilee', *The Outlook* (10 July 1915), 46–48.

71 'The Book of the Month', *Poetry Review*, I.3 (March 1912), 133.

72 *Loc. cit.*

73 *The Cerebralist*, 1 (December 1913), 34. The article is signed by the initials 'R.S.', a formula which has so far preserved its secret.

74 *Ibid.*, 35.

75 See his essay 'Christina Rossetti', *The Fortnightly Review*, LXXXIX N.S. 531 (March 1911), 422–29; and the references *passim* in his *The March of Literature* (London, 1938), 705–6 & 716.

76 He had a poem 'The Song of the Women: a Wealden Trio' in *The Savoy*, 4 (August 1896), 85–86.

77 F. M. Hueffer, 'Preface', *Collected Poems* (London [1914]), 9.

78 *Poetry*, IV.3 (June 1914), 111–20. Pound's own footnote to this review says: 'Mr. Hueffer is not an *Imagiste*, but an Impressionist. Comparison has arisen because of my inclusion of one of his poems in the Anthologie des Imagistes.' (*Ibid.*, 120 fn.) Pound had already

reviewed the volume in *The New Freewoman* I.13 (15 December 1913), 251.

79 Harvey's *Bibliography* (316–17) lists five reviews apart from those by Pound; one by Edward Thomas, one by Edward Shanks, and three anonymous. One of the latter is supposed to have been written by Norman Douglas.

80 Hueffer's poems are in his *Collected Poems* (1914) and *On Heaven and Poems Written on Active Service* (London and New York, 1918).

81 *Collected Poems*, 'Preface', 9.

82 *Ibid.*, 13.

83 Pound to Harriet Monroe, 23 May 1914. *Letters of Ezra Pound*, 37; letter 45.

84 Pound to William Carlos Williams. From a letter of uncertain date, written from St Elizabeth's Hospital, Washington. Probable limits of composition are 1946–54. Microfilmed June 1955; State University of New York, Buffalo.

85 In his review of *The New Poetry: An Anthology*. Edited by Harriet Monroe and Alice Corbin Henderson (New York, 1917). *The Egoist*, IV.10 (November 1917), 151.

86 'And Other Poems', *The Chicago Evening Post*. Quoted in Horace Gregory, *Amy Lowell: Portrait of the Poet in her Time* (New York, 1958), 78.

87 Horace Gregory, *ibid.*, 102.

88 For Amy Lowell's poems see *The Complete Poetical Works of Amy Lowell* [1955].

89 Both extracts are from a letter dated 29 August 1913. Original in the Library of the University of Chicago.

90 Quoted by Stanley K. Coffman, *Imagism* . . . , *loc. cit.*, 180.

91 Confirmed by his autobiography *Life Is My Song* (New York, 1937).

92 *The Dominant City* (1913), 19. And see Fletcher's *Selected Poems* (London, 1938). There is as yet no collected edition.

93 Fletcher's first published poems in his new manner appeared in *Poetry*. These are the poems sent to Harriet Monroe by Pound. 'Irradiations', *Poetry*, III.3 (December 1913), 85–91.

94 *Poetry*, IV.6 (September 1914), 211–15.

95 Unpublished letter, 27 June, 1917. University of Chicago.

96 See Lawrence's letter to H.D., 10 August 1929. In *The Collected Letters of D. H. Lawrence*. Edited with an introduction by Harry T. Moore (1962), II, 1175.

97 A typical example is his letter to Amy Lowell, 18 December 1914. *Ibid.* (1962), I, 297–300.

98 'A Still Afternoon': Dreams Old and Nascent, Discipline, Baby Movements, *The English Review*, III (November 1909), 561–65.

99 D. H. Lawrence to Blanche Jennings, 2 November 1909. *Ibid.*, I, 57.
100 D. H. Lawrence to Edward Garnett, 30 December 1913. *Ibid.*, I, 259.
101 D. H. Lawrence to A. W. McLeod, 21 December 1916. *Ibid.*, I, 495. She was J. R. Lowell's great-niece, not his daughter.
102 For Lawrence's poems see *The Complete Poems of D. H. Lawrence*. Collected and edited with an introduction and notes by Vivian de Sola Pinto and Warren Roberts. 2 vols. (London, 1964).
103 Dated 22 December 1913. *Collected Letters*, I, 258. Henry Savage was friend and editor of Richard Middleton (1882–1911), a belated nineties figure who committed suicide in Brussels. Some of Lawrence's early poems have a surprising resemblance to Middleton's work.
104 Postmarked 19 November 1913. *Ibid.*, I, 244.
105 R. F. Smalley, 'Futurism and the Futurists', *The British Review*, VII.2 (August 1914), 225.
106 From a letter to an unnamed recipient, 31 May 1922. Quoted S. Foster Damon, *Amy Lowell* (Boston and New York, 1935), 605.
107 Ezra Pound to Harriet Monroe, March 1913, *Letters of Ezra Pound*, 17, letter 15.
108 Pound to Harriet Monroe, 23 September 1913. *Ibid.*, 22, letter 23. Pound was simultaneously promoting both Fletcher and Lawrence. See this letter and no. 22, dated 13 August 1913.
109 Pound to Glenn Hughes, 26 September 1927, *Ibid.* 212, letter 225.

IV THE GOSSAMER WEB

1 T. E. Hulme, 'Romanticism and Classicism', *Speculations*, 123.
2 T. S. Eliot, review of Peter Quennell's *Baudelaire and the Symbolists: Five Essays*, *The Criterion*, IX.35 (January 1930), 357.
3 Edward Storer, 'An Essay', *Mirrors of Illusion*, 110.
4 In 'Notes on Language and Style'. Michael Roberts, *T. E. Hulme*, 287.
5 S. T. Colendge, *Biographia Literaria*. Edited Arthur Symons: Everyman's Library (London, 1906), 159–60.
6 Rémy de Gourmont, *La Culture des Idées*, 3ème édition (Paris, 1900), 93 & 100–101.
7 The poems collected under the title *In Hospital* are dated 1873–75. They appeared in Henley's *A Book of Verses* (London, 1888). *In Hospital* was published as a separate pamphlet in America by Thomas B. Mosher, *The Bibelot*, VII.1 (Portland, Maine, 1901), and reprinted in Henley's *Poems: Works* II (1908), 3–46. Henley shows

the effects of his reading of Heine's unrhymed poems in *Die Nordsee*, *1825–1826*, collected in Heinrich Heine, *Buch der Lieder* (Hamburg, 1827), 306–72. A study of these by P. Remer had the significant title *Die freien Rhythmen in Heinrich Heines Nordseebildern, Ein Beitrag zur neuen deutschen Metrik* (Heidelberg, 1889).

8 'Rhymes and Rhythms, XXI', *Poems: Works*, I (1908), 231–32.

9 W. E. Henley, 'London Voluntaries', II and III. *Poems*, Vol. II (1908), 77–87.

10 'Town Sky-Line' is strongly reminiscent of Herrick. Maybe Tancred encouraged Hulme in this taste. Against Hulme (in A. R. Jones, 179, 181 & 176) set Herrick's *Hesperides*, World's Classics Edition (London, 1902), 12 & 149.

11 'Notes on Language and Style', Roberts, 301.

12 From 'Cherry Valley', *The Mountainy Singer*, 3.

13 *Life for Life's Sake* (1968), 109.

14 Unpublished letter conjecturally dated 3 December 1912: F.5 in the Harriet Monroe Collection of the University of Chicago.

15 Ezra Pound to Homer L. Pound, 3 June 1913. *Letters of Ezra Pound*, 21, letter 20.

16 *The Letters of Gerard Manley Hopkins to Robert Bridges*. Edited Claude Colleer Abbott (London, rev. edn. 1955), 155, letter XC, 18 October 1882.

17 *Studies in Classic American Literature* (London edn., 1924), 168–69. With typical vehemence Lawrence also denounced Whitman as a 'post-mortem poet' (*ibid.*, 165 & 245).

18 Richard Aldington, 'Reviews', *The Egoist*, I.13 (1 July 1914), 247.

19 Thomas Burnett Swann, *The Classical World of H.D.* (Lincoln, Nebraska, 1962), 10.

20 Walter Pater. *Selected Works* (London and New York, 1948).

21 Ford Madox Hueffer, 'Thus to Revisit', vii, *The English Review* (March 1921), 221.

22 T. S. E[liot], 'A Commentary', *The Criterion*, XIII.52 (April 1934), 451.

23 'Belated Romanticism', *The New Age* (18 February 1909), 350.

24 On this see Alberto Frattini, *Da Tommaseo a Ungaretti* (Bologna, 1959), 91.

25 Unpublished letter Sir Herbert Read to G. S. Fraser, 21 January 1967.

26 Ezra Pound, 'Paris', *Poetry*, III.1 (October 1913), 29–30.

27 *The New Age*, XIII.19–25 (4 September—16 October 1913), 551–52 ff.

28 Taupin, *op. cit.*, 168.

29 Ezra Pound to Harriet Monroe, 28 March 1914. *Letters of Ezra*

*Pound*, 35, letter 42. Flint's 'Contemporary French Poetry' constituted a whole issue of *Poetry Review*, I.8 (August 1912), 355 ff.

30  F. S. Flint, 'The Appreciation of Poetry', 3 & 5.

31  *The New Age*, V.14 (5 August 1909), 288.

32  'The Approach to Paris: III: "Monsieur Romains, Unanimist"', *The New Age*, XIII.21 (18 September 1913), 607–9.

33  See M.-L. Bidal, *Les Écrivains de l'Abbaye* (Paris, 1938), 65.

34  *The New Age* (24 August 1911), 400. The omission of accents, etc., in the text follows Hulme or the printer throughout.

35  'A Lecture on Modern Poetry', Roberts, 262–63.

36  André Beaunier, *La Poésie Nouvelle*, 3ème edition (Paris, 1902), 39.

37  'A Lecture on Modern Poetry', *loc. cit.*, 260, 262–63.

38  *Premiers Poèmes* (*Avec une Préface sur le vers libre*), (Paris 1897), 23 ff. Kahn is quoting from his own article of 1888 in *Le Revue Indépendante* (*ibid.*, 31).

39  For Hulme and Guyau, see M. Guyau, *Les Problèmes de L'Esthétique, Contemporaine* (Paris, 1884), 175–76; and compare 'A Lecture', Roberts, 264. De Gaultier's views on language were similar to those of Rémy de Gourmont. See, for example, Jules de Gaultier, *Revue Blanche*, VI.31 (May 1894), 402; and compare the discussion of language in Hulme's 'Searchers after Reality. II. Haldane', *The New Age* (19 August 1909), 315–16. The last of Hulme's three articles in 'Searchers after Reality' dealt with de Gaultier. See 'Searchers after Reality. III. De Gaultier', *The New Age*, VI.5 (2 December 1909), 107–8.

40  Ribot develops these arguments in the investigation of 'L'Imagination mystique' included in his *Essai sur l'Imagination Créatrice* (Paris, 1900), 186 ff. See, too, Ribot on 'L'Imagination plastique', *ibid.*, 157–58.

41  'A Lecture', Roberts, 268–69. (And Compare Ribot, *op. cit.*, 195.] Hulme must have been satisfied with this argument. It is repeated, with slight modifications, in his essay on Haldane, *The New Age* (19 August 1909), 315–16, and in 'Romanticism and Classicism', *Speculations*, 134–35.

42  Ribot, *op. cit.*, 157.

43  'A Lecture', 266–67.

44  *Le Problème du Style*, 3ème édition (Paris, 1902); nouvelle édition (Paris, 1907), 33.

45  Miss Kate Lechmere, in conversation with the author, 1966.

46  'Notes on Language and Style', 274–75, and cf. *Le Problème du Style*, 36.

47  *Le Problème du Style*, 123.

48  'Notes on Language and Style', 296.

49 [C.-P.] Baudelaire, *Oeuvres Complètes*. Texte établi et annoté par Y.-G. Le Dantec. Bibliothèque de la Pléiade, No. 1/7 (Paris, 1961), 156, 99, 86.

50 In *La Pluie et le beau temps* (Paris, 1896), 72–73.

51 *Life for Life's Sake* (1968), 101.

52 *Ibid.*, 120.

53 Richard Aldington, 'The Imagists', *Bruno Chap Books*, II (Special Series), 5 (1915), 69–70.

54 Henri de Régnier, *La Sandale Ailée*: 1903–1905, 4ème édition (Paris, 1906), 127.

55 'Images—I', *Images 1910–1915* (1915), 12. There is a cross-current here. Storer's poem 'Venice', written *c.* 1919 and published in his *Terra Italica* (1920), 16 has the lines
> Cargoes of scented fruit
> Glide through the still canals,
> . . . .

56 Letter H.D. to Glenn Hughes. Quoted in Glenn Hughes, *Imagism and the Imagists*, 110–11.

57 Letter H.D. to T. B. Swann. Quoted in T. B. Swann, *The Classical World of H.D.*, 10.

58 'Ezra Pound in England', *Texas Quarterly* (Autumn 1964), 72.

59 See John J. Espey, *Ezra Pound's Mauberley: A Study in Composition* (Berkeley and Los Angeles, 1955), especially 25–48. Espey must be used with caution. He thinks, for example, that Gautier's 'Coquetterie Posthume' 'gives directions for his own laying out'! (*Ibid.*, 30.)

60 For example, *Guide to Kulchur* ([1938;] New York edn. 1952), 178–79; 227 & 293.

61 *Poetry*, III.1 (October 1913), 26–27.

62 Pound to W. C. Williams, 21 May 1909. *Letters of Ezra Pound*, 8, letter 4.

63 Pound to Harriet Monroe. *Ibid.*, 23, letter 24.

64 See 'The Approach to Paris, II', *The New Age*, XIII, 20 (11 September 1913), 577.

65 Pound to Harriet Monroe, January 1915. *Letters of Ezra Pound*, 48–49, letter 60.

66 Pound to Iris Barry, 27 July 1916. *Ibid.*, 89, letter 103.

67 Pound to Sarah Perkins Cope, 22 April 1934. *Ibid.*, 257, letter 277.

68 'The Approach to Paris. II', *The New Age* (11 September 1913), 577.

69 'Vorticism', *The Fortnightly Review* (1 September 1914), 467.

70 *Le Problème du Style*, 89.

71 Pound to Harriet Monroe, 2 October 1915. *Letters of Ezra Pound*, 64, letter 75.

72 Pound to René Taupin, May 1928. *Ibid.*, 218, letter 229.

73 *Poetry*, VIII.1 (April 1916), 38–43.

74 'Harold Monro', *The Criterion*, XI.45 (July 1932), 590.

75 Lionel Johnson, 'The Work of Mr. Pater', *The Fortnightly Review* (September 1894). Reprinted as 'Walter Pater. IV' in Lionel Johnson, *Post Liminium: Essays and Critical Papers*. Edited by Thomas Whittemore (London, 1911), 20.

76 De Régnier's poem is 'Promenade', first published in *La Renaissance Latine*, I.2 (15 June 1902), 167.

77 See G. Kahn, 'Mélopées: I, II, III, IV', *La Vogue*, 5 (1886), 162–63.

78 W. G. Tinckom-Fernandez, 'T. S. Eliot, "10"', *The Harvard Advocate*, 125 (December 1938), 8.

79 In *The Claims of French Poetry* (1907), 311.

80 'Verse', *The New Age*, VI.24 (14 April 1910), 567–69.

81 See Else Lasker-Schüler, 'Dirge', *Contemporary German Poetry*, 109. 'Eau-Forte' was published in *Some Imagist Poets* (1915), 63.

82 Bithell's work requires more investigation. He was a formidable scholar, and often a considerable translator, whose work between 1908 and 1914 has not been adequately evaluated. At that time he was in the provinces, a university lecturer in Manchester, and it is doubtful whether he had chance or inclination for ties with London and its literary circles.

83 F. S. Flint, 'Ripostes of Ezra Pound', *Poetry and Drama*, 1 (March 1913), 61.

84 Conversation Giuseppe Ungaretti and J. B. Harmer, Rome, August 1967.

85 'The History of Imagism', *op. cit.*, 70–71.

86 W. L. Schwartz, *The Imaginative Interpretation of the Far East in Modern French Literature 1800–1925* (Paris, 1927), 54. Outa (in English transliteration *uta*) is another name for the tanka.

87 'Introduction', *The Classical Poetry of the Japanese* (London, 1880), 18.

88 *Transactions of the Asiatic Society of Japan*, XXX.

89 As Part IV of *Japanese Poetry* (1911), 145–209.

90 *Ibid.*, 192.

91 *Ibid.*, 205.

92 *Ibid.*, vii.

93 *Ibid.*, no. 66; 216.

94 *B.E.F.E.O.* (1903), 723–29.

95 Schwartz, *op. cit.*, 160.

96 'Les Epigrammes Lyriques du Japon', *Les Lettres* (April and June–August 1906). Reprinted with some additions, in P-L. Couchoud, *Sages et Poètes d'Asie*, 2ème édition (Paris, 1916).

97 'Book of the Week. Recent Verse', *The New Age*, 722 (N.S. III.2) (11 July 1908), 212–13.

98 Couchoud, *Sages et Poètes d'Asie*, 124.

99 *Ibid.*, 106–07; 'Préface', 7 ff.

100 Quoted Earl Miner, *The Japanese Tradition in British and American Literature* (Princeton, New Jersey, 1958), 159.

101 Morikimi Megata, in *Richard Aldington: An Intimate Portrait*, 73.

102 *Nishikigi*. Translated from the Japanese of Motokiyo by Ernest Fenollosa. Edited by Ezra Pound. *Poetry*, IV.2 (May 1914), 34–48. See too 'The Classical Drama of Japan'. Edited from Ernest Fenollosa's manuscripts by Ezra Pound. *The Quarterly Review*, CCI.441 (October 1914), 450–77. 'Exile's Letter', the first of the poems in *Cathay* to be published, appeared in *Poetry*, V.6 (March 1915), 258–61.

103 The full note is reprinted in *Personae* (New York edn., 1956), 126.

104 Pound to John Quinn, 10 January 1917. *Letters of Ezra Pound*, 102, letter 115.

105 'Preface', *Some Imagist Poets 1916* (London 1916), viii.

106 *Japanese Poetry* (1911), 145 ff.

107 Ezra Pound, 'Vorticism', *op. cit.*, 467.

108 Ezra Pound, 'How I Began', *T.P.'s Weekly*, XXI.552 (6 June 1913), 707.

109 Ezra Pound, 'Vorticism', *op. cit.*, 467.

110 'Edward Wadsworth, Vorticist. An Authorised Appreciation', *The Egoist*, I.16 (15 August 1914), 306.

111 Quoted Earl Miner, *op. cit.*, 165. Amy Lowell, 'Foreword', *Pictures of the Floating World* (New York, 1919), vii–viii.

112 *The Complete Poetical Works of Amy Lowell*, 441–42 & 560.

113 Earl Miner, *op. cit.*, 174.

114 The British Museum copy is date-stamped 11 November 1912.

115 John Gould Fletcher, *Goblins and Pagodas* (Boston and New York, 1916), 'Preface', xvii.

116 J. G. Fletcher, *Japanese Prints* (Boston, 1918). 'Preface', 15–16.

117 Frank Livingstone Huntley, 'Zen and the Imagist Poets of Japan', *Comparative Literature*, IV.2 (Spring 1952), 170–78. He also mentioned Adelaide Crapsey, who died in 1914, but had no overt links with the Imagists. See her *Verse* (New York, 1915).

118 Unpublished letter Sir Herbert Read to G. S. Fraser, 21 January 1967.

119 See Charles Norman, *Ezra Pound*, 99–100.

120 See Alfred Kreymborg, *Troubadour*, 204–5.

121 Allen Upward, 'The Discarded Imagist', *The Egoist*, II.6 (1 June 1915), 98.

122 H. A. Giles, *A History of Chinese Literature* (1901), 'Preface', v. The first history of Japanese literature in a European language was

also the work of an Englishman. This was W. G. Aston's *A History of Japanese Literature* (London, 1899). Aston, like Giles, gave a selection of translations. He discussed the tanka and the 'haikai' (*ibid.*, 26–48 & 289–97).

123 On Pound and Fenollosa see Michael Reck, *Ezra Pound: A Close-up* (1968), 21–22, 119 & 166–75.

124 *Ibid.*, 119.

125 See A. C. Graham, 'The Translation of Chinese Poetry', *Poems of the Late T'ang* (1965), 32–36.

126 F. M. Ford, *The March of Literature*, 42; and see *ibid.*, 36–42 *passim*.

127 Pound to Iris Barry, June 1916. *Letters of Ezra Pound*, 82, letter 95.

128 Ernest Fenollosa, *The Chinese Written Character as a Medium for Poetry: An Ars Poetica*. With a Foreword and Notes by Ezra Pound (1936), 10–11; 12–14.

129 See his letter to John Quinn, 10 January 1917. *Letters of Ezra Pound*, 101, letter 115.

130 Ernest Fenollosa and Ezra Pound. 'The Chinese Written Character as a Medium for Poetry', *The Little Review*, VI.5–8 (September, October, November, December 1919), 62–64; 57–64; 55–60 & 68–72.

131 Ernest Fenollosa, *Epochs of Chinese and Japanese Art: An Outline History of East Asiatic Design*. Edited with a biographical notice of the author, by Mary McNeil Fenollosa (London, 1912), II, 6.

132 See T. S. Eliot, 'Classics in English', *Poetry*, IX.2 (November 1916), 101–2.

133 See Brigit Patmore, *My Friends When Young*, 66.

134 Note to 'Choruses from Iphigeneia in Aulis', *The Egoist*, II.11 (1 November 1915), 171.

135 H.D., *Choruses from Iphigeneia in Aulis* (London, 1915 edn.), prefatory note, 7.

136 Pound to W. C. Williams, 11 September 1920. *Letters of Ezra Pound*, 157, letter 170.

137 Richard Aldington, 'The Imagists', *Bruno Chap Books*, II (Special Series) 5 (1915), 70.

138 Who had turned Homer and Virgil into Augustan Englishmen. The Victorians put the Greeks into their own special brand of ornate drag.

139 H.D., quoted by Glenn Hughes, *op. cit.*, 110–11.

140 Benedicti Lampridii necnon Io. Bap. Amalthei, *Carmina* (Venice, 1550): Pars II. 'Io. Baptistae Amalthei. Eclogae, Elegiae, ac Epigrammata', 72 verso–74.

141 Nothing by Amaltheo (the more modern spelling is Amalteo) appears in the authoritative Austrian recension by P. A. Budik, *Leben und*

*Wirken des vorzüglichen lateinischen Dichter des XV–XVIII Jahrhunderts.* 3 Bände (Vienna, 1828).

142 See Alexander Pope's edition, *Selecta Poemata Italorum Qui Latine Scripserunt.* Cûra cujusdam Anonymi Anno 1684 congesta, iterum in lucem data, una cum aliorum Italorum operibus, Accurante A. Pope. (London, 1740), I, 26–28, 'Ecloga VII. Acon.' For a later edition see *Poemata Selecta Italorum,* Qui Seculo Decimo Sexto Latine Scripserunt, . . . (Oxford and London, 1808), 316–19, 'Acon'.

143 See A. Pope, *Selecta Poemata,* I, 23–25, 'Lycidas. Ecloga VI'.

144 For Amalteo's Italian poems see Il *Primo Volume Delle Rime Scelte Da Diversi Autori,* . . . (Venice, 1565), 201–19.

145 'The History of Imagism', *The Egoist, loc. cit.*

146 Ford Madox Hueffer, 'Thus to Revisit', vii, *The English Review* (March 1921), 218.

147 'Paris', *Poetry* (October 1913), 29.

148 In 'L'Influence Étrangère', his review of Adolphe Van Bever and Paul Léautaud's *Poètes d'Aujourd'hui.* Dated September 1900, and reprinted in *Le Problème du Style,* 157–68. See *ibid.,* 159.

149 On Hebrew poetics see H. Fuchs, *Universal Jewish Encyclopedia* (New York, 1942), VIII, 556–57; and Israel Davidson, *Jewish Encyclopedia* (New York, 1925), X, 93–100. The comments in the text relate to Classical Hebrew, by now almost a dead language. The Modern Hebrew of Israeli writers uses, as it wishes, rhyme, metre, and stanzaic formations.

V THE MOUNTAIN AND THE CLOUD

1 'The History of Imagism', *op. cit.,* 71.

2 T. S. Eliot, *On Poetry and Poets* (1957), 37.

3 T. E. Hulme, 'A Lecture on Modern Poetry', Roberts, 260.

4 'A Lecture on Modern Poetry', 258, 267–68.

5 Edward Storer, 'An Essay', *Mirrors of Illusion,* 107.

6 *Ibid.,* 110.

7 Arthur Symons, 'The Decadent Movement in Literature', *Harper's Monthly Magazine* (November 1893), 863.

8 It is mentioned in the manifesto of the Pléiade by Joachim du Bellay, who relates it to Petrarch. See L. E. Kastner, *A History of French Versification* (Oxford, 1903), 310–11.

9 'Notes and Announcements', *Poetry,* I.2 (November 1912), 65.

10 Discussed by C. M. Bowra, *Greek Lyric Poetry From Alcman to Simonides* (Oxford, 1936), 'Introduction', 1–15.

11 As first published, in *The Book of the Poets' Club* (1909), this poem

had an extra half-rhyme. The second line then read, 'And in the flash of gold heels on the pavement grey.' (*Ibid.*, 47.)

12 T. S. Eliot, 'Reflections on *Vers Libre*', *New Statesman* (3 March 1917), 519. Reprinted in *To Criticize the Critic*, 187.

13 'A Lecture on Modern Poetry', Roberts, 267.

14 *The Pisan Cantos* (London, 1949), 109.

15 Compare the reference in Ezra Pound, 'Vorticism', *The Fortnightly Review* (1 September 1914), 467, with the application of the concept to Homer in *Le Problème du Style* (1907), 88–90.

16 'German Chronicle', *Poetry and Drama*, 6 (June 1914), 228.

17 *Confessions of a Young Man* (London, 1888), 300–4.

18 'Reflections on Vers Libre', *New Statesman* (3 March 1917), 518–19. For the originals see S. Mallanmé, *Divagations* (Geneva, 1943), 15–20.

19 'A Lecture on Modern Poetry', Roberts, 268.

20 'Searchers after Reality. II. Haldane', *The New Age* (19 August 1909), 315–16. The Positivist view is already present in John Stuart Mill. See his 'Writings of Alfred de Vigny' (1838) in *Dissertations and Discussions in Mill's Essays on Literature and Society*. Edited J. B. Schneewind (New York, 1965), 236. The argument was developed in France by Taine and in England by F. Max Mueller, *Lectures on the Science of Language: Royal Institution, 1861–64* (2nd edn., London, 1889) and Herbert Spencer, *Philosophy of Style* (London, 1899), 27–34.

21 See Godfrey Lienhardt, *Social Anthropology* (London, 1964), 37.

22 Ezra Pound, 'Prologomena', *Poetry Review*, I.2 (February 1912), 76. The first phrase quoted was borrowed from Maurice Hewlett.

23 'A Few Don'ts By An Imagiste', *Poetry*, I.6 (March 1913), 201.

24 F. S. Flint, 'The Appreciation of Poetry', 17.

25 *Cantos LXXIV–LXXXIII: The Pisan Cantos* (1949), 116.

26 'Preface', *Some Imagist Poets: An Anthology* (Boston, New York and London, 1915), vi.

27 'Impressionism–Some Speculations. II', *Poetry*, II.6 (September 1913), 224. Reprinted, with some alterations, in the 'Preface' to Hueffer's *Collected Poems* [1914].

28 For Giles's translation, 'after Liu Ch'e', see H. A. Giles, *A History of Chinese Literature* (1901), 100. Pound's version, first published in *Des Imagistes*, is in *Personae* (New York, 1956 edn.), 108.

29 'German Chronicle', *Poetry and Drama* (June 1914), 228.

30 'An Essay', *Mirrors of Illusion*, 102–3.

31 'Prologomena', *Poetry Review* (February 1912), 73.

32 For a shrewd analysis of Pound's position, see Samuel Hynes, 'Pound and the Prose Tradition', *Yale Review*, LI.4 (June 1962), 532–46.

33 'Preface', *Some Imagist Poets* (1915), vii.

34 Ezra Pound, 'A Few Don'ts by an Imagiste', *Poetry* (March 1913), 201.

35 F. S. Flint, 'Verse Chronicle', *The Criterion*, XI.45 (July 1932), 686–87. Pound admitted as much in an unpublished letter: 'I made the word—on a Hulme basis—and carefully made a name that was not and never had been used in France.' Pound to Margaret Anderson, 17 November 1917. In Library of University of Wisconsin, Milwaukee.

36 F. S. Flint, 'Imagisme', *Poetry*, I.6 (March 1913), 199.

37 See Clarence DeWitt Thorpe, *The Aesthetic Theory of Thomas Hobbes* (New York, 2nd edn., 1964), *passim*.

38 See *Leviathan*, Pt I, Chs. 2–3, ed. A. R. Waller (Cambridge, 1904), 3–13.

39 '... nothing can appear more beautiful to me than the strength of those images which they condemn.' John Dryden, 'Defence of the Epilogue', *Essays of Dryden*, ed. W. P. Ker (Oxford, 1900), I, 186.

40 *The Task*, ii, lines, 290–91.

41 See De Quincey's comments on Hazlitt in his 'Essay on Charles Lamb', *North British Review* (1848). Reprinted in *The Collected Writings of Thomas De Quincey*, ed. David Masson (Edinburgh, 1889), V, 231–32.

42 Unsigned, 'Alfred Tennyson. An Essay. In Three Parts. Part I', *Oxford and Cambridge Magazine*, 1 (January 1856), 7.

43 George Brimley, 'Alfred Tennyson's Poems', *Cambridge Essays* (London, 1855), 229.

44 Unsigned, 'Recent Poems and Plays', *Oxford and Cambridge Magazine*, 12 (December, 1856), 718.

45 Quoted by F. S. Flint, 'The History of Imagism', *op. cit.*, 70.

46 'Searchers after Reality. II. Haldane', *The New Age* (19 August 1909), 315–16.

47 'A Lecture on Modern Poetry', Roberts, 266–67.

48 Ezra Pound, 'A Few Don'ts by an Imagiste', *Poetry* (March 1913), 200.

49 Ezra Pound, 'Vorticism', *The Fortnightly Review* (1 September 1914), 469.

50 'Affirmations—IV. As for Imagisme', *The New Age*, XVI.13 (28 January 1915), 349.

51 *Ibid.*, 350.

52 'Vorticism', *op. cit.*, 466.

53 *Ibid.*, 461–62.

54 The triple distinction phanopoeia, melopoeia, and logopoeia was first elaborated in Pound's article, 'A List of Books', *The Little Review* IV.11 (March 1918), 57. For an explanation of phanopoeia,

see his remarks 'On Criticism in General', *The Criterion*, I.2 (January 1923), 152.

55 'On Criticism in General', *op. cit.*, 152, 146.
56 'As for Imagisme', *op. cit.*, 349.
57 See T. E. Hulme, review of Tancrède de Visan, *The New Age* (24 August 1911), 400.
58 This view was held, with differing emphases, by Locke, Berkeley and David Hume. For a comment see John Holloway, *Language and Intelligence* (1955), especially Ch. I, 'Ideas and Images', 1–15 *passim*.
59 Étienne Souriau, *La Poésie Française et la Peinture* (London, 1966), 29.
60 T. E. Hulme, *The New Age* (24 August 1911), 400.
61 On the psychology of perception see David Wechsler, *The Range of Human Capacities* (New York, 1935), 135 & 134 fn.
62 F. S. Flint, 'The Appreciation of Poetry', 2.
63 'Mr. Hueffer and the Prose Tradition in Verse', *Poetry*, IV.3 (June 1914), 120.
64 A view substantiated by native Chinese speakers, in particular Mr C. Chan of Hong Kong. Also by William Empson: conversation, 26 July 1969.
65 More precisely, Middle Egyptian, the language of the Middle Kingdom.
66 For an admirable exposition of this see Alan Gardiner, *Egyptian Grammar* (Oxford, 1950), 1–29 & 428–33.
67 *Ibid.*, 8 fn.
68 T. E. Hulme, 'A Lecture on Modern Poetry', Roberts, 265.
69 By *The Daily Chronicle*. Quoted in Edward Storer, *The Ballad of the Mad Bird and Other Poems* (London, 1909), [42].
70 Lionel Johnson. Written *c.* 1895; but first published, edited by Katharine Tynan, in *The Dublin Review* CXLI.283 (October 1907), 337. Quoted in Pound's Preface to *Poetical Works of Lionel Johnson* (London, 1915), xi–xii. Reprinted in 'Lionel Johnson', *Literary Essays of Ezra Pound*, edited with an Introduction by T. S. Eliot (1954), 365.
71 Ford Madox Ford, *Joseph Conrad: A Personal Reminiscence* (London and Boston, 1924), 181–82.
72 'Impressionism—Some Speculations', *Poetry*, II.5 (August 1913), 178.
73 In his review of *High Germany*. 'The Book of the Month', *Poetry Review*, I.3 (March 1912), 133.
74 Pound to F. S. Flint, 30 January 1921. Unpublished letter. University of Texas Collection.
75 Richard Aldington, 'Modern Poetry and the Imagists', *The Egoist*, I.11 (1 June 1914), 203.

76 For a contrary opinion, argued persistently but unconvincingly, see Allan Rodway, *The Romantic Conflict* (London, 1963), ix–x.

77 Edmund Wilson, 'Wallace Stevens and E. E. Cummings', *The Shores of Light: A Literary Chronicle of the Twenties and Thirties* (New York, 1952), 54.

78 Michael Fordham, 'Reflections on Image and Symbol', *New Developments in Analytical Psychology* (London, 1957), 51–52.

79 See his 'Contemporary French Poetry', *Poetry Review*, I.8 (August 1912), 355 ff. And compare his 'French Chronicle', *Poetry and Drama*, II.7 (September 1914), 303.

80 This was first published, posthumously, in Hulme's *Speculations*, 111–40.

81 'Romanticism and Classicism', *Speculations*, 113. Herbert Read thought this was the manuscript of an essay. It is more likely the draft of a lecture, perhaps the lecture advertised in *Poetry Review*, I.7 (July 1912), ii: '*Poetry Review* Lectures: on July 15 at 9 p.m. Mr. T. E. Hulme will lecture on 'The New Philosophy of Art as Illustrated in Poetry' at Clifford Inn Hall, Fleet Street, E.C.' The manuscript from which Herbert Read assembled it is lost, as are all the documents from which he constructed *Speculations*. See *ibid.*, 125 & 133.

82 *Ibid.*, 114.

83 *Ibid.*, 119–20.

84 *Ibid.*, 134.

85 Phyllis Bottome, in *This Week* (2 December 1935). Expanded in her *From the Life* (London, 1944), 72.

86 T. E. Hulme, 'Romanticism and Classicism', *Speculations*, 125.

87 Letter Ezra Pound to Louis Untermeyer. *EP to LU* (Bloomington, Ind., 1963), 17.

88 Wyndham Lewis, 'Introduction', *Wyndham Lewis and Vorticism* (Tate Gallery Catalogue, 1956), 4.

89 Lewis, *loc. cit.*

90 Apollinaire's manifesto is dated 20 June 1913. It is reprinted in *La Cultura italiana del'900 attraverso le riviste*, vol. 4º *Lacerba La Voce (1914–1916)*. A cura di Gianni Scalia (Turin, 1961), 192–93.

91 The first mention I have found is in *The Tramp*, I (August 1910), 487–88, where Marinetti's initial manifesto in *Le Figaro* is translated and discussed by an anonymous writer (Flint?).

92 See *Exhibition of Works by the Italian Futurist Painters*, The Sackville Gallery (1912). Marinetti's 'Initial Manifesto of Futurism' is translated in this catalogue: see 3–6 & 8. Among the painters was Umberto Boccioni, an artist of great ability, killed in the war.

93 R. F. Smalley, 'Futurism and the Futurists', *The British Review*

(August 1914), 224. '. . . two principal and one or two minor exhibitions of Futurist art in Bond Street.'

94 *Manifestes Futuristes, 1909–23* (Milano: Movimento futurista, N.D.) 'Vital English Art', *Futurist Manifesto*, N.P.

95 *Poetry and Drama*, I.3 (September 1913), 262–64; 291–305; 319–26; I.4 (December 1913), 389–91.

96 Ezra Pound, 'Vorticism', *The Fortnightly Review* (September 1914), 461–70.

97 Unpublished letter 7 August 1914. Collection of the University of Chicago.

98 See his 'The London Group 1915 (March),' *Blast*, 2 (July 1915), 97–99.

99 See T. E. Hulme, 'Modern Art. III. The London Group', *The New Age*, XIV.21 (26 March 1914), 661.

100 See Wyndham Lewis, 'A Review of Contemporary Art', *Blast* 2, 38–42.

101 'Vorticism', *op. cit.*, 464.

102 Quoted in Donald Hall, 'Ezra Pound: An Interview', *Paris Review*, 28 (Summer-Fall 1962), 30.

103 'Vorticism', *loc. cit.*, 471. Pound's Vorticist terminology may owe something to Hulme. See T. E. Hulme, 'Modern Art. II. A Preface Note and Neo-Realism', *The New Age*, XIV.15 (12 February 1914), 467–69; and 'Modern Art. III. The London Group', *The New Age*, XIV.21 (26 March 1914), 661–62.

104 The phrase is Shelley's. He called his plays 'a series of lyric pictures'. *The Poetical Works of Percy Bysshe Shelley*, edited by Edward Dowden (London and New York, 1890), 432.

105 'Vorticism', *op. cit.*, 471 fn.

106 Private communication: Miss Kate Lechmere to author.

107 Its 'official' date of publication, 20 June 1914, represented aspiration rather than fact.

108 In his *The New Age under Orage* (Manchester and New York, 1967), 189.

109 R. F. Smalley, 'Futurism and the Futurists', *The British Review* (August 1914), 224.

110 Quoted in 'The Later Yeats', *Poetry*, IV.2 (May 1914), 67, 65. 'The Magi' was published in *Responsibilities* (Churchtown, Dundrum, 1914), following its first printing in the *New Statesman* (9 May 1914). Reprinted in *The Collected Poems of W. B. Yeats* (London, 1950), 141.

111 D. W. Theobald, *The Concept of Energy* (1966), 22. Dr Theobald is a physicist.

112 Yeats to George Russell (Æ), *c.* May 1900. *The Letters of W. B. Yeats* (1954), 343.

113 Edward Storer, 'An Essay', *Mirrors of Illusion*, 110.

VI THE PUNISHED GROUND

1 Arthur Symons, *Aubrey Beardsley*. New Edition Revised & Enlarged (London, 1905), 17.
2 Ford Madox Hueffer, 'Thus to Revisit', vi, *The English Review*, 32 (February 1921), 116.
3 William Burroughs, *The Naked Lunch*. The Traveller's Companion Series, No. 76 (Paris, 1959), 216.
4 Ernest Hemingway, *In Our Time* (London, 1926), 71.
5 Richard Aldington to F. S. Flint. Unpublished letter, 20 September 1922. In Collection of Humanities Research Center, Austin, Texas.
6 Emyr Humphreys, radio broadcast. Quoted by Hugh MacDiarmid, 'The Return of the Long Poem', in *Ezra Pound : Perspectives*, 108.
7 Aldous Huxley to Julian Huxley, 3 August 1917. *Letters of Aldous Huxley*. Edited by Grover Smith (London, 1969), 132.
8 Baker Brownell, 'Post-Martial Emotion', *Poetry* XIX.3 (December 1921), 162–65.
9 Jim Morrison, *The Lords and the New Creatures* (New York, 1970), 99.

# Select Bibliography

THE WRITINGS OF THE IMAGISTS
A. PUBLISHED WORKS

Aldington, Richard.
'Reviews', *The Egoist*, I.13 (1 July 1914).
'Free verse in England', *The Egoist*, I.17 (1 Sept. 1914).
'The Imagists', *Bruno Chap Books*, II (Special Series) 5, 1915.
*Images 1910–1915*. London [1915].
*Images of War*. London [1919].
*A Fool i' the Forest: a Phantasmagoria*. London, 1925.
*Rémy de Gourmont. A Modern Man of Letters*. University of Washington Chapbooks, No. 13. Seattle, Wash., 1928.
*Rémy de Gourmont. Selections from All His Works*. New York, 1929; London, 1932.
*Collected Poems 1915–1923*. New York, 1928; London, 1929; 1933.
*A Dream in the Luxembourg* (American title *Love and the Luxembourg*). New York and London, 1930.
*The Poems of Richard Aldington*. Garden City, N.Y., 1934.
*Life for Life's Sake: a Book of Reminiscences*. New York, 1941; London, 1968.
*Poetry of the English-speaking World*. Chosen and edited by Richard Aldington. London and Toronto, 1947.
*The Complete Poems*. London, 1948.

Campbell, Joseph.
*The Rushlight*. Dublin, 1906.
*The Mountainy Singer*. Dublin, 1909.
*Irishry*. Dublin, 1913.
*Earth of Cualann*. Dublin and London, 1917.
*The Poems of Joseph Campbell*. Edited with an Introduction by Austin Clarke. Dublin, 1963.

Doolittle, Hilda [H.D.].
'Notes to Choruses from Iphigeneia in Aulis', *The Egoist*, II.11 (1 Nov. 1915).
*Choruses from Iphigeneia in Aulis*. Poets' Translation Series, London, 1915.
*Sea Garden*. London and Boston, 1916.

Review of J. G. Fletcher *Goblins and Pagodas*, *The Egoist*, III.12 (Dec. 1916).
*Hymen*. London and New York, 1921.
*Collected Poems of H.D.* New York, 1925; sixth printing 1940.
*The Usual Star*. London and Dijon, 1930.
*The Walls Do Not Fall*. London, 1944.
*Tribute to Freud*. New York, 1956; South Hinksey, 1971.
*Selected Poems*. New York and London, 1957.
*Bid Me To Live*. New York, 1960.

Fletcher, John Gould.
*The Dominant City*. London, 1913.
*Irradiations: Sand and Spray*. Boston, New York and London, 1915.
*Goblins and Pagodas*. Boston and New York, 1916; London, 1918.
*Japanese Prints*. Boston, 1918.
'Some Contemporary American Poets', *The Chapbook*. A Monthly Miscellany. Nov. 1920.
*Life is My Song*. New York, 1937.
*Selected Poems*. New York, 1938.

Flint, F. S.
'Recent Verse', *The New Age*, IV.5 (26 Nov. 1908).
*In the Net of the Stars*. London, 1909.
'Book of the Week. Recent Verse', *The New Age*, IV.16 (11 Feb. 1909).
Review of Émile Verhaeren, *Les Heures Claires*, *The New Age*, V.14 (5 Aug. 1909).
Review of *Contemporary German Poetry* (Ed. Jethro Bithell), *The New Age*, VI.24 (14 April 1910).
'Moods—I and II', *The Tramp*, II (Nov. 1910).
'Contemporary French Poetry', *Poetry Review*, I.8 (Aug. 1912).
'Imagisme', *Poetry*, I.6 (March 1913).
'The History of Imagism', *The Egoist*, II.5 (1 May 1915).
*Cadences*, London [1915].
*Otherworld: Cadences*. London, 1920.
'Verse Chronicle', *The Criterion*, XI.45 (July 1932).
'The Appreciation of Poetry'. (Unpublished typescript of lecture, Southport 1940.) Humanities Research Center, University of Texas.

Hueffer [later *Ford*], Ford Madox.
*Songs from London*. London, 1910.
*The Critical Attitude*. London, 1911.
'Christina Rossetti', *The Fortnightly Review*, LXXXIX N.S. 531 (March 1911).
'Impressionism—Some Speculations', *Poetry*, II.5–6 (Aug.–Sept. 1913).
*Collected Poems*. London, 1914 [1913].

'Literary Portraits—XVI: Mr. Arthur Symons and *The Knave of Hearts*', *The Outlook*, XXXII (27 Dec. 1913).

'Literary Portraits—XXXV: Les Jeunes and "Des Imagistes" ', *The Outlook*, XXXIII (9 May 1914).

'A Jubilee', *The Outlook*, XXXVI (10 July 1915).

*Antwerp*. With decorations by Wyndham Lewis. London, 1915.

*On Heaven and Poems Written on Active Service*. London and New York, 1918.

'Thus to Revisit', *The English Review*, XXXII (Feb. and March 1921).

*Joseph Conrad: a Personal Reminiscence*. London and Boston, 1924.

*Collected Poems*. New York, 1936.

*The March of Literature*. New York, 1938; London, 1939.

*Buckshee* [Last poems]. With introductions by Robert Lowell and Kenneth Rexroth. Cambridge, Mass., 1966.

Hulme, T. E.

'Belated Romanticism', *The New Age*, IV.17 (18 Feb. 1909).

'Bergson and Bax', *The New Age*, V.12 (22 July 1909).

'Searchers after Reality. II. Haldane', *The New Age*, V.17 (19 Aug. 1909).

'Searchers after Reality. III. De Gaultier', *The New Age*, VI.5 (2 Dec. 1909).

Review of Tancrède de Visan, *L'Attitude du Lyrisme Contemporain*, *The New Age*, IX.17 (24 Aug. 1911).

'The Complete Poetical Works of T. E. Hulme', *The New Age*, X.13 (25 January 1912).

'Mr. Epstein and the Critics', *The New Age*, XIV.8 (25 Dec. 1913).

'Modern Art II. A Preface Note and Neo-Realism', *The New Age*, XV.15 (12 Feb. 1914).

'Modern Art. III. The London Group', *The New Age*, XIV.21 (26 March 1914).

'German Chronicle', *Poetry and Drama*, II.6 (June 1914).

*Speculations*. Ed. Herbert Read. London and New York, 1924.

'Notes on Language and Style', ed. Herbert Read, *The Criterion*, III.12 (July 1925).

*Language and Style*. Manuscript in the collection of the University of Keele. Incomplete, with some errors, appears as Appendix III, 'Notes on Language and Style', in Michael Roberts, *T. E. Hulme*, London, 1938.

'A Lecture on Modern Poetry'. In Michael Roberts, *T. E. Hulme*, London, 1938, Appendix II.

*Further Speculations*. Ed. Sam Hynes. Minneapolis, Minn. [1955]; rev. edn. Lincoln, Neb., 1962.

'The Poetical Works of T. E. Hulme'. In Alun R. Jones, *The Life and Opinions of T. E. Hulme* (London, 1960), Pt. II.

*Imagist Anthology* 1930. With an introduction by Ford Madox Ford. London, 1930.

Lawrence, D. H.
*Love Poems and Others*. London and New York, 1913.
*Amores*. London and New York, 1916
*Look! We Have Come Through!* London, 1917; New York, 1918.
*New Poems*. London, 1918; New York, 1920.
*Birds, Beasts and Flowers*. New York and London, 1923.
*Studies in Classic American Literature*. New York, 1923; another edition London, 1924.
*The Collected Poems of D. H. Lawrence*. 2 vols. London, 1928; New York, 1929.
*The Collected Letters of D. H. Lawrence*. Ed. Harry T. Moore. 2 vols. New York and London, 1962.
*The Complete Poems of D. H. Lawrence*. Collected and edited with an Introduction and notes by Vivian da Sola Pinto and Warren Roberts. 2 vols. London and New York, 1964.

Lowell, Amy.
*A Dome of Many-Coloured Glass*. Boston and New York, 1912.
*Sword Blades and Poppy Seeds*. New York and London, 1914.
*Six French Poets: Studies in Contemporary Literature*. New York, 1915.
*Men, Women and Ghosts*. New York, 1916.
*Tendencies in Modern American Poetry*. New York, 1917.
*Can Grande's Castle*. New York, 1918; Oxford, 1920.
*Pictures of the Floating World*. New York, 1919.
*Fir-Flower Tablets*. Boston, 1921; London, 1922.
*The Complete Poetical Works of Amy Lowell*. Boston [1955].

Pound, Ezra [Loomis].
*A Lume Spento*. Venice, 1908.
*A Quinzaine for this Yule*. London, 1908.
*Personae*. London, 1909.
*Exultations*. London, 1909.
*Canzoni*. London, 1911.
'I Gather the Limbs of Osiris', *The New Age*, X.5–17 30. (Nov. 1911–22 Feb. 1912).
'Prologomena', *Poetry Review*, I.2 (Feb. 1912).
*Patria Mia*. Chicago, 1950; London, 1962. First published in *The New Age* (5 Sept.–14 Nov. 1912).
*Ripostes*. London, 1912; Boston, 1913.
'Status Rerum', *Poetry*, I.4 (Jan. 1913).
'A Few Don'ts by an Imagiste', *Poetry*, I.6 (March 1913).

'The Approach to Paris. I–VII', *The New Age*, XIII.19–25 (4 Sep.-16 Oct. 1913).

[Pound, Ezra (ed.)] *Des Imagistes*. New York and London, 1914.

'Edward Wadsworth, Vorticist. An Authorised Appreciation', *The Egoist*, I.16 (15 Aug. 1914).

'Vorticism', *The Fortnightly Review*, XCVI N.S. 573 (1 Sept. 1914).

'The Classical Drama of Japan.' Edited from Ernest Fenollosa's manuscripts. *The Quarterly Review*, CCI.441 (Oct. 1914).

'Affirmations'—IV. As for Imagisme'. *The New Age*, XVI.13 (28 Jan. 1915).

*Cathay*. London, 1915.

(Ed.) *Catholic Anthology: 1914–1915*. London, 1915.

'Status Rerum—the Second', *Poetry*, VIII.1 (Apr. 1916).

*Lustra*. London, 1916.

*Gaudier-Brzeska: A Memoir*. London and New York, 1916.

*Pavannes and Divisions*. New York, 1918.

'A List of Books', *The Little Review*, IV.11 (March 1918).

*Quia Pauper Amavi*. London, 1919.

*Hugh Selwyn Mauberley*. London, 1920.

*Umbra: The Early Poems of Ezra Pound*. London, 1920.

'On Criticism in General', *The Criterion*, I.2 (Jan. 1923).

'Harold Monro', *The Criterion*, XI.45 (July 1932).

(Ed.) *Profile: An Anthology Collected in MCMXXXI*. Milan, 1932.

'This Hulme Business', *The Townsman*, II.5 (Jan. 1939).

*Guide to Kulchur*. London and New York, 1938; new edn., 1952.

'Ford Madox (Hueffer) Ford: Obit.' *Nineteenth Century and After*, CXXVI.750 (Aug. 1939).

*The Pisan Cantos*. New York, 1948; London, 1949.

*The Letters of Ezra Pound 1907–1941*. Ed. D. D. Paige, with a Preface by Mark van Doren. New York, 1950; London, 1971. Another edn. London, 1951.

*Literary Essays of Ezra Pound*. Ed. with an Introduction by T. S. Eliot. London, 1954.

*Personae: the Collected Poems of Ezra Pound*. New York, 1956.

'National Culture: A Manifesto—1938', in *Impact: Essays on Ignorance and the Decline of American Civilization*. Ed. Noel Stock. Chicago, 1960.

*EP to LU: Nine Letters. . . .* Ed. J. A. Robbins. Bloomington, Ind., 1963.

*The Cantos of Ezra Pound*. London, 1964; New York, 1965.

*A Lume Spento and Other Early Poems*. London and New York, 1965.

*Collected Shorter Poems*. 2nd edn. London, 1968.

*Some Imagist Poets: An Anthology*. Boston, New York and London, 1915, 1916, 1917.

Storer, Edward [Augustine].
*Inclinations*. London [Nov. 1907].
*Mirrors of Illusion*. London [1908].
*The Ballad of the Mad Bird and Other Poems*. London, 1909.
*Narcissus*. London, 1913.
Review of *Some Imagist Poets*, *The British Review*, XI.3 (Sept. 1915).
*Terra Italica*. London, 1920.
'Grotesques of Pirandello', *Forum* (Oct. 1921).
*I've Quite Forgotten Lucy*. London, 1932.


B. UNPUBLISHED MANUSCRIPTS

Doolittle, Hilda [H.D.].
Letters. Harriet Monroe Collection, Modern Poetry Library, University
of Chicago.

Fletcher, John Gould.
Letters, etc. Harriet Monroe Collection, University of Chicago.

Flint, F. S.
Letters, mss. and notebooks, etc. Humanities Research Center, University
of Texas.

Hulme, T. E.
Mss. collections. University of Keele.
Letters to F. S. Flint. Humanities Research Center, University of Texas.

Pound, Ezra.
Letters. Harriet Monroe Collection, University of Chicago.
Letters. Yale University Library.
Letters to William Carlos Williams. Lockwood Memorial Library,
State University of New York, Buffalo.
Letters to F. S. Flint. Humanities Research Center, University of Texas.

Storer, Edward.
Letters to F. S. Flint. Humanities Research Center, University of Texas.

OTHER WORKS
A. BOOKS AND PAMPHLETS.

Anderson, Margaret. *My Thirty Years' War*. New York, 1930.
Annand, J. A. 'The Image and Precision of Meaning in Poetry: Theory
and Practice, 1789–1834'. B.Litt. Thesis. Oxford, 1951.
Archer, William. *Poets of the Younger Generation*. London and New York,
1902.
Beaunier, André. *La Poésie Nouvelle*. 3rd edn. Paris, 1902.

224

Bergonzi, Bernard. *Heroes' Twilight*. London, 1965.

Bergson, H. L. *An Introduction to Metaphysics*. Trs. T. E. Hulme. London, 1913.

Bianchi, Ruggero. *La Poetica dell'Imagismo*. Milan, 1965.

Bithell, Jethro. *Contemporary German Poetry*. Trs. and with introduction by Jethro Bithell. London, 1909.

Bithell, Jethro. *Contemporary Belgian Poetry*. Trs. and with introduction by Jethro Bithell. London, 1911.

Bithell, Jethro. *Contemporary French Poetry*. Trs. and with introduction by Jethro Bithell. London, 1912.

Bogan, Louise. *Achievement in American Poetry, 1900–1950*. Chicago, 1951.

*The Book* [*The Second Book, the Third Book*] *of the Poets' Club*. London, 1909, 1911, 1913.

Brooks, Cleanth. *Modern Poetry and the Tradition*. Chapel Hill, 1939; London, 1948.

Bryher [A. W. Ellerman]. *The Heart to Artemis: A Writer's Memoirs*. London, 1963.

Chamberlain, Basil Hall. *The Classical Poetry of the Japanese*. London, 1880. Revised and enlarged edn. (as *Japanese Poetry*). London, 1911.

Chisolm, L. W. *Fenollosa: the Far East and American Culture*. New Haven, Conn. and London, 1963.

Clough, Rosa T. *Futurism: The Story of a Modern Art Movement. A New Appraisal*. New York, 1961.

Coffman, Stanley K. Jr. *Imagism: A Chapter for the History of Modern Poetry*. Norman, Okla., 1951.

Coleridge, Samuel Taylor. *Biographia Literaria*. Ed. Arthur Symons, London, 1906.

Colum, Padraic. *Wild Earth*. Dublin, 1907.

Colum, Padraic. *Wild Earth and Other Poems*. Dublin, 1916.

Colum, Padraic. *Poems*. London, 1932.

Crane, Stephen. *The Collected Poems of Stephen Crane*. Ed. Wilson Follett. New York, London, 1930; 1966.

Davis, Earle R. *Vision Fugitive: Ezra Pound and Economics*. Lawrence, Kans. and London, 1968.

de Bosschère, Jean. *The Closed Door*. Trs. F. S. Flint. London and New York, 1917.

Dédéyan, Charles. *Rilke et la France*. 3 vols. Paris, 1960, 1961, 1963.

de Gourmont, Rémy. *Le Latin Mystique*. Préface de J.-K. Huysmans. 2nd edn. Paris, 1892.

de Gourmont, Rémy. *La Culture des Idées*. 3rd edn. Paris, 1900.

de Gourmont, Rémy. *Le Problème du style*. 3rd edn. Paris, 1902; new edn. 1907.

de Nagy, N. C. *The Poetry of Ezra Pound: the Pre-Imagist Stage*. Cooper Monographs 4 (Berne, 1960).

de Nagy, N. C. *Ezra Pound's Poetics and Literary Tradition: the Critical Decade*. Cooper Monographs 11 (Berne, 1966).

de Régnier, Henri. *La Sandale Ailée: 1903–1905*. 4th edn. Paris, 1906.

de Souza, R. *Le Rythme Poétique: Questions de Métrique*. Paris, 1892.

de Souza, R. *Du Rythme en Français*. Paris, 1912.

Dickinson, Emily. *Poems*. Ed. Mabel Loomis Todd and T. W. Higginson. 3 vols. Boston, 1890–96.

Dowson, Ernest. *Decorations*. London, 1899.

Duhamel, Georges, and Vildrac, Charles. *Notes sur la Technique Poétique*. Paris, 1910.

Eliot, T. S. *On Poetry and Poets*. London and New York, 1957.

Eliot, T. S. *To Criticize the Critic*. London and New York, 1965.

Espey, John J. *Ezra Pound's Mauberley. A Study in Composition*. Berkeley and London, 1955.

Farr, Florence. *The Music of Speech*. London, 1909.

Farr, Florence. *The Solemnization of Jacklin*. London, 1912.

Fenollosa, Ernest. *Epochs of Chinese and Japanese Art: An Outline History of East Asiatic Design*. Ed. with a biographical notice by Mary McNeil Fenollosa. 2 vols. New York, 1911; London, 1912.

Fenollosa, Ernest. *The Chinese Written Character as a Medium for Poetry: an Ars Poetica*. With a Foreword and Notes by Ezra Pound. London and New York, 1936; San Francisco, 1964.

Gallup, Donald. *A Bibliography of Ezra Pound*. London, 1963, 1969.

Garnett, David. *The Golden Echo*. London, 1953.

Giles, H. A. *Gems of Chinese Literature*. London and Shanghai, 1884.

Giles, H. A. *A History of Chinese Literature*. London, 1901.

Goldring, Douglas. *South Lodge*. London, 1943.

Graham, A. C. *Poems of the Late T'ang*. Harmondsworth, 1965.

Grant, Joy. *Harold Monro and the Poetry Bookshop*. London, 1967.

Gregory, Horace. *Amy Lowell: Portrait of the Poet in Her Time*. New York, 1958.

Greene, E. J. H. *T. S. Eliot et la France*. Paris, 1951.

Guyau, M. *Les Problèmes de l'Esthétique Contemporaine*. Paris, 1884.

Hardy, Barbara G. 'Coleridge's Theory of Communication.' M.A. thesis. London, 1949.

Harvey, David Dow. *Ford Madox Ford 1873–1939: A Bibliography of Works and Criticism*. Princeton, N.J., 1962.

Hassall, Christopher. *Rupert Brooke: A Biography*. London, 1964.

Henley, W. E. *Poems: Works* I & II. London, 1908.

Hoffman, Frederic J. and Harry T. Moore. *The Achievement of D. H. Lawrence*. Norman, Okla. 1953.

Holloway, John. *Language and Intelligence*. London, 1955.

Hughes, Glenn. *Imagism and the Imagists*. Stanford, 1931.

Hunt, J. H. Leigh. Imagination and Fancy. London, 1846; rptd. 1907.

Hunt, Violet. *The Flurried Years* (American title *I Have This to Say*). London and New York, 1926.

Jackson, Thomas H. *The Early Poetry of Ezra Pound*. Cambridge, Mass., 1968.

Jones, Alun R. *The Life and Opinions of T. E. Hulme*. London, 1960.

Jones, Peter (ed.) *Imagist Poetry*. Harmondsworth, 1972.

Jung, C. G. *Synchronizität als ein Prinzip akausaler Zusammenhänge. Studien aus dem C.G. Jung-Institut. IV.* Zürich, 1952.

Kahn, Gustave. *Premiers poèmes (Avec une Préface sur le vers libre)*. Paris, 1897.

Kenner, Hugh. *The Invisible Poet: T. S. Eliot.* New York, 1959; London, 1960.

Kenner, Hugh. *The Pound Era*. Berkeley, 1971; London, 1972.

Kermode, Frank. *Romantic Image*. London, 1957.

Kershaw, Alister and Frédéric-Jacques Temple, ed. *Richard Aldington: An Intimate Portrait*. Carbondale and Edwardsville, Ill., 1965.

Kreymborg, Alfred. *Troubadour*. New York, 1925.

Lewis, [P.] Wyndham. 'The Enemy of the Stars', *Blast*, I (1914). Rev. edn. London, 1932.

Liu, James J. Y. *The Art of Chinese Poetry*. London, 1962.

Mallarmé, S. 'Un coup de Dès', *Cosmopolis*, VI.17 (1897). Definitive text: *Un Coup de Dès Jamais N'abolira Le Hasard*. Paris, 1914.

*Manifestes Futuristes, 1909–23*. Milan, n.d.

Marinetti, F. T. 'Initial Manifesto of Futurism' in *Exhibition of Works by the Italian Futurist Painters*. The Sackville Gallery, London, 1912.

Martin, Marianne W. *Futurist Art and Theory 1909–1915*. Oxford, 1968.

Martin, Wallace. *The New Age under Orage*. Manchester and New York, 1967.

Merrill, Stuart. *Pastels in Prose*. New York, 1890.

Miner, Earl. *The Japanese Tradition in British and American Literature*. Princeton, N.J., 1958.

Monroe, Harriet and Alice Corbin Henderson, ed. *The New Poetry*. New York, 1917.

Monroe, Harriet. *A Poet's Life: Seventy Years in a Changing World*. New York, 1938.

Mullins, Eustace. *This Difficult Individual, Ezra Pound*. New York, 1961.

Nevinson, C. R. W. *Paint and Prejudice*. London, 1937.

Norman, Charles. *Ezra Pound*. New York, 1960; rev. edn. London, 1969.

Pater, Walter. *Walter Pater: Selected Works*. ed. Richard Aldington. London and New York, 1948.

Patmore, Brigit. *My Friends When Young: The Memoirs of Brigit Patmore*. Ed. with an Introduction by Derek Patmore. London, 1968.

Pattee, Fred Lewis. *A History of American Literature since 1870*. New York, 1915; rptd. 1968.

Pratt, William C. *The Imagist Poem: modern poetry in miniature*. Edited and with an Introduction by William Pratt. New York, 1963.

Read, Herbert. *Collected Poems*. London and New York, 1966.

Reck, Michael. *Ezra Pound: A Close-Up*. New York, 1967; London, 1968.

Rhys, Ernest. *Everyman Remembers*. London, 1931.

Ribot, T. *Essai sur l'Imagination Créatrice*. Paris, 1900.

Roberts, Michael. *Critique of Poetry*. London, 1934.

Roberts, Michael. *T. E. Hulme*. London, 1938.

Ross, Robert H. *The Georgian Revolt, 1910–1922. Rise and fall of a poetic ideal*. Carbondale and Edwardsville, Ill., 1965; London, 1967.

Sagar, Keith. *The Art of D. H. Lawrence*. Cambridge, 1966.

Schneidau, Herbert N. *Ezra Pound: The Image and the Real*. Baton Rouge, La, 1969.

Schwartz, W. L. *The Imaginative Interpretation of the Far East in Modern French Literature 1800–1925*. Paris, 1927.

Starkie, Enid. *From Gautier to Eliot. The Influence of France on English Literature, 1851–1939*. London, 1960.

Stead, C. K. *The New Poetic: Yeats to Eliot*. London, 1964; New York, 1966.

Stock, Noel, ed. *Ezra Pound: Perspectives*. Chicago, 1965.

Stock, Noel. *The Life of Ezra Pound*. London, 1970.

Sullivan, J. P. *Ezra Pound and Sextus Propertius: A Study in Creative Translation*. Austin, Tex., 1964; London, 1965.

Swann, Thomas Burnett. *The Classical World of H.D.* Lincoln, Neb., 1962.

Symons, Arthur. *Poems*. 2 vols. London, 1901.

Symons, Arthur. *The Symbolist Movement in Literature*. London, 1899. Rev. edn. London, 1908.

Taupin, René. *L'Influence du Symbolisme Français sur la Poésie Américaine de 1910 à 1920*. Paris, 1929.

Ueda, Makoto. *Zeami, Bashō, Yeats, Pound. A Study in Japanese and English Poetics*. The Hague, 1965.

Van Bever, Adolphe and Paul Léautaud. *Poètes d'Aujourd'hui: Morceaux Choisis*. 2 vols. Paris, 1900.

Verhaeren, Émile. *The Love Poems of Émile Verhaeren*. Trs. F. S. Flint. London and Boston, 1916.

Vildrac, Charles. *Le Verslibrisme. Étude critique sur la forme poétique irrégulière*. Ermont, Seine-et-Oise, 1902.

Vildrac, Charles. *Images et mirages*. Paris, 1907.

Wagner, Geoffrey. *Wyndham Lewis: a Portrait of the Artist as the Enemy.* London and New Haven, 1957.

Wees, William C. *Vorticism and the English avant-garde.* Toronto and Manchester, 1972.

Whitman, Walt. *Poems.* Selected and ed. by W. M. Rossetti. London, 1868.

Willey, Basil. *Coleridge on Imagination and Fancy.* Wharton Lecture, 1946.

Wilson, Edmund. *Axel's Castle: A Study in the Imaginative Literature of 1870–1930.* New York, 1931; 1961.

Witemeyer, Hugh H. *The Poetry of Ezra Pound: forms and renewal, 1908–1920.* Berkeley and Los Angeles, 1969.

Yeats, W. B. *Autobiographies.* London, 1926.

Yeats, W. B. *The Letters of W. B. Yeats.* Ed. Allan Wade. London and New York, 1954.

Yip, Wai-lim. *Ezra Pound's Cathay.* Princeton, N.J., 1969.

Ziff, Larzer. *The American 1890s.* New York, 1966; London, 1967.


B. ARTICLES AND ESSAYS.

'A Mock Funeral. An Undergrad "Sent Down"', *The Tatler*, XI.144 (30 March 1904).

Abercrombie, Lascelles. 'Poetry', *The Blue Review*, I (June 1913).

Apollinaire, Guillaume. 'L'Anti-tradition Futuriste', Rptd. in *La cultura italiana del 900 attraverso le riviste*. Vol. 4. *Lacerba; La Voce (1914–16)*. A cura di Gianni Scalia. Turin, 1961.

Breunig, Leroy C. 'F. S. Flint, Imagism's "Maître d'Ecole"', *Comparative Literature*, IV.2 (Spring 1952).

Brownell, Baker. 'Post-Martial Emotion', *Poetry*, XIX.3 (Dec. 1921).

Chamberlain, Basil Hall. 'Bashō and the Japanese Poetical Epigram', *Transactions of the Asiatic Society of Japan*, XXX (1902).

Couchoud, P-L. 'Les Epigrammes Lyriques du Japon', *Les Lettres* (Apr., June–Aug. 1906). Rptd. with some additions in P-L. Couchoud, *Sages et Poètes d'Asie*. 2nd edn., Paris, 1916.

Eliot, T. S. 'Reflections on Vers Libre', *New Statesman*, VIII.204 (3 March 1917). Rptd. in *To Criticize the Critic*. London and New York, 1965.

Eliot, T. S. Introduction to E. Pound's *Selected Poems*. London, 1928.

Eliot, T. S. Review of Peter Quennell, *Baudelaire and the Symbolists: Five Essays. The Criterion*, IX.35 (Jan. 1930).

E[liot], T. S. 'A Commentary', *The Criterion*, XIII.52 (Apr. 1934).

Fenollosa, Ernest and Ezra Pound. 'The Chinese Written Character as a

229

Medium for Poetry', *The Little Review*, VI. 5–8 (Sept., Oct., Nov., Dec. 1919).

Fordham, Michael. 'Reflections on Image and Symbol', *New Developments in Analytical Psychology*, London, 1957.

Frattini, Alberto. 'Marinetti e il Futurismo', *Letteratura Italiana: I Contemporanei*, I (Milan, 1963).

'Futurism: Literature', *The Tramp*, I (Aug. 1910).

G., E. W. 'A Plea for Certain Exotic Forms of Verse', *The Cornhill Magazine*, XXXVI (July 1877).

Hall, Donald. 'Ezra Pound: An Interview', *Paris Review*, 28 (Summer–Fall 1962).

Hart, Bernard. 'The Conception of the Unconscious'. In *Subconscious Phenomena*, ed. H. Münsterberg [1910].

Hendry, J. F. 'Hulme as Horatio', *Life and Letters Today*, XXXV.64 (Dec. 1942).

'The conscious artist'. *Times Literary Supplement* (15 June 1962). [About F. M. Hueffer.]

Huntley, Frank Livingstone. 'Zen and the Imagist Poets of Japan', *Comparative Literature*, IV.2 (Spring 1952).

Hynes, Samuel. 'Pound and the Prose Tradition', *Yale Review*, LI.4 (June 1962).

Ishiguro, Hide. 'Imagination', *British Analytical Philosophy*, ed. Bernard Williams and Alan Montefiore. 1966.

Izzo, Carlo. 'Lettere inedite di Ezra Pound', *Nuova Corrente*, 5–6 (Jan.–June 1956).

Jones, Alun R. 'Notes towards a History of Imagism', *South Atlantic Quarterly*, LX (Summer 1961).

Kamerbeek, J. 'T. E. Hulme and German Philosophy: Dilthey and Scheler', *Comparative Literature*, XXI.3 (Summer 1969).

Lewis, [P] Wyndham. 'The London Group 1915 (March)', *Blast*, II (July 1915).

Lewis, Wyndham. 'Modern Caricature and Impressionism', *Blast*, II (July 1915).

Lewis, Wyndham. 'Note for a Catalogue', *Vorticist Exhibition: Catalogue*. London, 1915.

Lewis, Wyndham. 'A Review of Contemporary Art', *Blast*, II (July 1915).

Lewis, Wyndham. 'Introduction'. *Wyndham Lewis and Vorticism*. Tate Gallery Catalogue. London, 1956.

Middleton, Christopher. 'Documents on Imagism from the Papers of F. S. Flint', *The Review*, 15 (April 1965).

Monro, Harold, ed. *The Chapbook*. London, 1919–1925.

Nevinson, C. R. W. 'Vital English Art', *Lacerba*, II.14 (15 July 1914). Reprinted in *Manifestes Futuristes, 1909–23* [Milan, n.d.]

O'Connor, Frank. 'A Gambler's Throw', *The Listener*, (17 Feb. 1966).

Pater, Walter. 'Aesthetic Poetry'. First pub. as 'Poems by William Morris' in *Westminster Review*, N.S. 34 (Oct. 1868). Pub. in U.S.A. by Thomas B. Mosher in *Two Appreciations, The Bibelot*, V.10 (Portland, Maine, 1899).

Patmore, Brigit. 'Ezra Pound in England', *Texas Quarterly*, VII.3 (Autumn 1964).

Rexroth, Kenneth. 'Poetry, Regeneration and D. H. Lawrence', *Bird in the Bush: Obvious Essays*. Norfolk, Conn. and New York, 1959.

Rexroth, Kenneth. 'The Influence of French Poetry on America', *Assays*. Norfolk, Conn., 1961.

'S., R.' 'The Imagistes', *The Cerebralist*, 1 (Dec. 1913).

Schneidau, Herbert N. 'Pound and Yeats: The Question of Symbolism', *ELH*, XXXII.2 (June 1965).

Smalley, R. F. 'Futurism and the Futurists', *The British Review*, VII.2 (Aug. 1914).

Symons, Arthur. 'Mr. Henley's Poetry', *The Fortnightly Review*, LII N.S. 308 (1 Aug. 1892).

Symons, Arthur. 'The Decadent Movement in Literature', *Harper's Monthly Magazine*, XXVI (European edn.) LXXXVII (American edn.) 522 (Nov. 1893).

Taupin, René. 'The Example of Rémy de Gourmont', *The Criterion*, X.41 (July 1931).

Thomas, Edward. 'Two Poets', *The English Review*, II.3 (June 1909).

Tinckom-Fernandez, W. G. 'T. S. Eliot, 10', *The Harvard Advocate*, (Dec. 1938).

Tomlin, E. W. F. 'The Criterion', *The Townsman*, II.6 (April 1939).

*Tripod, The*. Nos. 1, 2, 4 & 5 [Futurist documents]. Cambridge, 1912.

Upward, Allen. 'The Discarded Imagist', *The Egoist*, II.6 (1 June 1915).

Ward, Patricia A. 'Coleridge's Critical Theory of the Symbol', *Texas Studies in Literature and Language*, VIII.1 (Spring 1966).

Wees, William C. 'Pound's Vorticism: Some New Evidence and Further Comments', *Wisconsin Studies in Contemporary Literature*, VII.2 (Summer 1966).

Wilson, Edmund. 'Wallace Stevens and E. E. Cummings', *The Shores of Light: a literary chronicle of the Twenties and Thirties*. New York, 1952.

Yeats, W. B. 'Introduction', *Oxford Book of Modern Verse: 1892–1935*. Oxford, 1936; New York, 1937.

# Index

90; *High Germany*, 84; 'On Heaven
87, 89; *Parade's End*, 89; *Some
Do Not*, 89; 'The Old Houses Of
Flanders', 89; 'The Three-Ten',
85; 'When the World Crumbled',
89
Hughes, Glen, 103, 143
Hulme, T. E., 18–27, 29–31, 32–34,
38, 40, 47, 52–57, 112; Imagist
group, 17–35, 110; and F. S. Flint,
19–22, 32–33, 34; on poetry,
29–30; sources, 106–8, 115–9;
Japanese influence, 126; on form,
148–9, 151, 154, 182, 186; on
metaphor, 155–6; on language,
156, 157, 158–9; on the image,
161, 163–5; on Impressionism,
169; on neo-classicism, 174–7;
'Above the Dock', 33, 53; 'A City
Sunset', 19, 55; *An Introduction
to Metaphysics*, 34; 'At Night', 56,
107; 'Autumn', 19, 20, 55, 108,
147; *Book of the Poets' Club*, 24;
'Complete Poetical Works', 33,
37, 55, 155; 'Conversion', 53; 'In
the City Square', 119, 130; 'In the
Quiet Land', 56; 'Language and
Style', 30, 118, 119; 'Lecture on
Modern Poetry', 24–25, 30, 115,
116, 148, 154, 164, 169; 'Mana
Aboda', 33, 55; 'Over a large table
—smooth', 107; *Ripostes*, 126;
'Sunset', 54; 'The Embankment',
55, 151, 155
Humphreys, Emrys, 187
Huneker, James G., 13
Huxley, Aldous, 188

Ideology, 169–72
Image, 161–9
Imagists and Imagism, 7, 8, 13,
42–43, 57, 103–4, 140; definition,
17, 45–47; development, 17, 27,
184–93; American compared with
English, 105; sources and
influences, 106–46; French
influence, 106–26; Japanese
influence, 126–36; Chinese
influence, 136–40; Greek influence,

140–2; Latin influence, 142–4;
Bible, 144–6; theories, 147–83
Imagiste Group (Pound), 17, 35–43,
57, 62, 83, 120, 150–1
Impressionism, 59, 85, 169–73
Irish Literary Society, 32–33, 49

James, Henry, 158
Jammes, Francis, 121, 125
Japanese influence, 106, 126–36, 147
Johnson, Lionel, 2, 3, 4, 5, 169
Jones, A. R., 52
Jones, Alun, 53
Joyce, James, 38, 125; 'I Hear an
Army', 38; *Chamber Music*, 38;
*Ulysses*, 125, 184

Kahn, Gustave, 112, 115, 116, 117,
118, 125, 145, 146; *Premiers
Poèmes*, 116
Kant, Emanuel, 162
Keats, John, 90
Kipling, Rudyard, 6, 7, 16; 'Danny
Deever', 7; 'Recessional', 7;
'Cities and Thrones and Powers', 7
Kreymborg, Alfred, 37

Laforgue, 125, 146
Laing, R. D.: *The Divided Self*, 54
Language, 1–2, 24–25, 155–60
Latin influence, 142–4
Lawrence, D. H., 1, 8, 23, 41, 43,
99–103, 110, 112; on Imagists,
99–100; and Hueffer, 99–100;
form, 152; 'All of Roses', 101;
*Birds, Beasts and Flowers*, 101,
103; 'Erinnyes', 99–100; 'Gloire
de Dijon', 101; 'Green', 101;
*Lady Chatterley's Lover*, 101;
'Mosquito', 103; 'Song of a Man
Who Has Come Through', 152;
'The Snapdragon', 100; 'Violets',
102
Léautaud, Paul, 19
Lechmere, Kate, 61, 118
Leavis, F. R., 82
Li-Po, 138
Locke, 161–2; *Essay concerning
Human Understanding*, 162